walking with purpose

Dear Friend,

Welcome to *Opening Your Heart: The Starting Point*! How I wish I could be sitting across from you, hearing your thoughts and insights about all the things we're going to delve into during this study. You are about to begin an exciting journey closer to the heart of God. No previous experience with Bible study is necessary. You can come as you are—with your questions, doubts, joys, and hopes.

If you are doing this study with a group of women, I am praying that you'll find it to be a safe place to let down your guard. I'm asking God to surround you with women who want to encourage you, and walk alongside you as you all explore the basics of our faith. No question is dumb, no confidence will be shared outside the group, and masks can be dropped at the door. This is a place where you get to be real.

Each one of us comes to this study from a different place spiritually. Some will find that the questions in the study cause us to think about things that are new concepts to us. Others might find that much is a review. God meets each one of us where we are, and is always faithful to take us to a deeper, better place, regardless of where we come from.

So much of a woman's time is spent giving to others, which is a beautiful gift and sacrifice. But we can only give what we have received ourselves, and if we don't take the time to replenish and refresh our souls, it won't be long before we are running on empty. God waits for you each morning, and wants to fill you up—to shower you with His mercy, tenderness, and love. He utterly adores you. You are His precious daughter, and He is thrilled that you have decided to take this time to get to know Him better!

"The Lord, your God, is in your midst, a mighty savior, who will rejoice over you with gladness, and renew you in his love, who will sing joyfully because of you!" (Zephaniah 3:17)

With prayers for you as you open your heart to the One who loves you best ~

Lisa Brenninkmeyer
Founder and Chief Purpose Officer, Walking with Purpose

Opening Your Heart
The Starting Point

www.walkingwithpurpose.com

Authored by Lisa Brenninkmeyer
Cover and page design by True Cotton
Production management by Christine Welsko

IMPRIMATUR   + William E. Lori, S.T.D., Archbishop of Baltimore

The recommended Bible translations for use in Blaze and Walking with Purpose studies are: The New American Bible, which is the translation used in the United States for the readings at Mass; The Revised Standard Version, Catholic Edition; and The Jerusalem Bible.

Any internet addresses (websites, blogs, etc.) in this book are offered as a resource, and may change in the future. Please refer to www.walkingwithpurpose.com as the central location for corresponding materials and references.

Reprinted: July 2018

ISBN: 978-1-943173-00-6

Opening Your Heart

TABLE OF CONTENTS

INTRODUCTION

LESSONS

APPENDICES

ANSWER KEY

PRAYER PAGES

Welcome to Walking with Purpose

You have many choices when it comes to how you spend your time—thank you for choosing Walking with Purpose. Studying God's Word with an open and receptive heart will bring spiritual growth and enrichment to all aspects of your life, making every moment that you've invested well worth it.

Each one of us comes to this material from our own unique vantage point. You are welcome as you are. No previous experience is necessary. Some of you will find that the questions in this study cause you to think about concepts that are new to you. Others might find much is a review. God meets each one of us where we are, and He is always faithful, taking us to a deeper, better place spiritually, regardless of where we begin.

The Structure of *Opening Your Heart*

Opening Your Heart is a twenty-two-session Bible study that integrates Scripture with the teachings of the Roman Catholic Church to point us to principles that help us manage life's pace and pressure while living with calm and steadiness.

This Bible study is designed for both group discussion and interactive personal study.

If you are going through *Opening Your Heart* with a small group in your parish, most weeks will be spent in the group discussing one of the lessons from the *Opening Your Heart Study Guide*. Once a month you'll gather for a Connect Coffee, which consists of social time, a DVD presentation of one of the related Bible study talks, and small group discussion of selected questions that relate to the talk.

If you're going through this study either on your own or in a small group, you are welcome to order the DVDs, but you might find it simpler to watch the talks online. The URL for each talk is listed on the Connect Coffee Talk outline within the study guide.

Study Guide Format and Reference Materials

The *Opening Your Heart Study Guide* is divided into three sections:

The first section comprises twenty-two lessons. Most lessons are divided into five "days" to help you form a habit of reading and reflecting on God's Word regularly. If you are a woman who has only bits and pieces of time throughout your day to accomplish tasks, you will find this breakdown of the lessons especially helpful. Each day focuses on Scripture readings and related teaching passages, and ends with a Quiet Your Heart reflection. In addition, Day Five includes a Saint's Story; a lesson conclusion; a resolution section, in which you set a goal for yourself based on a theme of the lesson; and short clips from the *Catechism of the Catholic Church*, which are referenced throughout the lesson to complement the Scripture study.

For the Connect Coffee Talks in the series, accompanying outlines are offered as guides for taking notes. Included are questions to help direct group discussion following the talks, as well as URLs for those who would like to view the talks online.

The second section, the appendices, contains supplemental materials referred to during the study, and includes an article about Saint Thérèse of Lisieux, the patron saint of Walking with Purpose (Appendix 1). In Appendix 2, you'll find letterhead stationery for your letter to Jesus, which you'll write in Lesson 2. Appendix 3 is the article "Conversion of Heart," which offers supplemental materials for Lesson 3. Appendix 4 is an excellent article, "Confession by the Numbers," which accompanies Lesson 11.

The third section contains the answer key. You will benefit so much more from the Bible study if you work through the questions on your own, searching your heart, as this is your very personal journey of faith. The answer key is meant to enhance small group discussion, and provide personal guidance or insight when needed.

Two memory verses have been chosen for *Opening Your Heart*, and we encourage you to memorize them as you move through the Bible study. Illustrations of the two verses can be found at the end of Lesson 7, and color versions and phone lock screens can be downloaded from our website. More explanation of memorizing Scripture will be covered in Lesson 7.

At the end of the book are pages on which to write weekly prayer intentions.

Walking with Purpose™ Website

Please visit our website at www.walkingwithpurpose.com to find additional free content, supplemental materials that compliment our Bible studies, as well as a link to our online store for additional Bible studies, DVDs, book and more!

WWP Scripture Printables of our exclusively designed verse cards that compliment all Bible studies. Available in various sizes, lock screens for phones, and a format that allows you to e-mail them to a friend.

WWP Bible Study Playlists of Lisa's favorite music accompany each Bible study.

WWP Videos of all Connect Coffee Talks by Lisa Brenninkmeyer.

WWP Blog by Lisa Brenninkmeyer you are welcome to come here to find a safe place where the mask can drop and you can be real. Subscribe for updates.

WWP Leadership Development Program
We are here to help you take your leadership to the next level! Through our training, you'll discover insights that help you achieve your leadership potential. You'll be empowered to step out of your comfort zone and experience the rush of serving God with passion and purpose. We want you to know that you are not alone; we offer you encouragement and the tools you need to reach out to a world that desperately needs to experience the love of God.

Links to WWP Social Media

Twitter, Pinterest, Facebook, Instagram

NOTES

Lessons

NOTES

Walking with Purpose is a community of women growing in faith – together! This is where women are gathering. Join us!

www.walkingwithpurpose.com

Lesson 1: Connect Coffee Talk

FOUR STEPS TO WALKING WITH PURPOSE

Accompanying DVD can be viewed by disc or please visit our website at walkingwithpurpose.com/videos and select *Opening Your Heart* Bible Study, click through to select Videos.

Key verse:

"I'm not saying that I have this all together, that I have it made. But I am well on my way, reaching out for Christ, who has so wondrously reached out for me. Friends, don't get me wrong: By no means do I count myself an expert in all of this, but I've got my eye on the goal, where God is beckoning us onward—to Jesus. I'm off and running and I'm not turning back. So let's keep focused on that goal, those of us who want everything God has for us." (Philippians 3:12–15, The Message translation of the Holy Bible)

Four Steps to Walking with Purpose:

1. **Discover God's Love for You**

   God sees that you aren't perfect, but that doesn't make you any less the apple of His eye. No matter what your parents or other people may have said to you, and no matter what your husband, friends, neighbors, or coworkers have said to you (or about you), God is completely captivated by you. He loves you. He is on your side. There is nothing that He would not do for you as long as it is for your good.

2. **Determine What Drives You**

   The apostle Paul said, "I do not understand what I do. For what I want to do I do not do, but what I hate, I do." (Romans 7:15)

   Are you driven by . . .

9

Pride

Vanity

Sensuality

3. Decrease Distractions

Rick Warren writes in *The Purpose Driven Life*, "It is impossible to do everything people want you to do. You have just enough time to do God's will. If you can't get it all done, it means you're trying to do more than God intended for you to do (or, possibly, that you're watching too much TV)."[1]

4. Develop an Eternal Perspective

Horatio Spafford penned, "When peace, like a river, attendeth my way, when sorrow like sea billows roll; whatever my lot, Thou hast taught me to say, it is well, it is well with my soul."[2]

---

[1] Rick Warren, *The Purpose Driven Life: What on Earth Am I Here For?* (Grand Rapids, MI: Zondervan, 2002), 31.

[2] Horatio G. Spafford, "It Is Well with My Soul," Timeless Truths, http://library.timelesstruths.org/music/It_Is_Well_with_My_Soul/.

Lesson 2

WHO IS JESUS CHRIST?

Introduction

Who is Jesus Christ? It may seem strange to begin with such a seemingly simple question, but it's one that even Jesus asked His disciples: "Who do the crowds say that I am?" (Luke 9:18) The disciples answered by telling Jesus how people of the day were describing Him. Some were saying Jesus was "John the Baptist, others, Elijah; still others, 'one of the ancient prophets has arisen.'" (Luke 9:19) In our current culture, some people describe Jesus as a great teacher, a moral leader, and someone who showed us how to love.

We know from the Bible that Jesus was fully human. He had a human body, which grew tired (John 4:6) and got hungry (Matthew 4:2). Jesus had human emotions; He expressed anger (Mark 11:15–17), love (Mark 10:21), and sadness (John 11:32–36). He can relate to us because of His human experiences such as temptation (Mark 1:13), learning (Luke 2:46–52), work (Mark 6:3), obedience (Luke 2:51), and suffering (the Passion).

Was He more than a man? Was He more than a great teacher and a moral leader? To avoid the mistake of worshipping a god of our own making—a god of our imagination—we need to look at how Jesus described Himself.

"I am the bread of life." (John 6:35)
"I am the light of the world." (John 8:12)
"I am the resurrection and the life." (John 11:25–26)
"I am the way, the truth, and the life." (John 14:6)
"Receive me; receive God." (Matthew 10:40)
"To have seen me is to have seen God." (John 14:9)

Author C. S. Lewis wrote:

> A man who was merely a man and said the sort of things Jesus said wouldn't be a great moral teacher, he'd either be a lunatic—on a level with a man who says he's a poached egg—or else he'd be the devil of hell. You must make your choice. Either this man was and is the Son of God, or else a madman or something worse. . . . But don't let us come up with any patronizing nonsense about his being a great human teacher. He hasn't left that open to us. He didn't intend to.[3]

Day One
JESUS THE ANSWER

Read John 14:1–10 and the following commentary on that passage.

> From ancient times philosophers have summed up the human condition as a quest to answer three fundamental queries: What should I do? What can I know? What can I hope for? Jesus Christ answers them all, not merely with doctrine, but with his very person. "I am the way" can translate into: What should you do? Follow me! Do what I have done. "I am the truth" means: What can you know? You can know everything, if only you know me. Knowing me, you know the truth; you know the secret behind the workings of the whole universe and the yearnings of the human heart. "I am the life" means: What can you hope for? In me, through me, you can hope for and expect the fullness of life that you long for, even though you may not be able to put that longing into words. Christ is truly the living water that quenches every thirst. He is truly the light that scatters every kind of darkness. The quest of every man and woman to satisfy the heart's deepest needs is the quest to seek his face, and it leads either to Christ and the place he has prepared for us in heaven or to a dead end[4].

1. According to the commentary, what is Jesus telling us when He says, "I am the way, the truth, and the life".

---

[3] C. S. Lewis, *Mere Christianity*, rev. ed. (New York: Macmillan/Collier, 1952), 55.

[4] John Bartunek, *The Better Part: A Christ-Centered Resource for Personal Prayer* (Hamden, CT: Circle Press, 2007), 936.

A. "I am the way" means:

B. "I am the truth" means:

C. "I am the life" means:

2. How would you explain Jesus Christ to someone who has never heard of Him? Describe Him in three or four sentences.

3. Using the letterhead stationery in Appendix 2, write a letter to Jesus. Correspond with Him as you would a friend. Share with Him your dreams and what you are hoping for, your fears and how you need His help. Tell Him what He means to you. Note: These letters are meant to be private. No one should be asked to share any portion of her letter in a group setting.

Quiet your heart and enjoy His presence. . . . He holds the answers to the deepest longings of your heart.

At a time when Western women have more privilege and opportunity than ever before, our feelings of discontent and dissatisfaction have skyrocketed. Could it be that we are looking for answers to our longings in the wrong places? Could it be that we have become seekers of comfort instead of seekers of truth? Take some time to ask the Lord to help you to be open to Him when He shows you the way to go, instead of insisting on your own way. Ask Him to give you the humility to set down your preconceived notions of who He is and what is true, in order to hear and accept His perspective. Ask Him to replace your complacency or your willingness to settle for being comfortable instead of truly living the life you were created for. He is the way, the truth, and the life. Your heart's deepest longings will be satisfied only through a relationship with Him.

Day Two
JESUS THE FULFILLMENT

"[Jesus] said to them, 'These are my words that I spoke to you while I was still with you, that everything written about me in the law of Moses and in the prophets and psalms must be fulfilled.' Then he opened their minds to understand the scriptures." (Luke 24:44–45)

The Old Testament is filled with several dozen major prophecies regarding "the anointed one" ("Messiah" in Hebrew), the deliverer who was to be sent by God at some point in the future to rescue His people. These prophecies were hints of what was to come, which would make it easier to identify whether a person was the true Messiah or an impostor.

Spoiler alert: Jesus nailed every single one of them. Some of us take that fact at face value, but others have a bit more of a skeptical streak. Didn't Jesus already know what was said in the Old Testament, so couldn't He just choose to fulfill each one? Actually, no. Many of the prophecies were tied to events (some historical, some personal) that a person just couldn't control.

Next objection: Wasn't the Bible just put together to make Jesus look good? Couldn't the New Testament writers just have worked the facts to make it all fit? For example, there was an Old Testament prophecy that said the Messiah's bones wouldn't be broken, so couldn't the writer of the Gospel of John have just *said* that the legs of the two thieves on either side of Jesus were broken, but that Jesus was already dead so the soldiers didn't break His? A number of things make it unlikely that one of the Gospel writers would have fabricated the facts. Why would they later have been willing to be martyred for the honor of someone who was a fake messiah? Why wouldn't the Jewish community (full of eyewitnesses) have jumped all over falsified facts? While the Jewish Talmud never refers to Jesus positively, it also doesn't refute that the fulfillment of the prophecies took place. On that subject, there is silence.

It's OK to hash out our doubts, questions, and objections. But let's ask the Lord to help us have the openness to really listen to His words—to *His* perspective on what took place. Let's seek truth wholeheartedly.

1. Read the following prophecies found in Isaiah 53 regarding the suffering Messiah, and note the New Testament fulfillments found in the verses that follow. Note: These prophecies were made more than five hundred years before Jesus' birth.

Isaiah 53

1 Who would believe what we have heard? To whom has the arm of the LORD been revealed?

2 He grew up like a sapling before him, like a shoot from the parched earth; He had no majestic bearing to catch our eye, no beauty to draw us to him.

3 He was spurned and avoided by men, a man of suffering, knowing pain, Like one from whom you turn your face, spurned, and we held him in no esteem.

4 Yet it was our pain that he bore, our sufferings he endured. We thought of him as stricken, struck down by God and afflicted,

5 But he was pierced for our sins, crushed for our iniquity. He bore the punishment that makes us whole, by his wounds we were healed.

6 We had all gone astray like sheep, all following our own way; But the LORD laid upon him the guilt of us all.

7 Though harshly treated, he submitted and did not open his mouth; Like a lamb led to slaughter or a sheep silent before shearers, he did not open his mouth.

8 Seized and condemned, he was taken away. Who would have thought any more of his destiny? For he was cut off from the land of the living, struck for the sins of his people.

9 He was given a grave among the wicked, a burial place with evildoers, though he had done no wrong, nor was deceit found in his mouth.

10 But it was the LORD's will to crush him with pain. By making his life as a reparation offering, he shall see his offspring, shall lengthen his days, and the LORD's will shall be accomplished through him.

11 Because of his anguish he shall see the light; because of his knowledge he shall be content; My servant, the just one, shall justify the many, their iniquity he shall bear.

12 Therefore I will give him his portion among the many, and he shall divide the spoils with the mighty, Because he surrendered himself to death, was counted among the transgressors, Bore the sins of many, and interceded for the transgressors.

Luke 17:25 (fulfillment of Isaiah 53:3)

2 Corinthians 5:21 (fulfillment of Isaiah 53:4–5)

Mark 15:4–5, Luke 23:8–9, John 1:29 (fulfillment of Isaiah 53:7)

"God has thus brought to fulfillment what he had announced beforehand through the mouth of all the prophets, that his Messiah would suffer." (Acts 3:18)

2. Read the following Old Testament prophecies, and note how Jesus fulfills them in the Gospel of Matthew.

   "Therefore the Lord himself shall give you a sign. Behold a virgin shall conceive, and bear a son, and his name shall be called Emmanuel." (Isaiah 7:14)

   Matthew 1:22–23

   "But you, Bethlehem . . . least among the clans of Judah, From you shall come forth for me one who is to be ruler in Israel; whose origin is from old, from ancient times." (Micah 5:1, NAB)

   Matthew 2:1

   Other Old Testament prophecies include the massacre of the innocents in Bethlehem (Jeremiah 31:15, Matthew 2:18) and Jesus bringing light to Galilee (Isaiah 9:1–2, Matthew 4:12–16), being sent to heal the brokenhearted (Isaiah 61:1–2, Luke 4:1–19), being betrayed (Psalm 41:10, Luke 22:47–48), being falsely accused (Psalm 35:11, Mark 14:57–58), and being betrayed for thirty pieces of silver (Zechariah 11:12–14, Matthew 27:9–10).

Quiet your heart and enjoy His presence. . . . The One who holds history in His hands is listening to you.

Was this prophetic fulfillment just some kind of an accident? Analysis by mathematician Peter W. Stoner concludes that the probability of someone fulfilling just eight of the prophecies is one chance in one hundred million billion.[5] And Jesus fulfilled far, far more than eight! What do we do with numbers like that? We can't even wrap our heads around them. The response it should evoke in us is wonder and awe. At the very least, we should be pretty impressed with the fact that sending Jesus as

---

[5] Peter W. Stoner, *Science Speaks* (Chicago: Moody Press, 1969), 109.

the Messiah was God's intention from the get-go, and He didn't miss a detail in bringing it to pass exactly as He'd planned. Take a few minutes to praise God for being so far beyond anything we can wrap our heads around. Don't expect to figure Him out—just let Him know you find Him amazing.

Day Three
JESUS THE SAVIOR

1. According to CCC 430, what is the meaning of the name Jesus?

2. Before we delve into why Jesus is the Savior, it's worth addressing the question, do we need saving? If we are basically good people, if our good deeds outweigh our bad, then aren't we doing just fine on our own? Explore this subject through the questions that follow.

   Can any of us claim to be without sin? See Romans 3:23 and 1 John 1:8.

   Why do you think we find it so easy to rationalize our mistakes?

   What is the consequence of sin—any sin, even a small one? See Romans 6:23.

The consequence of sin isn't the only thing that is a concern for us. Sin also has power—it can leave us feeling incapable of being the kind of people we long to be. We can get stuck—trapped—in patterns of behavior that we know are destructive. Sin also divides. It puts up a wall between us and God. This is a very big deal, because we were created to have a relationship with Him. Close friendship with Him will be the only thing that brings us true satisfaction and fulfillment.

3. The punishment for sin is death, the power of sin leaves us trapped, and the division of sin keeps us from God. But God never intended to leave us in a hopeless situation like this. What solution does He offer? Is this offer made only to those who have cleaned themselves up and proven to be worthy? See Romans 5:6–8.

4. When Jesus died on the cross, "God was reconciling the world to himself in Christ, not counting [our] trespasses against [us]." (2 Corinthians 5:19) What motivated Him to do this? See John 3:16.

Quiet your heart and enjoy His presence. . . . "If the Son makes you free, you will be free indeed." (John 8:36)

Without a savior, we wouldn't be able to experience freedom from the grip of sin. Meditate on the words of this beautiful song, "Lord, I Need You," by Matt Maher, from the album All the People Said Amen. *Even better, listen to it and make these words your prayer.*

Lord, I come, I confess
Bowing here, I find my rest
Without You, I fall apart
You're the One that guides my heart

Lord I need You, oh, I need You
Every hour I need You
My one defense, my righteousness
Oh God, how I need You
Where sin runs deep Your grace is more
Where grace is found is where You are
And where You are, Lord I am free
Holiness is Christ in me

Lord I need You, oh, I need You
Every hour I need You
My one defense, my righteousness
Oh God, how I need You

Teach my song to rise to You
When temptation comes my way
And when I cannot stand I'll fall on You
Jesus, You're my hope and stay

Lord, I need You, oh, I need You
Every hour I need You
My one defense, my righteousness
Oh God, how I need You[6]

Day Four
JESUS THE LORD

"[Jesus] reflects the glory of God and bears the very stamp of his nature, upholding the universe by his word of power." (Hebrews 1:3, RSV)

1. What did Saint Paul have to say about Jesus? Read his words from Colossians 1:15–20. After each section, put what you've read into your own words.

    "[Jesus] is the image of the invisible God." (Colossians 1:15)

    "For in [Jesus] were created all things in heaven and on earth, the visible and invisible, whether thrones or dominions or principalities or powers; all things were created through him and for him." (Colossians 1:16)

    "[Jesus] is before all things, and in him all things hold together." (Colossians 1:17)

---

[6] Matt Maher, "Lord, I Need You," *All the People Said Amen* (Franklin, TN: Provident Label Group, 2013), compact disc.

"[Jesus] is the head of the body, the church. [Jesus] is the beginning, the firstborn from the dead, that in all things he himself might be preeminent." (Colossians 1:18)

"For in [Jesus] all the fullness [of God] was pleased to dwell." (Colossians 1:19)

2. What did the apostle John (eyewitness of Jesus' time on earth) have to say about Jesus? Read the following words from Saint John found in John 1. After each section, put what you've read into your own words.

"[Jesus] was in the beginning with God. All things came to be through him, and without him nothing came to be." (John 1:2–3)

"And the Word [Jesus] became flesh and made his dwelling among us, and we saw his glory, the glory as of the Father's only Son, full of grace and truth." (John 1:14)

"No one has ever seen God. The only Son, God, who is at the Father's side, has revealed him." (John 1:18)

3. According to CCC 84, what is the meaning of the title Lord? How did Jesus reveal His divine sovereignty or Lordship over all?

Quiet your heart and enjoy His presence. . . . "[Jesus] is the Lord of the world and of history, the only One to whom we must completely submit our personal freedom." (CCC 84)

Submit your personal freedom. It's a pretty tall order, especially when we humans really like to be the ones in control. We'd be crazy to hand over our freedom to someone weak, someone we didn't trust, someone unreliable, someone selfish, someone driven by ego. But what would it feel like to submit our personal freedom to someone who had proven Himself to be utterly trustworthy, who promised to never leave us, who was completely selfless to the point of death, whose humility was incomparable, and who was the supreme power in the universe? What if we weren't meant to bear the weight and pressure of trying to stay in control all the time? What if there were a safe place to let down our guard? What if there were someone who was just waiting to guide us to the best place to experience joy and fulfillment?

Take a few moments to talk to God about what scares you when you think of submitting your personal freedom to Him. Then tell Him five things about Himself that remind you of His goodness and greatness, and write them down.

Day Five
SAINT'S STORY

Saint Victoria Wins the Victory of Love

Everyone wants a savior, but few people want a lord. Christ is both Savior and Lord. He is the one Savior: "Only in him is there salvation; for of all the names in the world given to men, this is the only one by which we can be saved." (Acts 4:12) And He is the one Lord: "And for this God raised him high, and gave him the name which is above all other names; so that all beings in the heavens, on earth and in the underworld, should bend the knee at the name of Jesus and that every tongue should acknowledge Jesus Christ as Lord, to the glory of God the Father." (Philippians 2:9–11) Jesus gave His life on the cross so that through Him we could experience the meaning for which we long, both here on earth and forever in heaven. He longs for our love, and when we get a glimpse of His beauty and a taste of the meaning His love can give to our life (". . . whose power, working in us, can do infinitely more than we can ask or imagine" [Ephesians 3:20]), we long to give it to Him. Saint Victoria had a particularly dramatic adventure of love once she decided to follow Christ.

Victoria lived in North Africa in a pagan family around the year 300, when severe legal persecution against the Christians was frequent and violent. As a teenager, she converted to the Christian faith, though her family remained pagan. Soon she fell so in love with Christ that she desired to give her whole life up to Him, and made a vow of virginity.

Her parents were furious, because she was their only daughter and they had arranged a profitable and honorable marriage for her. They refused to accept her denials and forced her to go through with the marriage. But when the wedding day came, she put her trust completely in Jesus, and instead of going downstairs to be received by her husband, she said a prayer and then leaped out the upper-story window of her room. Landing safely, she fled to a nearby church and started serving Jesus and His kingdom full-time.

One Sunday morning a few years later, when she was in her early twenties, she was with a group of about fifty Christians attending a Mass being celebrated in a private home. Suddenly, a platoon of imperial soldiers burst in, broke up the Mass, and arrested the whole group.

Victoria and her companions (of every age and both sexes) stood trial, professing their faith courageously and eloquently in the face of torture. They were stretched on the rack, torn with iron hooks, and beaten with cudgels—just to make them renounce their faith in Christ and give due worship to the false pagan gods of the Roman Empire.

Victoria especially impressed both the public and the judges. Her brother (still a pagan) actually attended the trial and pleaded for her release on the grounds of insanity, but she debated so intelligently with the judge that she disproved the charge. The judge was so moved by her valor and poise that when his arguments and cajolery failed to shake her fidelity, he stepped down from his judgment seat, removed his robe of office, and pleaded with her, merely as a friend, not to throw her life away. She responded, "I have already told you. I am a Christian. And I attended the Mass."

Eventually, with all the Christians having firmly held their faith, the authorities lost patience and threw them into prison, where one by one, after long days of suffering that they bore with faith, hope, and love, they entered into the everlasting joy of their beloved Lord.

Saint Victoria knew who Christ was: the Lord who had given her both life and the hope for eternal life. And so He was the one Lord who deserved the gift of her life in return.

Are there times in your life when you don't stand firm in your faith, when you downplay your Christianity to fit in? What have you learned from Saint Victoria's story to help you in those situations?

Jesus always supplies the grace we need to do His will. If Saint Victoria's story disturbs you, remember that she was equipped with the grace and courage sufficient for the suffering she endured. God gives us the grace we need *when we need it*, not when we're worrying about something that might happen in the future.

Conclusion

Have you ever tried to wrap your head around who God is, what He's really like? Jesus reveals God to us. Not that Jesus can be put into a box and neatly defined; He will always be more than our minds can comprehend. But would we want to worship someone so understandable and predictable that He'd just be a nicer version of us? Don't we long for something more—someone so much greater than we are that He can surmount the things that perplex us, bringing peace to our chaos?

May the many facets of Jesus fill us with wonder and awe whenever we think of Him.

May theologian John Piper's words increase our appreciation of who Jesus is:

> We admire Christ for his transcendence, but even more because the transcendence of His greatness is mixed with submission to God. We marvel at him because his uncompromising justice is tempered with mercy. His majesty is sweetened by meekness. In his equality *with* God he has a deep reverence *for* God. Though he is worthy of all good, he was patient to suffer evil. His sovereign dominion over the world was clothed with a spirit of obedience and submission. He baffled the proud scribes with his wisdom, but was simple enough to be loved by children. He could still the storm with a word, but would not strike the Samaritans with lightning or take himself down from the cross.[7]

---

[7] John Piper, *Seeing and Savoring Jesus Christ* (Wheaton, IL: Crossway Books, 2001), 29–30.

Who is Jesus Christ? He is the lover of your soul. He is the eternal God, the Creator of the world, all-powerful and all-knowing, and He loves you personally. How did He prove His love? It was through His suffering and death on the cross that He proved once and for all your worth to Him. In the words of Father John Bartunek, "It's like sitting in the electric chair in place of the man who murdered your children so that he doesn't have to suffer and die—crazy love, incalculable love, unfathomable love. And that is God's glory: making known God's love."[8]

He is the answer to our deepest questions.

He is the fulfillment of all our longings.

He is the Savior who rescues us.

He is the Lord who can be trusted with our freedom.

There never was, and never will be, anyone like Jesus.

My Resolution

"My Resolution" is your opportunity to write down one specific personal application from this lesson. We can take in a lot of information from studying the Bible, but if we don't translate it into action, we have totally missed the point. In James 1:22, we're told that we shouldn't just hear the Word of God; we are to "do what it says." So what qualities should be found in a good resolution? It should be **personal** (use *I*, *me*, *my*, *mine*), it should be **possible** (don't choose something so far-fetched that you'll just become discouraged), it should be **measurable** (a specific goal to achieve within a specific time period), and it should be **action oriented** (not just a spiritual thought).

In what specific way will I apply what I learned in this lesson?

Examples:

1. During the prayer after the Eucharist this week, instead of mindlessly singing the Communion song, I will think about how Jesus showed His love for me by suffering in my place on the cross.

---

[8] Bartunek, *The Better Part*, 932–33.

2. I'll take fifteen minutes this week to journal about the difference between Jesus being my Lord and being my Savior. I'll reread the first paragraph of the Saint's Story to aid my understanding. I'll identify one area of my life in which it is hard to let Jesus be in charge (being my Lord). I will pray that God will help me relinquish control of this area of my life.

3. Each morning, I'll reread the five things that remind me of God's goodness and greatness in the Quiet Your Heart section of Day Four.

My Resolution:

Catechism Clips

The following Catechism quotes are taken from the *Compendium of the Catechism of the Catholic Church.*[9]

81. What is the meaning of the name "Jesus"?
Given by the angel at the time of the Annunciation, the name "Jesus" means "God saves." The name expresses his identity and his mission "because he will save his people from their sins" (Matthew 1:21). Peter proclaimed that "there is no other name under heaven given to men by which we can be saved" (Acts 4:12).

82. Why is Jesus called "Christ"?
"Christ" in Greek, "Messiah" in Hebrew, means the "anointed one." Jesus is the Christ because he is consecrated by God and anointed by the Holy Spirit for his redeeming mission. He is the Messiah awaited by Israel, sent into the world by the Father. Jesus accepted the title of Messiah but he made the meaning of the term clear: "come down from heaven" (John 3:13), crucified and then risen, he is the Suffering Servant "who gives his life as a ransom for the many" (Matthew 20:28). From the name Christ comes our name of Christian.

---

[9] The *Compendium of the Catechism of the Catholic Church* is a summarized version of the *Catechism of the Catholic Church.*

84. What is the meaning of the title "Lord"?

In the Bible, this title regularly designates God as Sovereign. Jesus ascribed this title to himself and revealed his divine sovereignty by his power over nature, over demons, over sin, and over death, above all by his own Resurrection. The first Christian creeds proclaimed that the power, the honor, and the glory that are due to God the Father also belong to Jesus: God "has given him the name which is above every other name" (Philippians 2:9). He is the Lord of the world and of history, the only One to whom we must completely submit our personal freedom.

Lesson 3

WHY IS JESUS CHRIST INTERESTED IN MY FRIENDSHIP?

Introduction

We all desire true friendship—relationships characterized by trust, affection, and support. A true friend wants what is best for the other. She is motivated by care and concern, not self-interest.

So why is Jesus Christ interested in your friendship? Is He lacking in some way? Does He need something from you? Does He want a relationship with you because He is lonely?

Jesus doesn't need anything. He was never lonely. So why did He create you and then desire closeness to you? The answer to this secret is shared in the *Catechism of the Catholic Church*, 221: "God has revealed his innermost secret: God himself is an eternal exchange of love, Father, Son, and Holy Spirit, and he has destined us to share in that exchange."

For all eternity, there has been an exchange of love going on between God the Father, Jesus, and the Holy Spirit. So why did He create people, especially when He knew how much it would cost—when He knew it would cost Jesus His life? In the words of author and speaker Christopher West, "Because love wants to share itself. True love wants to expand its communion. All the hunger we have for love, for union, for happiness are given by God to lead us to Him. The difference between a saint and the greatest sinner is where they go to satisfy that hunger."[10]

Jesus wants to satisfy your inner hunger and emptiness through a friendship with Him. He does this for many reasons, four of which we'll explore in this lesson:

---

[10] Christopher West, *An Introduction to the Theology of the Body* (West Chester, PA: Ascension Press, 2008).

1. He loves you
2. He wants you to fulfill your purpose in life
3. He knows you were made for more
4. He wants to spend eternity with you

Because Jesus knows you so well, He knows what you need. Because He loves you so much, He wants to give you what you need. What you need is *Him*. So He offers you His friendship.

"Christ alone is the cornerstone on which it is possible solidly to build one's existence. Only Christ—known, contemplated and loved—is the faithful friend who never lets us down, who becomes our traveling companion, and whose words warm our hearts." —Saint John Paul II

Day One
HE LOVES YOU

Read Psalm 139:1–16 below:

> 1 Lord, you have probed me, you know me: 2 you know when I sit and stand; you understand my thoughts from afar. 3 You sift through my travels and my rest; with all my ways you are familiar. 4 Even before a word is on my tongue, Lord, you know it all. 5 Behind and before you encircle me and rest your hand upon me. 6 Such knowledge is too wonderful for me, far too lofty for me to reach. 7 Where can I go from your spirit? From your presence, where can I flee? 8 If I ascend to the heavens, you are there; if I lie down in Sheol, there you are. 9 If I take the wings of dawn and dwell beyond the sea, 10 Even there your hand guides me, your right hand holds me fast. 11 If I say, "Surely darkness shall hide me, and night shall be my light"—12 Darkness is not dark for you, and night shines as the day. Darkness and light are but one. 13 You formed my inmost being; you knit me in my mother's womb. 14 I praise you, because I am wonderfully made; wonderful are your works! My very self you know. 15 My bones are not hidden from you, when I was being made in secret, fashioned in the depths of the earth. 16 Your eyes saw me unformed; in your book all are written down; my days were shaped, before one came to be.

1. Underline verses 13 to 16 as you reread them.

2. God created you with careful attention to every specific detail of your being. You are His masterpiece. He looks at you, His precious daughter, with delight and love. Does this truth agree or clash with your image of God's heart toward you?

3. Underline verses 7 to 12 as you reread them. Will God ever leave you alone? Where can you go to escape His loving presence? Is He with you now?

4. How is God's love for you described in CCC 220?

Quiet your heart and enjoy His presence. . . . Rest in His steadfast love.

The Bible tells us that Jesus loves you so much that "the very hairs on your head are all numbered." (Luke 12:7) He knows everything about you—the good, the bad, the innermost secrets—and nothing diminishes that limitless love. While other people may evaluate you according to how you perform, what you achieve, or what you look like, Jesus cares for you simply because you belong to Him.

"God proves his love for us in that while we were still sinners Christ died for us." (Romans 5:8) He didn't wait until we were all cleaned up and deserving of His mercy. He proved His love when we were still a hot mess. And while this love is broad enough to reach every person, it is also intensely personal. In the words of Saint Augustine, "God loves each of us as if there were only one of us."

Take a few moments to thank God for His relentless love. If you find His love for you hard to fathom, ask Him for the grace to see yourself through His eyes of mercy.

Day Two
HE WANTS YOU TO FULFILL YOUR PURPOSE IN LIFE

"[For my determined purpose is] that I may know Him [that I may progressively become more deeply and intimately acquainted with Him, perceiving and recognizing and understanding the wonders of His Person more strongly and more clearly]." (Philippians 3:10)

"Why did God make you? God made me to know Him, to love Him, and to serve Him in this world, and to be happy with Him for ever in heaven." (Baltimore Catechism No. 1)

1. We are invited to know Jesus personally, which is not the same as knowing *about* Him or knowing *of* Him. Write down the name of someone you know *of.* Then write the name of someone you know personally. What aspects of your relationship with the person you know personally have allowed that friendship to grow deeper?

2. Our friendship with Jesus grows deeper in much the same way that any earthly relationship develops. It doesn't happen automatically—we have to invest time and heart. Read the following verses and share insights into ways that we can get to know Jesus better.

   Jeremiah 29:13

   Proverbs 3:5–6

   John 14:23

3. Even when we realize that our true purpose in life is to know God, things can get in the way of that pursuit. Distractions, other loves, apathy, pride, and busyness are some of the obstacles we face. What do you find to be the biggest hindrance to growing closer to God through knowing Him better?

Quiet your heart and enjoy His presence. . . . There's nothing more important than sitting at His feet.

Every single circumstance we face is an opportunity to know Jesus in a fresh, new way. Hidden within every heartache and every joy is a revelation of Him. Are you hungry to know God better? Do you want to fulfill the purpose He created you for? Then go at life with this perspective. As you reflect on the obstacles you are facing today, ask the Lord, "What are you trying to teach me here? What aspect of who you are is being revealed to me right now?" Then listen for His gentle guidance.

Day Three
HE KNOWS YOU WERE MADE FOR MORE

Jesus knows that you were made for more than self-centered living. Because He created you, He knows what will ultimately satisfy and fulfill you. That *more* you are longing for is Jesus. So He offers you His friendship.

But let's be real here—it's hard to understand how to have a friendship with someone you can't see or touch. Without meaning to, you may end up developing a relationship with "imaginary friend Jesus."

In the words of Father Dwight Longenecker, the "Jesus" you are having a relationship with may simply be "a projection of [your] own desires, [your] own culture or values, goals and dreams of [your] own context . . . The real Jesus is bigger and more dangerous than your pleasant emotional experiences."[11]

---

[11] Dwight Longenecker, "A Personal Relationship with Jesus," Patheos.com, http://www.patheos.com/blogs/standingonmyhead/a-personal-relationship-with-jesus.

The only way we are going to experience the *more* we were created for is if we forge a relationship with the real Jesus. The following verses will point us in the right direction to do just that.

1. A. What will we do if we are truly Jesus' friends? See John 15:14.

    B. How would you summarize Jesus' commands? See Matthew 22:37–38.

2. Scripture makes it clear that Jesus isn't content with "Christmas card friends." He wants the real thing. Friendship with Jesus requires following hard after Him. How is this described in Luke 9:23?

When you are friends with Jesus, He shows up in every area of your life. And here's the hard truth: He doesn't really care whether or not everyone agrees with you, whether you feel comfortable, or whether you get every little thing your heart desires. He does care about where you spend your money, the words that come out of your mouth, and the attitudes in your heart. But more than anything, He is utterly consumed with love for you, and it's the real kind of love that truly wants you to *thrive*. That's why He gets into all those details of your life. He'd rather see you uncomfortable and passion filled than bored and purposeless.

3. When we hold an area of our life back from Jesus, when we say, "This is off-limits and stays under *my* control," we are very likely to miss out on something really beautiful that He has planned for us. Can you identify an area of your life that you are holding back from Jesus, that just might be holding you back from living the *more* you were created for?

Quiet your heart and enjoy His presence. . . . He longs to give you more than you can imagine.

In the classic book The Lion, the Witch and the Wardrobe, *Lucy is preparing to meet the lion, Aslan, who represents Jesus in the story. She's frightened at the thought, and asks Mr. Beaver if Aslan is safe. He replies: "Who said anything about being safe? 'Course he isn't safe. But he's good. He's the King, I tell you."*

The same could be said of Jesus. He isn't safe. But He's good. The life He leads us to isn't predictable, easy, or comfortable. But it is fulfilling, peace filled, and purposeful. The key word is full. *Being a friend of the real Jesus, following Him wherever He leads, always fills the emptiness that so many of us feel inside.*

Are you tired of feeling empty? Are you longing for purpose? Do you need something (or someone) to pull together the mess in your life and create something full of meaning? Then ask Jesus to give you more of Himself. This is a prayer He just waits to answer with a resounding yes.

Day Four
HE WANTS TO SPEND ETERNITY WITH YOU

Have you ever asked yourself, "Is this all there is?" Have you pursued the things you've been told matter most (a good degree, position, reputation, résumé, home, clothes, body, etc.) only to find that achieving them doesn't satisfy as much as you expected? These things weren't meant to satisfy us, because God knows that when we die, each and every one of them will disintegrate into nothingness. Make no mistake—just because you receive the world's applause doesn't mean you've made the right choices.

This is one of the things Jesus wants to teach us through a friendship with Him. He wants to lead us to the choices that ultimately satisfy and matter in eternity. The most important choice you will ever make is one for or against a relationship with Jesus. Nothing will impact your eternity more than this choice.

1. How is heaven described in John 14:2–3?

"Christ's words reveal that our destiny involves both a place and a person. The place is the Father's house, a place which will contribute to happiness; but being there comes from knowing a person—Christ Himself." —Keith Krell

2. According to John 3:16 and 5:24–29 (spoken by Jesus), how can we receive eternal life? What is the alternative?

Ralph Martin, President of Renewal Ministries, addresses this important decision with the following words:

> Christianity is not a game. It's not a literary theme designed to enrich us. It's not a philosophical puzzle for the intellectually inclined to ponder. It's a cry of love and warning from the God who made us, who sees the desperate predicament we're in because of our own sins, who has gone to incredible lengths to rescue us from that predicament, and who is urgently concerned that we not overlook the only means by which we can be saved. Why be a Christian? Because Christianity is the truth. Because without that truth, life makes no sense and has no meaning. Because becoming a Christian makes an eternal life-and-death difference to each of us.[12]

3. Jesus offers us eternal life as a gift, but it's up to us to receive it. Read Appendix 3, "Conversion of Heart." Have you experienced conversion of heart? Journal your thoughts below.

Quiet your heart and enjoy His presence. . . . There's no better time to surrender to the One who loves you and waits for you.

"The Lord does not delay his promise, as some regard delay, but he is patient with you, not wishing that any should perish but that all should come to repentance." (2 Peter 3:9)

---

[12] Ralph Martin, "Why Be a Christian?" ChristLife, http://christlife.com/resources/articles/whybeachrtn.html.

God is patient. He waits for us to accept His gift of eternal life. But He doesn't wait forever. Death comes to all of us at some point, and its timing is unpredictable. Jesus longs to spend eternity with you, and it's going to be so incredible there! It'll be worth any sacrifice made here.

". . . no eye has seen, nor ear heard, nor the heart of man conceived, what God has prepared for those who love him." (1 Corinthians 2:9) Will you offer Him your heart?

If you aren't ready to do that, perhaps you could start to pray every day, "Jesus, if you are real, please come and get me." He understands that you feel lost. He knows that finding Him in the midst of the confusion in your heart feels impossible. So invite Him to come. Ask Him to find you. This is a prayer He loves to answer, but you have to ask. No one can do it for you.

Day Five
SAINT'S STORY

Kateri Tekakwitha

Why is Jesus interested in raising lilies from thorns? And why does He care about the hidden stories of little souls?

It is because each of us is the Father's gift to the Son. Each of us is an unrepeatable, unique marvel of God's creation, forged in darkness. No matter how humble or undesirable our circumstances are by the world's standards, God loves us with an unquenchable, everlasting love.

Kateri Tekakwitha's story is a humble one, yet she experienced closeness to God and was honored by the Church by being canonized a saint. She was born in 1656 to a Mohawk chief and a Catholic Algonquin mother, but a smallpox epidemic left her orphaned, permanently scarred, and partially blind at the age of four. She was a hidden soul in many ways, often shielding herself under blankets from the mean stares of other villagers and from the harsh light of the sun.

She spent much time alone, working in the fields and tending to crops, or in the woods collecting firewood and roots for dyes and medicines. During this time she would lift her heart to God, listening for Him to speak through the rustling of the leaves. She experienced God's presence, and always found Him ready to talk with her and to comfort her in her distress.

She was baptized at the age of twenty, and incurred the wrath of the village for her faith. She refused to work on Sundays and was in turn refused food. Children threw stones, and she was threatened with torture if she did not renounce her faith. She endured this suffering nobly, offering her love for Christ, thinking of all that He had suffered to win her soul for heaven. Kateri Tekakwitha knew from a young age that Jesus Christ, Son of the Blessed Virgin Mary, was watching over her with a bridegroom's interest.

Eventually, she fled on a two-month journey two hundred miles away to the mission of Saint Francis Xavier in the Christian colony of Indians in Canada. There, she received her first Holy Communion, on Christmas Day 1677, and devoted her life to prayer, penance, and care for the weak. She did these tasks as acts of love to the One who loved her first. Living a life of pure love for Jesus is how she became known as the Lily of the Mohawks.

We wonder sometimes why Jesus is interested in our friendship, and why He cares for us in our littleness. We are not the great ones of the earth. We do not start wars or conquer nations. We do not command the multitudes. We are small. Our daily chores and fallen nature are struggle enough. And yet, we still dare to dream. We dream of a great and endless love; we dream of One who is always listening, who bends with infinite tenderness over our misery and washes away the ugliness we find in ourselves.

If you wonder why Jesus desires your friendship, ask Him. Ask Him in prayer before the Blessed Sacrament, where He lays down His life for you every day, hidden in the silence and darkness of the tabernacle. Ask Him. And listen. And do it every day.

Kateri Tekakwitha lived a short life, dying at the age of twenty-four. But in that time she learned that Jesus desires not just our friendship, but our love. He wants to take care of us and claim us for Himself. Each flower, no matter how small, has a secret center that belongs to God alone. It is already His, and it always will be His. If we surrender and open up to Him, we will come to understand what He told us about the lilies of the field: "Not even Solomon in all his splendor was robed like one of these." (Matthew 6:29)

What did Saint Kateri Tekakwitha do to discover Jesus' desire for her friendship? What can you learn from her life to experience a similar discovery?

Conclusion

"Why would the Creator of the universe be interested in friendship with me? I'm not a person with power and great influence. Why does He care about me?"

To understand why God pursues friendship with you, it's necessary to recognize what He sees when He looks at you. He doesn't see someone of insignificance. He sees the masterpiece that He created. He sees His precious daughter.

What an incredible honor it is that the One who holds the world in His hands, who knows all and controls all, cares about every detail of your life. Not only does He know you completely; He wants to be known by you. He wants an intimate friendship. He has proven what a trustworthy friend He is. He gave up everything for you.

" . . . though he was in the form of God, he did not regard equality with God something to be grasped. Rather, he emptied himself, taking the form of a slave, coming in human likeness; and found human in appearance, he humbled himself, becoming obedient to death, even death on a cross." (Philippians 2:6–8)

Jesus became one of us in order to be the bridge to connect us to God. Other religions are characterized by man reaching up to God. Only in Christianity does God reach down to man.

If we could only see ourselves through the eyes of God, never losing sight of His unconditional love for us, how amazing our lives would be! We would do everything with the right motive: out of gratitude for all He has given us. We wouldn't spend so much time trying to please all the different people in our lives, living for their approval. We wouldn't constantly search for fulfillment through shopping, food, or pleasure. Jesus would be enough.

This is my prayer for you (and me!): That you, "rooted and grounded in love, may have strength to comprehend with all the holy ones what is the breadth and length and height and depth, and to know the love of Christ that surpasses knowledge, so that you may be filled with all the fullness of God." (Ephesians 3:17–19)

My Resolution

In what specific way will I apply what I have learned in this lesson?

"'For I know the plans I have for you,' declares the Lord, 'plans to prosper you and not to harm you, plans to give you hope and a future.'" (Jeremiah 29:11)

Examples:

1. I'll tape an index card with the verse Jeremiah 29:11 on the dashboard of my car to remind me throughout the day of this important truth.

2. Each time I wash my hair, I'll remember that "the very hairs on [my] head are all numbered" by Him (Luke 12:7) and will dwell on God's personal love for me.

3. Knowing that Jesus desires my friendship and wants to spend time with me, I'll do my lesson each day, using it as a springboard to prayer, instead of rushing through the whole lesson in one sitting.

My Resolution:

Catechism Clips

CCC 220 God's love is "everlasting": "For the mountains may depart and the hills be removed, but my steadfast love shall not depart from you." Through Jeremiah, God declares to his people, "I have loved you with an everlasting love; therefore I have continued my faithfulness to you."

CCC 221 But St. John goes even further when he affirms that "God is love": God's very being is love. By sending his only Son and the Spirit of Love in the fullness of time, God has revealed his innermost secret: God himself is an eternal exchange of love, Father, Son, and Holy Spirit, and he has destined us to share in that exchange.

Lesson 4

WHY AND HOW SHOULD I PRAY?

Introduction

When faced with a decision, do you like to run your thoughts by a friend to receive her input? I have a close friend, Janet, who is so amazing at decorating—especially picking out paint colors—that I can't make a decision in my house without her seal of approval. If I want her advice about something as simple as the color of my kitchen walls, you can be sure that I like to talk through big decisions with her as well.

Can you imagine how your relationship with a friend would diminish if you never spoke to her? As women, we need to share our hearts with one another—our concerns, our joys, our hopes—if we want our friendships to deepen. In that same way, we need to spend quality time talking to God, or our relationship with Him will remain shallow and we'll miss out on the incredible guidance He offers.

I remember sitting in Sunday school as a little girl, holding a plastic telephone, along with each of the other children in my class. "Prayer is just picking up the telephone and giving Jesus a call," the teacher said. "He's your best friend, and He always wants to hear from you. I promise you'll never get a busy signal!" We would then all practice picking up the phone and giving Jesus a call.

Sometimes we think that prayer is something we have to be good at in order to do it, when actually, it's one of those things we learn by doing regularly. Although there is great value in reading about prayer, ultimately, we need to just "pick up the phone" and have a conversation with God. He doesn't need us to impress Him with big words and eloquent phrases. It isn't about how articulate we are. We can come messy and just be ourselves.

While it's the time we spend in prayer that transforms us, unfortunately all sorts of things make it hard for us to pray. In this lesson, we'll look at three of these difficulties and explore ways we can get past them to grow in our friendship with Christ.

Day One
DIFFICULTY NO. 1: "I AM TOO BUSY TO PRAY"

Do you ever feel you just can't find the time to pray? We're so busy, and although prayer sounds good in theory and we have a strong sense that we'd be better people if we did more of it, we get up and get moving and there doesn't seem to be any room in the day to slow down and talk to God.

That's the reason we often give for not praying. But I don't believe it's truly the underlying issue. I'm not saying that our schedules aren't busy. I just believe that we make time for whatever is important to us. If I'm honest, when I don't pray, it's usually because I simply don't feel like it. There's something else that I'd rather do. I think I'm going to feel more satisfied by doing something else.

If we want to be transformed into the women God created us to be, we need to explore what's holding us back from prayer. Let's be real and dig deep.

1. What obstacles most often keep you from praying?

   Time

2. What role do your feelings play in your prayer life? Are they important? Why or why not?

Our feelings will always encourage us to do what's comfortable. But true love isn't always comfortable. Authentic love often requires doing something *despite* our feelings. This is true of all human relationships, and it's true of our relationship with God.

3. According to CCC 2725, why is prayer a "battle," and why is it worth fighting through the barriers to pray?

Quiet your heart and enjoy His presence. . . . He is near to all who call on Him. (Psalm 145:18)

We live in a culture that values productivity, results, and performance. Because prayer, just like love, can't be measured in that way, it's tempting to put it on the back burner. Sometimes it just feels more satisfying to check some things off the to-do list than to sit quietly in prayer.

Whether or not we feel like praying should not determine whether we pray. We shouldn't pray to get something from God; we should pray simply in order to be with Him. Our willingness (or unwillingness) to "waste" time with Him says a lot about how much we love Him.

Dear Lord,

I want to love you more, I truly do. But if I'm honest, spending time sitting with you is hard. I can't see you. I can't feel you. I ask you a question and I only hear silence. This holds my attention for about ten seconds. Help me to switch my thinking regarding prayer. Help me to see that even if I don't feel like I'm having a mind-blowing spiritual experience, you are just excited that I'm turning my face toward yours. This is a little hard for me to believe. Do you honestly love me so much that my attention means that much to you? If I believe what the Bible says, then I have to believe that yes, this is how much you love me. Help me to love you in return with the gift of my time.

Day Two
DIFFICULTY NO. 2: "I WANT TO BE SELF-SUFFICIENT"

I hate to be weak and dependent. When a friend brings dinner to my family, I want to pay her back quickly with a favor so that things aren't uneven. Feeling indebted makes me feel like I can't get my act together. The irony is that one of my top love languages[13] is "acts of service." So the very thing that makes me feel loved makes me feel like I need to balance the scales. It's a little messed up.

This desire to be self-sufficient bleeds into my relationship with God. I want to come to Him cleaned up, like a member of His A-team, the one He can count on to bring home the win. Left unchecked, this strong tendency of mine really gets in the way of a fruitful prayer life and blocks me from experiencing His love. I'll never fully give God

---

[13] *The 5 Love Languages* is a great book by Gary Chapman. In it, he outlines the five primary ways we express our love: physical touch, acts of service, quality time, words of affirmation, and gifts. The premise of the book is that the way we express love is the way we want it expressed to us. We can love someone in our love language, but if the other person's love language is different, he or she won't feel the love being expressed as much as we'd like.

my heart (which is what He wants more than anything) if I don't know He loves me and is for me. So clearly, this prayer difficulty is an important one to work through.

1. A. Why is self-sufficiency such a block to a vibrant prayer life?
    See Matthew 18:1–4.

    B. What are qualities found in children that you think please Jesus?

2. What childlike quality of prayer is described in Luke 11:5–8 and 18:1–8?

Why did the friend who needed bread and the widow who needed justice receive what they asked for? Was it because of their strength? No. It was because of their weakness and desperation. They were so needy that they asked, and asked, and asked. They knew, beyond a doubt, that help could be given, that power was there, and they determined not to give up until they received what they hoped for. When we come to God in weakness and desperation, He can't but help us. He knows exactly what will help us, and He has the power to do it. Don't give up. Keep asking. Don't quit praying just before the miracle happens.

3. When children ask for what they need, they ask *big*. They ask with boldness. God wants our prayers to be filled with the faith that believes the impossible can happen, because when we tame them we are saying that God isn't all that powerful, or that He doesn't really care about our dreams and our needs. This kind of attitude saddens His heart. He wants us to bring our most audacious hopes and passions and our deepest hurts and disappointments and confidently ask for His power to pour out, for the miracle to come.

The alternative to praying big things is to reduce what we're dreaming of to something small enough that we think we can accomplish it on our own. This absolutely robs God of the chance to show us just how wonderful, powerful, creative, and amazing He is.

So what are your dreams? What are your big, audacious hopes? What are three things well beyond your reach that you wish would come true? List them here, and turn those hopes and dreams into a prayer. Ask God to do the impossible for you.

Quiet your heart and enjoy His presence. . . . Your prayers are evidence of your confidence in God.

"Ask and it will be given to you; seek and you will find; knock and the door will be opened to you. For everyone who asks, receives; and the one who seeks, finds; and to the one who knocks, the door will be opened. Which one of you would hand his son a stone when he asks for a loaf of bread, or a snake when he asks for a fish? If you then, who are wicked, know how to give good gifts to your children, how much more will your heavenly Father give good things to those who ask him." (Matthew 7:7–11)

Our heavenly Father is the giver of all good things, and He delights to give. He encourages us to ask, seek, and knock, and He waits to shower us with just what we need. It's important to note that this passage does not say that no matter what we ask for, we will get it. He says He'll "give good things to those who ask him." He knows better than we do what we truly need, and what the best timing is for us to receive those good gifts.

Let's not miss out on any of the blessings God is ready and waiting to give us. "Let us confidently approach the throne of grace to receive mercy and to find grace for timely help." (Hebrews 4:16)

Take some time to ask God for what you need. Don't forfeit a blessing just because you never prayed about it or you gave up too soon.

Day Three
DIFFICULTY NO. 3: "I'VE GIVEN UP HOPE"

It can be hard to hope. Have you ever prayed for something and believed with all your heart that God would come through for you? And then you waited. And all you heard was silence. And all you felt was discouragement. And the promise in John 14:14 ("Ask anything of me in my name, I will do it") started to feel like a cruel joke, a bait and switch.

When this has been our experience, many of us allow our hearts to grow a little bit cynical. We don't want to be naive. We're smarter than that. We can see the obstacles. We're very good at assessing our reality, and adjusting our expectations accordingly. We've decided that it's better not to get our hopes up, so our prayers become stale or nonexistent. Spiritually, we are just going through the motions.

In the words of Paul E. Miller, author of *A Praying Life*, "It's a short trip from determination to despair, when you realize that you aren't going to change the situation, no matter what you do. It hurts to hope in the face of continued failure, so you try to stop hurting by giving up on hope."[14]

If this is where you are, then you might have had a really hard time answering question 3 on Day Two. I understand what that feels like. I've been there. It's very hard to reopen a dream when you've spent a while lowering your expectations. Just as I said in Quiet Your Heart on Day Two, God doesn't promise to give us whatever we want whenever we want it. But I believe that when we have given up hope, it isn't just an issue of us learning to deal with disappointment. We run the risk of developing an inaccurate view of the heart of the Father. We start to think that He's holding out on us instead of lavishly loving us.

1. I realize that when we talk about unanswered prayers, we are treading on sacred ground. This is the place where hearts lie shattered, and tenderness is needed. But even as I say that, I think it's important to share an essential truth: At the core of our disappointment lies a lack of gratitude. True, God has not given what was specifically asked for. But what *has* He given? Read the following verses and what God has given in each.

   John 3:16

   Ephesians 1:7

   Ephesians 1:13

---

[14] Paul E. Miller, *A Praying Life: Connecting with God in a Distracting World* (Colorado Springs: NavPress, 2009), 182.

1 Peter 1:3–4

I could list pages of Scripture references that would reflect even more gifts from God, but I think you get the point. Please know that when I have you look up those passages, I am preaching these truths to myself, as well. All too often, I forget or take these things for granted.

In a season of my life when I had given up hope, God led me to a Bible verse that pierced my heart. As I read Galatians 4:15, I felt He was speaking to me. It read, "What has happened to all your joy?" It stopped me in my tracks, because I knew that my joy was *gone*. And I thought about people who had so much less than I, yet simply having salvation through Christ was enough to fill them with gratitude. And I knew something was wrong, and the one with the problem wasn't God.

2. The best antidote to lack of hope is a cultivated spirit of gratitude. The key word is *cultivated*, because gratitude doesn't come naturally to most of us. We have to actively look for evidence of His grace at work in our lives. Take some time to write down the ways in which God has taken care of you and blessed you (in ways you might be taking for granted).

Quiet your heart and enjoy His presence. . . . Cast your hopelessness at His feet.

Come to God in your need. Ask for His help to grow in gratitude. Allow His words to become your own. When you pray the words of Scripture, you are praying God's heart back to Him. Take the following personalized versions of these Bible verses and turn them into prayers.

Dear Lord, "Restore to me the joy of my salvation." (Psalm 51:12, RSV)

"May You, the God of hope, fill me with all joy and peace in believing, so that I may abound in hope by the power of the Holy Spirit." (Romans 15:13)

"May the eyes of my heart be enlightened, that I may know what is the hope that belongs to Your call, what are the riches of glory in Your inheritance among the holy ones, and what is the surpassing greatness of Your power for me who believes." (Ephesians 1:18–19)

Lord, "I do believe, help my unbelief." (Mark 9:24)

Day Four
PRAY BOLDLY. SURRENDER COMPLETELY.

1. After reading Matthew 19:26, what do you think Jesus would have to say about hesitant, doubt-filled, tame prayers?

When we pray boldly, it isn't because we see God as a genie in a bottle who exists to do our bidding or to ensure our personal comfort. We pray boldly because in doing so, we are acknowledging that there is absolutely nothing that God can't do. The question is not *can* He answer the prayer in this way, but *will He choose* to answer the prayer in this way. This brings us to the second point: Surrender completely.

2. In Mark 14:35–36, how did Jesus model praying boldly yet surrendering completely?

3. When we surrender to God's will in prayer, we are following Christ's example. What's another reason this is an important way to pray? See Isaiah 55:8.

Quiet your heart and enjoy His presence. . . . Let your desires be shaped by Him.

"From the end of the earth will I cry unto thee, when my heart is overwhelmed; lead me to the rock that is higher than I." (Psalm 61:2)

There is a rock higher than you. His thoughts are not your thoughts, and His ways are not your ways. But He is not distant. He is very near, and utterly attentive to your cry. He hopes that you will pray big and bold prayers. He hopes that you will see His limitless power, and ask accordingly. But at the same time, He hopes you are able to humbly recognize that you don't have a mind equal to His. You are finite, and He knows better than you what is best.

Can you trust that your heavenly Father knows what is best for you? This is such an important question—so essential to our prayer life that it's included in the Compendium of the Catechism of the Catholic Church, *575: "Filial trust is tested when we think we are not heard. We must therefore ask ourselves if we think God is truly a Father whose will we seek to fulfill, or simply a means to obtain what we want. If our prayer is united to that of Jesus, we know that He gives us much more than this or that gift. We receive the Holy Spirit who transforms our heart."*

In Psalm 37:4, we read the promise: "Take delight in the Lord, and he will give you the desires of your heart." Something very interesting happens when we delight in the Lord when we pray. The very desires that God wants us to have are birthed in our souls. Slowly but truly, we become more like Jesus as we begin to want what He wants, when He wants it, how He wants it. We are changed. We are transformed.

Take some time to share your desires with the Lord. Dream wildly. Pray boldly. But never lose sight of the fact that your heavenly Father loves you, and will only give you good gifts. And only He knows which gifts are the best.

Day Five
SAINT'S STORY

Saint Elizabeth of Portugal Rules from Her Knees

Prayer is simply speaking with God or, as Saint Teresa of Ávila put it, having a conversation with the "one who I know loves me." We can pray in the midst of our other activities simply by lifting our hearts and minds to God, thanking Him for His blessings, and asking for His help. But since our relationship with Jesus really is a *relationship*, we also need to spend quality time exclusively with the Lord, reflecting on His Word, letting Him pour His grace gently into our minds and hearts, and contemplating His goodness. When Jesus told us to "Seek first the Kingdom of God and his righteousness, and all these other things will be given to you as well," (Matthew 6:33) that's what He meant. If we put God first (which is what prayer is all about), He will guide us in all things and make our lives into beautiful works of art. Saint Elizabeth of Portugal exemplified this truth in a remarkable way.

Elizabeth lived in the 1300s. She was the daughter of a Spanish king, and as a child, she lapped up the lessons of self-discipline, modesty, and elegance that were taught in her father's court. She learned to be a model Catholic princess, though she learned it through simple, ordinary means. She was taught to conscientiously care for her appearance, since she was the daughter of a king (and of the King), but never to flaunt her beauty, lest she become proud or lead men into sin. She learned self-control and self-discipline by abstaining from spontaneous snacks and following a detailed daily schedule. She learned love for God and for her neighbor by participating in works of charity and in the sacred liturgy from a very young age.

When she was twelve she was married to the King of Portugal (Denis was his name), who admired her beauty and nobility of birth much more than her virtue. Denis was a cruel and unfaithful husband, but Elizabeth loved him with Christian charity and served with undying devotion, hoping and praying constantly for his return to a life of grace, and bathing him in cheerful and sincere attention. She ran the royal household with such generosity and good sense that Denis was free to dedicate himself entirely to putting his realm in order, and he was an effective ruler. Elizabeth found time to give constant service to the poor, and even to defuse political powder kegs. Twice, in fact, she rode right out into the middle of battlefields to reconcile opposing forces. When Denis died after a long illness, through which Elizabeth nursed him unwearyingly, she longed to retire into a convent of Poor Clares that she had built, but she was convinced she was to remain engaged in court life, much to the benefit of her children and other relations—not to mention the people of her country.

When we hear about such extraordinary Christians as Saint Elizabeth of Portugal, sometimes we can think that they were just born that way. But Saint Elizabeth's secret was found somewhere else—in her simple but constant and sincere prayer life. She regularly rose early enough to begin her day with morning prayer and meditation, and went to daily Mass as often as she could, receiving Holy Communion regularly. And in the evening, in spite of her obligations and duties, both pleasant and unpleasant, as queen, she always made time to spend another ten or twenty minutes in her private oratory, speaking with the Lord about her family, her affairs, and His divine will for her life.

Prayer is not complicated, which is why children understand it so spontaneously. What's complicated is convincing ourselves that God really does deserve first place in our lives. As Saint John Chrysostom taught, "Nothing is equal to prayer; for what is impossible, it makes possible; what is difficult, easy. . . . For it is impossible, utterly impossible, for the man who prays eagerly and invokes God ceaselessly ever to sin." (CCC 2744)

How can Saint Elizabeth's model of a simple, constant, and sincere prayer life help your own prayer life?

Conclusion

"Whoever remains in me and I in him will bear much fruit, because without me you can do nothing." (John 15:5)

There is such a difference between a faraway, impersonal God and the One who remains within our hearts offering us a personal relationship with Him.

I see the difference, but I don't always live it. I have spent far too many days worrying and anxious. I can spend a ton of time and energy concerned about everything that I have to do, making lists and feeling exhausted simply anticipating what is to come. At other times, I simply lay it all out in front of God in prayer, asking that He will engineer events, making the crooked places straight and giving me the energy and help I need one day at a time. It's amazing how much easier everything becomes when I let my schedule "remain in Him."

I have found that I cannot remain in Him throughout the day unless that is how I have started it. The beginning of my day sets the tone for the rest of it. One of the first times I was exposed to the importance of starting my day with some time remaining in Christ was when I read a book called *Disciplines of the Beautiful Woman*. The author, Anne Ortlund, had a wonderfully organized desk, purse, closet, life . . . and her book told her readers how they could duplicate that organization in their lives. Anne showered each morning and then went to a coffee shop, where a person could see the real secret of her life. Not a day went by when she didn't begin with prayer and Bible reading, remaining in Christ. While I really wanted to be able to emulate her self-discipline, I remember thinking, "Well, wouldn't that be great if I had time to go to a coffee shop each morning! I've got kids who wake up sometimes before six, who need me constantly. I'm exhausted. Do I need to get up at four a.m. in order to remain in Christ?"

The answer is no. You don't have to go to a coffee shop daily, nor do you need to give up all your sleep. But you can watch for the first quiet opportunity. There have been times in my life when I could get up at six a.m. daily and have an hour alone with God. There have been seasons, especially when I was nursing a new baby, when I desperately needed my sleep. I would then look for the first spot of quiet and claim it for God—not for phone calls, cleaning, or TV. I wasn't always able to set a specific time, but I learned to watch for a pocket of quiet, recognize it when it came along, and reserve it for God.

Building a stronger friendship with Christ through prayer does take time, but don't get discouraged if you are in a season of life when time alone seems elusive. We can also take time to pray when our children are with us! A friend of mine shared the story of how her mother taught her to pray through her example: "Anytime we were anywhere near a church, she'd say, 'Let's pop in and say hi to Jesus.' When we were little, she'd tell us to kneel down in front of the tabernacle and blow Him a kiss. As we got older, she'd encourage us to tell Him we loved Him. Start to finish, it was probably three minutes long; it never felt like an inconvenience. In high school and college, the first place I'd go when I needed help was to the adoration chapel or the church. I didn't know what I was going to say, but I just knew that was where I needed to go."

One of the most esteemed sons of the Church, Brother Lawrence, has a lot to teach us about finding time to pray when taking care of all that life demands of us. When he would go to the kitchen to begin his duties as a cook with the Carmelite monks, he would pray, "Oh, my God, since thou art with me, and I must now, in obedience to thy commands, apply my mind to these outward things, I beseech thee to grant me the grace to continue in thy presence; and to this end do thou prosper me with thy assistance."

Was Brother Lawrence praying while attending Mass? No. He was communing with God in the midst of washing dishes. He went on to write, "And in the noise and clatter of my kitchen, while several persons are at the same time calling for different things, I possess God in as great tranquility as if I were upon my knees at the Blessed Sacrament."[15] Also, he asked God to give him "grace to continue" to remain in Christ. He didn't try to do it in his own strength; he understood the pointlessness of it, just as it says in John 15:4: "As the branch cannot bear fruit by itself, unless it abides in the vine, neither can you, unless you abide in me."

Do you find it hard to pray? Is it a struggle to find the time? Ask God to help you. He is always listening and calling to your heart.

---

[15] Brother Lawrence, *The Practice of the Presence of God* (Old Tappan, NJ: Revell, 1958), 9.

My Resolution

In what specific way will I apply what I have learned in this lesson?

Examples:

1. I will set my alarm fifteen minutes earlier so that I can *get up* (praying in bed doesn't tend to go so well) and pray before distractions get in the way of my time with God.

2. This week I will look for an extra opportunity to pray, perhaps while I am in the car, taking a shower, or washing the dishes.

3. When I sit down to pray, I'll make sure my cell phone is somewhere else, because it's such a distraction.

My Resolution:

Catechism Clips

Note: Both Catechism Clips are from the *Compendium of the Catechism of the Catholic Church*.

575. How may we strengthen our filial trust?
Filial trust is tested when we think we are not heard. We must therefore ask ourselves if we think God is truly a Father whose will we seek to fulfill, or simply a means to obtain what we want. If our prayer is united to that of Jesus, we know that He gives us much more than this or that gift. We receive the Holy Spirit who transforms our heart.

2725. Why is prayer a "battle"?
Prayer is a gift of grace, but it always presupposes a determined response on our part because those who pray "battle" against themselves, their surroundings, and especially the Tempter who does all he can to turn them away from prayer. The battle of prayer is inseparable from progress in the spiritual life. We pray as we live because we live as we pray. Prayer increases our trust in God.

NOTES

Lesson 5: Connect Coffee Talk
GOD – FIRST PLACE IN ALL THINGS

Accompanying DVD can be viewed by disc or please visit our website at walkingwithpurpose.com/videos and select *Opening Your Heart* Bible Study, click through to select Videos.

Key verse:

"He is also head of the body, the church; and He is the beginning, the firstborn from the dead, so that He Himself will come to have first place in everything."
(Colossians 1:18)

Put God first when . . .

1. **You don't know if you trust Him.**

2. **You're tired and weary.**

   A. Don't rely on your emotions.

   B. Rest in the understanding that God loves and accepts you.

   C. Remember, you are the glove; He is the hand.

3. **Life isn't what you thought it would be.**

   A. Jesus weeps with us.

   B. God never gives us more than we can endure.

   C. Our hearts must avoid ingratitude.

4. **You have a crazy busy life.**

QUESTIONS FOR DISCUSSION

1. What do you most hope to get out of Walking with Purpose this year?

2. What is keeping you from making God the highest priority in your life? Is it a lack of trust? Is it weariness? Is it disappointment in what life has dealt you? Is it because you are so busy that even though you love God in your heart, you fail to love Him in your schedule? Which of these four areas are hardest for you?

3. What commitment could you make for the next thirty days in order to allow God to become a higher priority in your life?

Lesson 6

WHO IS THE HOLY SPIRIT?

Introduction

Are you distressed today?
Are you facing a major decision?
Do you need relief from your responsibilities?
Do you have a broken relationship?
Do you find yourself falling into the same patterns of sin again and again?

I remember well a period of my life when I was overwhelmed with loneliness. I had moved as a young bride to Germany, leaving behind family, friends, a language I understood, and all things familiar. My husband traveled Monday through Friday, and I sat at home, nauseated with morning sickness. It was during this time that I began to really get to know the third person of the Trinity, the Holy Spirit.

I had not learned to fully appreciate Him until He was my only companion throughout the day. I couldn't afford to talk to my mom on the phone whenever I felt like it. But I could pick up a phone spiritually and talk to God whenever I needed or wanted to. I didn't feel like I was accomplishing anything in terms of a career or moving forward in building my new life overseas, but I was able to devote many hours to studying Scripture and growing in that area of my life. I didn't have access to wonderful Bible teachers or exciting Sunday homilies, but the Holy Spirit was a wonderful teacher, and I learned how to study the Bible and hear God's voice while I sat alone in my home. When Jesus promised the disciples that He was going to send the Holy Spirit to them, He described the Spirit as "the paraclete." The translation of *paraclete* is "he who is called to one's side" and "consoler." (CCC 692) When I opened my heart to Christ, He in turn sent the One who was called to my side. He consoled me in my loneliness and never left me.

Perhaps God is working in your life right now in the midst of circumstances that really hurt. Could it be that you now have an opportunity to get to know the Holy

Spirit on a more personal level as you come face-to-face with your loneliness, your emptiness, or your brokenness, and your need of Him?

Day One
GOD'S PERSONAL BREATH

Before we delve into what we can learn about the Holy Spirit, it's important to understand that we will never completely figure Him out. He is God, the third person of the Trinity. He can't be put in a little box of a definition and tied with a bow of complete understanding. As it says in Deuteronomy 29:28 NAB, "The hidden things belong to the Lord our God." We have to accept that we'll never comprehend the hidden things. But the second part of the verse offers encouragement for us: "But the revealed things are for us and for our children forever." So we're going to study the revealed things that are ours. God has made these things known to us and wants us to know the Holy Spirit so He can help us grow closer to Him and more like His Son.

1. Is the Holy Spirit equal to God the Father and Jesus? See CCC 685. Note: The word *consubstantial* means "of the same substance or essence."

2. Let's take a look at the Holy Spirit's first appearance in the Bible. What action took place in Genesis 1:2?

The phrase used in this passage, "a mighty wind," is a translation of the Hebrew word *ruah*. According to CCC 691, "The term 'Spirit' translates the Hebrew word *ruah*, which in its primary sense, means breath, air, wind. Jesus indeed uses the sensory image of the wind [to describe] him who is personally God's breath, the divine Spirit." This means that just before the world was created, the Holy Spirit was sweeping over the unformed earth, breathing over and stirring the waters. He was there at the very beginning and was fully involved in creation.

3. One could certainly describe God as a long-term planner. Even in the moment that Adam and Eve sinned, God was preparing to launch His rescue plan.[16] Exactly how the rescue would take place and who specifically would be the Savior (the Messiah) wasn't clear to the people of the Old Testament. This "hiddenness" is described in CCC 702: "From the beginning until 'the fullness of time,'[17] the joint mission of the Father's Word [Jesus] and [the Holy] Spirit remains *hidden*, but it is at work. God's Spirit prepares for the time of the Messiah."

As the Holy Spirit continued to work in "hidden" ways, the people of the Old Testament waited and watched for the promised rescue—for the arrival of the Messiah. The Holy Spirit was at work, filling particular people to empower them for specific things. Bezalel was filled with the Holy Spirit, giving him supernatural artistic and creative ability to make the temple beautiful (Exodus 31:1–5). Gideon "was clothed with the spirit of the LORD" (Judges 6:34) to give him the strength and leadership skills needed for victory in battle. The Holy Spirit filled the prophet Isaiah so he could speak God's words prophetically to God's people (Isaiah 61:1–3). The Holy Spirit filled specific people for specific tasks, but His filling was not there for the asking. The average follower of God had no access to the Holy Spirit.

The Holy Spirit continued the hidden work of preparing God's people for their Messiah. A foundation had been laid and God had taught countless lessons about what it meant to be in His family. After that long period of preparation, something totally new was promised. Read the following Old Testament prophecies regarding what was to come for God's people. Describe the promise and record what you think they might have felt hearing these words:

"I will give you a new heart, and a new spirit I will put within you. I will remove the heart of stone from your flesh and give you a heart of flesh. I will put my spirit within you so that you walk in my statutes, observe my ordinances, and keep them." (Ezekiel 36:26–27)[18]

---

[16] See Genesis 3:15 for this first prophecy about God's rescue of His people. This is called the protoevangelium—the first Gospel.

[17] This is a description used for the time when Jesus came to earth in human form (the Incarnation).

[18] I realize Ezekiel is a very difficult book to find. I promise you, it is in there. (I bought Bible indexing tabs and it makes all this flipping around the Bible *much* easier.)

"It shall come to pass, I will pour out my spirit upon all flesh. Your sons and daughters will prophesy, your old men will dream dreams, your young men will see visions. Even upon your male and female servants, in those days, I will pour out my spirit." (Joel 3:1–2, NAB)

Quiet your heart and enjoy His presence. . . . Let the breath of heaven surround you.

I wonder if you feel a little bit like the Old Testament followers of God felt. Do you look at the Holy Spirit as someone reserved for the special few, those somehow marked by God for a mission and a purpose that you think must not include you? Does He feel out of reach? If that's the case, listen to these words:

"Through his grace, the Holy Spirit is the first to awaken faith in us and to communicate to us the new life, which is to 'know the Father and the one whom he has sent, Jesus Christ.'" (CCC 684)

Do you know what this means? It means that if you are seeking God, if you feel faith beginning to awaken in your heart, you can be assured that the Spirit's breath is near. He is wooing you to come closer. He wants you. Can you take a little step nearer to Him by sharing with Him your needs? Ask Him to fill your emptiness with Himself.

Day Two
THE HUMBLE UNVEILING

God had promised that He was going to pour His Holy Spirit into the hearts of His people, but the waiting continued. These prophecies remained unfulfilled for at least three hundred years. Why so long? We are told in Galatians 4:4, "when the fullness of time had come, God sent his Son." God alone knew the perfect time for Jesus' arrival. During that perfect time when God became man—when Emmanuel, *God with us,* arrived—the Holy Spirit became very active. This stirring of the Spirit indicated something big was coming.

1. Read the following verses and describe the Holy Spirit's activity.

Luke 1:15 (This verse is describing John the Baptist, whose life's mission was to point the way to Jesus.)

Luke 1:34–35

Luke 3:21–22

2. Read CCC 687, and underline every phrase that refers to the Holy Spirit's actions and purpose. Then circle any phrase that reveals the Holy Spirit's humility.

"No one comprehends the thoughts of God except the Spirit of God." Now God's Spirit, who reveals God, makes known to us Christ, his Word, his living Utterance, but the Spirit does not speak of himself. The Spirit who "has spoken through the prophets" makes us hear the Father's Word, but we do not hear the Spirit himself. We know him only in the movement by which he reveals the Word to us and disposes us to welcome him in faith. The Spirit of truth who "unveils" Christ to us "will not speak on his own." Such properly divine self-effacement explains why "the world cannot receive [him], because it neither sees him nor knows him," while those who believe in Christ know the Spirit because he dwells with them.

3. John the Baptist; Mary, the Blessed Mother; and Jesus all were filled with the Holy Spirit. Read the following verses and describe each one of them according to the passage.

John the Baptist: John 3:30

Mary, the Blessed Mother: Luke 1:47–48

Jesus: Philippians 2:6–8

Which character quality of the Holy Spirit do you see reflected in each one of them?

4. If you are looking for evidence of the Holy Spirit's presence, then look for humility. We can achieve great things (in both the secular and the spiritual realm), but the mark of the Holy Spirit isn't achievement or fame. When the Holy Spirit is the One at work, everything will point to Christ. *He* will be unveiled. *He* will be the One lifted up.

    This sounds good in theory, but in reality, human nature resists this kind of self-effacement. Sure, it's easy to *say* that we want Christ to be center stage, but then we work behind the scenes to ensure that we are noticed a little bit, too.

    Ann Voskamp, author of the *New York Times* best seller *One Thousand Gifts*, knows what it feels like to be noticed and suddenly listened to with great interest. But she points us all toward the path of humility with these words:

    > No one is meant to stand really on platforms. Sure, everyone's got a platform under them—every artist, every businessperson, every person with a message, a service, a product, a community. And the movers and shakers would have us thinking that a platform is what elevates your visibility above the crowd so your message finds its audience. But there's a deeper current of Truth running through the cosmos: "He must increase, but I must decrease." A platform is whatever one finds under one's self—and the only thing that is meant to be under a Christian is an altar. The only call on a Christian is not to pick up a microphone, not to pick some stairs to some higher platform, but to pick up a cross . . . The only call on a Christian is to build every platform into the shape of an altar, to shape every platform into the form of sacrificial service.[19]

---

[19] Ann Voskamp, "Every Platform an Altar," The High Calling, http://www.thehighcalling.org/articles/daily-reflection/every-platform-altar.

And when we see sacrificial service pouring out of someone who doesn't ask to be noticed, we are seeing the Holy Spirit at work. Christ is being humbly unveiled in the life of His servant.

Humility doesn't come naturally to us. In which area of your life is this a struggle? Where are you wishing your contribution would be noticed or recognized? Where are you finding it hard to serve sacrificially?

Quiet your heart and enjoy His presence. . . . He is meek and humble of heart. (Matthew 11:29)

The Holy Spirit is meek and humble, and He will not force His way into your heart. Revelation 3:20 says that He "stand[s] at the door and knock[s]. If anyone hears [His] voice and opens the door, then [He] will enter." He waits to be invited in.

If we do invite Him in, one of the things the Holy Spirit does is search our hearts. One of the reasons He does this is to know how best to pray for us. So often we are blind to what is going on inside us. We're pretty quick to justify our actions, but the Holy Spirit searches us, and intercedes for us based on what we truly need. "And the one who searches hearts . . . intercedes for the holy ones according to God's will." (Romans 8:27)

Will you open the door and invite the Holy Spirit in? Will you ask Him to search your heart and bring to the surface things that you might not recognize within yourself? I promise you, as He reveals them, He'll do so gently. And then He'll be right there, giving you the strength and the courage to ask for forgiveness. And He'll provide all you need for transformation in the very areas of your greatest struggle. Invite Him in.

Day Three
CLOTHED WITH POWER

While He walked on earth, Jesus showed by His example what it looked like to be filled with the Holy Spirit. Then, just before He ascended into heaven, He told His disciples, "I am sending the promise of my Father upon you; but stay in the city until you are clothed with power from on high." (Luke 24:49) They probably didn't need a whole lot of convincing to stay put. Jesus' arrest and crucifixion had shaken them to the core. When Jesus was arrested and people suggested Peter was one of His disciples, terrified Peter denied even knowing Jesus. After the Resurrection, Jesus found the disciples huddling and hiding in the upper room where they had celebrated the Last Supper. Jesus stayed with them for forty days afterward, and that certainly would have buoyed their emotions, but they were all too aware of how dangerous it was to be allied with Jesus. Staying in the city, waiting in the upper room and praying sounded like a pretty good plan.

But everything was about to change. Read the story in Acts 2:1–39. I know it's long. But it's juicy and worth reading every word.

1. What change was seen in Peter after he was filled with the Holy Spirit at Pentecost?

God had fulfilled His promise! The waiting was over. He poured His Holy Spirit straight into the hearts of His people.

The impact of the Holy Spirit in Peter made him a bold preacher, and also revealed a growth in humility. In Mark 14:31, Jesus told Peter that he was going to deny Him three times. Peter's reply revealed his self-confidence: "Even though I should have to die with you, I will not deny you!" We all know how that story turned out. In his speech at Pentecost, Peter stepped off the platform that highlighted his own abilities, and instead simply pointed to Christ.

2. When the people were cut to the heart by Peter's words, what did Peter tell them to do? What did he promise would happen if they did this? See Acts 2:37–38.

3. Whom was the promise of Acts 2:38 made for? See Acts 2:39.

Do you ever feel far off from God? Be encouraged! You are not excluded from this promise. It is for you! If you have been baptized, in that moment, the Holy Spirit took up residence in your soul. He wants to work within you to *be in you* all that you need. Your part is to clear the cobwebs between you and God by repenting of your sin. This clears the way for Him to fill you with Himself.

4. In what area of your life do you need boldness or power?

Quiet your heart and enjoy His presence. . . . Repent and be filled with the Holy Spirit.

"Not by might, and not by power, but by my Spirit, says the Lord of hosts." (Zechariah 4:6)
Is there something you are facing that feels overwhelming? Does the mountain you need to climb look terribly steep, and does it appear impossible to reach its summit with all the burdens you are carrying on your back?

God urges you to keep going, to keep climbing. But He doesn't expect you to do it by relying on your own might and power. He wants you to rely on the power of the Holy Spirit. Lay your concerns at His feet. Spread out the obstacles before Him. Ask the Holy Spirit to search your heart for any way in which the obstacles are rooted in unconfessed sin. If He reveals something, confess it on the spot. Then ask that the power of the Holy Spirit would fill you.

Day Four
WHAT DIFFERENCE DOES HE MAKE IN OUR LIVES?

After Pentecost, more and more followers of Christ were baptized and filled with the Holy Spirit. Some of them, inspired by the indwelling Holy Spirit, became the authors of the New Testament. Many of the books they wrote were actually letters written to the early Church communities to encourage and teach them. The beauty of Scripture is that it was written in such a way that it had relevance then, yet can speak to us today.

Each of the following verses shows us a way that the Holy Spirit helps us. Once we understand what the Holy Spirit does in a general sense, we can think about how that *impacts us personally*. So as you read these verses, write down how the Holy Spirit can affect your daily life.

The first is given as an example:

Romans 8:14–16 (The Holy Spirit confirms that we are God's children.)

"For those who are led by the Spirit of God are children of God. For you did not receive a spirit of slavery to fall back into fear, but you received a spirit of adoption, through which we cry, 'Abba, Father!' The Spirit itself bears witness with our spirit that we are children of God."

Answer: I sometimes question who I am and where I'm going. When I read this verse, I'm reminded that God sent the Holy Spirit to live in my heart to remind me from within that I am His—that I am His child, His beloved daughter. If I live my life from that identity, I'm so much more likely to make the right choices, instead of doing things to please other people.

1. **Galatians 5:22–23** (The Holy Spirit makes us holy.)

2. **Romans 8:26** (The Holy Spirit helps us pray.)

3. **Luke 12:12** (The Holy Spirit helps us speak.)

4. **John 14:16–17** (The Holy Spirit remains with us.)

Quiet your heart and enjoy His presence. . . . Let Him intersect your daily life and transform you.

The Holy Spirit is willing to do so much for us, but He is a gracious guest, and waits to be invited. He leaves it up to you. You can decide to just keep Him in the entryway of your heart, or you can invite Him to come all the way in. It all depends on how much power and transformation you really want to experience. Unfortunately, too many of us are afraid to throw open all the doors of our hearts to Him. We say that certain rooms are off-limits. When we do this, we miss out. The rooms we close off are often ones that contain pain that He is just waiting to heal. Or perhaps they are places where we're stuck in bad patterns of behavior, and He wants to set us free. Take some time to pray about the rooms that you are keeping closed off to the Holy Spirit. Can you open the door a crack and invite Him to enter? I promise you, the breath of His presence will be sweet and gentle.

Day Five
SAINT'S STORY

Saint Elizabeth Ann Bayley Seton

For those who suffer, the Holy Spirit is the invisible consoler, the friend who lifts us up again and again, giving us the strength to carry on even when we have lost everything.

It is easy for us to think of saints as a pretty picture on a holy card: serene face, radiant eyes, folded hands. But that is often not the whole story. For some, there are dark nights filled with tears, moments of confusion and anguish and uncertainty, sudden shocks of tragedy, gray days of tedium and dryness.

It is in those dark days that we most need the light and support of the Holy Spirit, our consoler, advocate, and guide. It is through Him that a deep yes is forged under the shadow of the cross.

Elizabeth Ann Bayley Seton's life was marked by suffering, even though she was a child of privilege, born in 1774 to a prominent Anglican family in New York. Despite her high-society upbringing, Elizabeth's childhood was quiet, and she spent much of her time reading, especially the Bible.

She became acquainted with suffering early on in life when her mother died and her stepmother rejected the children of her husband's first marriage. When Elizabeth's father traveled, her stepmother sent her and her sister to live with their uncle. Later, her stepmother divorced her father. The social stigma of divorce at this time caused a shadow to fall on their family, and Elizabeth plummeted into a dark period of depression.

She married William Seton when she was nineteen, and the couple had five children. When William's father passed away, he left his family to the care of his son, during a time when William's business was struggling to stay afloat. The Setons eventually went bankrupt, and to make matters worse, William began showing signs of tuberculosis.

In hopes of improving William's health, the Seton family traveled to Italy to visit their friends, the Filicchis. Upon the Setons' arrival, the Italian officials were nervous about William's sickness, so they quarantined the family in a cold stone lazaretto. A few months later, William died. A widow at age twenty-nine with five small children under the age of eight, Elizabeth lived out all the worst stresses and anxieties that come with being a single mother who has to provide for her family.

It was during this time that Elizabeth began attending Mass with the Filicchis, completely taken by the Catholic faith. There, working in secret and in silence, the Holy Spirit was leading her soul to the fullness of truth. Elizabeth eventually returned home to the United States and was confirmed in the Catholic Church in the early years of the nineteenth century.

Her American family was horrified to discover her Catholic conversion. More alone than ever, she continually went to prayer with a sense of utter desolation, reaching out for God because she had no one else to turn to. There, too, the Holy Spirit helped her find light, encouragement, and strength. He brought her to Jesus and gave her new life again and again.

Feeling called to start a Catholic school for children, Elizabeth found all her efforts met with failure, so strong was the anti-Catholic sentiment at the time. Finally, after many disappointments, she established a religious order, the Sisters of Charity, with the help of a bishop, and then founded a school for needy girls. From those humble beginnings in a small stone farmhouse came a great work of God: Catholic education in America was born.

God's will is difficult to understand, but the Holy Spirit can help us to say yes to it anyway. We don't have to understand everything that God does in our lives. We simply have to offer ourselves like Mary, the spouse of the Spirit, and say, "Let it be done unto me."

In a letter Elizabeth wrote to a friend on March 26, 1810, she gave the following encouragement: "Faith lifts the staggering soul on one side, hope supports it on the other, experience says it must be, and love says let it be."

And where is the Holy Spirit in this struggle to follow God? He is the wind beneath our wings.

What fruits and gifts of the Holy Spirit did Saint Elizabeth Ann Bayley Seton's life reveal?

Conclusion

"Now the Lord is the Spirit, and where the Spirit of the Lord is, there is freedom." (2 Corinthians 3:17)

There are so many times in our lives when we whisper, "I can't."

I can't be more patient with my kids.
I can't forgive him.
I can't keep going.
I can't bear this loss.
I can't give any more.

The Holy Spirit comes to us in those moments and whispers:

I know you can't. I see. I see your limitations. I see your hurts. I see what's been done to you. But even though you can't, I can. I have come to break all the chains that keep you from living the life of freedom that you were meant to live. You were made for more, daughter of God. I am here for you. I am for you. My love for you is relentless.

I am your **Comforter** (one who relieves another of distress).
I am your **Counselor** (one whose profession it is to give advice and manage causes).
I am your **Helper** (one who furnishes another with relief or support).
I am your **Intercessor** (one who acts between parties to reconcile differences).
I am your **Strengthener** (one who causes you to grow, become stronger, endure, and resist attacks).

Is there a place in your life where you are not living in freedom?

Do you feel chained to old habits of behavior and powerless to change?

Do you feel bound by lies about your identity—lies that say you are worthless, or ugly, or stupid?

Do you feel stuck in the rat race, unable to slow down, unable to breathe?

These are the very places where you need to invite me to come and set you free.

Don't treat me as an interesting character in a book. Ask me to jump off the pages of the Bible and into your heart.

My Resolution

In what specific way will I apply what I have learned in this lesson?

Examples:

1. This week I will start every day by reading Romans 8:14–16. I'll remind myself who I am. I am God's beloved daughter. The Holy Spirit in my heart confirms it.

2. This week I'll pray God's own words back to Him by turning this verse into a daily prayer:

   "Teach me to do your will, for you are my God. May your kind Spirit guide me on ground that is level." (Psalm 143:10)

3. I'll choose one of the fruits of the Holy Spirit listed in Galatians 5:22–23 and focus on growing in that area this week, through the help of the Holy Spirit.

My Resolution:

Catechism Clips

CCC 691 "Holy Spirit" is the proper name of the one whom we adore and glorify with the Father and the Son. The Church has received this name from the Lord and professes it in the Baptism of her new children.

The term "Spirit" translates the Hebrew word *ruah*, which in its primary sense, means breath, air, wind. Jesus indeed uses the sensory image of the wind to suggest to Nicodemus the transcendent newness of him who is personally God's breath, the divine Spirit. On the other hand, "Spirit" and "Holy" are divine attributes common to the three divine persons. By joining the two terms, Scripture, liturgy, and theological language designate the inexpressible person of the Holy Spirit, without any possible equivocation with other uses of the terms "spirit" and "holy."

CCC 692 When he proclaims and promises the coming of the Holy Spirit, Jesus calls him the "Paraclete," literally, "he who is called to one's side," *ad-vocatus*. "Paraclete" is commonly translated by "consoler," and Jesus is the first consoler. The Lord also called the Holy Spirit "the Spirit of truth."

CCC 685 To believe in the Holy Spirit is to profess that the Holy Spirit is one of the persons of the Holy Trinity, consubstantial with the Father and the Son: "with the Father and the Son he is worshipped and glorified." For this reason, the divine mystery of the Holy Spirit was already treated in the context of Trinitarian "theology." Here, however, we have to do with the Holy Spirit only in the divine "economy."

CCC 687 "No one comprehends the thoughts of God except the Spirit of God." Now God's Spirit, who reveals God, makes known to us Christ, his Word, his living Utterance, but the Spirit does not speak of himself. The Spirit who "has spoken through the prophets" makes us hear the Father's Word, but we do not hear the Spirit himself. We know him only in the movement by which he reveals the Word to us and disposes us to welcome him in faith. The Spirit of truth who "unveils" Christ to us "will not speak on his own." Such properly divine self-effacement explains why "the world cannot receive [him], because it neither sees him nor knows him," while those who believe in Christ know the Spirit because he dwells with them.

CCC 702 From the beginning until "the fullness of time," the joint mission of the Father's Word and Spirit remains hidden, but it is at work. God's Spirit prepares for the time of the Messiah. Neither is fully revealed but both are already promised, to be watched for and welcomed at their manifestation. So, for this reason, when the Church reads the Old Testament, she searches there for what the Spirit, "who has spoken through the prophets," wants to tell us about Christ.

> By "prophets" the faith of the Church here understands all whom the Holy Spirit inspired in living proclamation and the composition of the sacred books, both of the Old and the New Testaments. Jewish tradition distinguishes first the Law (the first five books or Pentateuch), then the Prophets (our historical and prophetic books) and finally the Writings (especially the wisdom literature, in particular the Psalms).

NOTES

Lesson 7

WHY SHOULD I READ THE BIBLE?

Introduction

"Know this first of all, that there is no prophecy of scripture that is a matter of personal interpretation, for no prophecy ever came through human will; but rather human beings moved by the Holy Spirit spoke under the influence of God." (2 Peter 1:20–21)

"God is the author of Sacred Scripture because he inspired its human authors; he acts in them and by means of them. He thus gives assurance that their writings teach without error his saving truth." (CCC 136)

The Bible is unlike any other book you will ever read. It is the most popular, most powerful, and most precious book in existence. "No one really knows how many copies of the Bible have been printed, sold, or distributed. The Bible Society's attempt to calculate the number printed between 1816 and 1975 produced the figure of 2,458,000,000. A more recent survey, for the years up to 1992, put it closer to 6,000,000,000 in more than 2,000 languages and dialects. Whatever the precise figure, the Bible is by far the bestselling book of all time."[20]

The Bible is the most powerful book because it transforms, convicts, inspires, and teaches us. Within the pages of Scripture we can find the answers to life's most important questions: Why am I here? What is the purpose of my life? Why is there suffering in the world? What happens after I die? How can I get to heaven? It also addresses practical questions: How can I be a good wife? How can I be a great mother? How can I be a better friend? We can spend our lives wasting time, chasing after things that don't really matter in the end. We can allow the ever-shifting moral

---

[20] Russell Ash, *The Top Ten of Everything 1997* (New York: Dorling Kindersley Publications, 1996), 112–13.

guidelines of our world to lead us, or we can turn to the truth found only in Scripture, and start building our lives on a solid foundation.

During this lesson, you will see an example of how precious the Bible was to Saint Irene and many others. This same appreciation for Scripture can be found today. Mark Hart, the executive vice president of Life Teen International, said, "How can we make time to read the daily papers or our e-mails and not God's love letter to us on a daily basis?" The Bible is God's truth, written in the form of a letter to us, His children. Although written by human hands, it was composed under the inspiration of the Holy Spirit, as if He were whispering in the ear of the writer.

How can we ignore such an amazing gift? In the words of Saint Jerome, "Ignorance of Scripture is Ignorance of Christ." He puts it pretty strongly! But he's right. If we want to really know Christ and move beyond a religion that's only in our heads to something that penetrates our hearts and changes us, we have to be willing to take the time to read the Bible.

Day One
IT'S WORTH READING BECAUSE IT'S TRUSTWORTHY

For a lot of us, it's hard to be enthusiastic about cracking open the Bible because we wonder whether it's relevant and true, or just a bunch of stories that are more mythical than historical. Can it be trusted?

This is an essential question to wrestle with, because two things are needed if reading the Bible is to really benefit us. First, we have to believe that what's written in it is reliable and true, and then we need to give the Bible's truths the chance to sink deep into our hearts and minds and impact our thoughts and behaviors.

1. What did you think about the Bible as you were growing up? Did you have doubts about its relevance or truth? Remember, this is the safe place to record your thoughts. There are no right or wrong answers to this question.

2. In order to embrace the Bible as truth, we have to believe that what we hold in our hands is an accurate version of what was originally written. Otherwise, it's as if we're the last person to be whispered to in the "telephone" game and the final message is mixed up.

The following chart compares respected historical texts. How often do you doubt the validity of Caesar's or Aristotle's writing? How do you feel the Bible measures up? Does this impact your opinion of the trustworthiness of Scripture?

Unparalleled Manuscript Support[21]

Author	When Written	Earliest Copy	Time Span	Number of Copies
Caesar	100–44 BC	900 AD	1,000 years	10
Tacitus	100 AD	1100 AD	1,000 years	20
Suetonius	75–160 AD	950 AD	800 years	8
Herodotus	480–425 BC	900 AD	1,300 years	8
Aristotle	384–322 BC	1100 AD	1,400 years	49
New Testament	45–100 AD	Fragment: 125 AD; Full copies: 3rd and 4th centuries	Fragment: 25 years; Full copies: 200–300 years	24,000

3. Read the following supports for the trustworthiness of Scripture:

Archaeological Proof

There isn't room here to document the many archaeological discoveries that have shed light on the validity of the truths of Scripture. Nelson Glueck, a renowned archaeologist who uncovered more than fifteen hundred ancient sites during his lifetime, said, "No archaeological discovery has ever controverted [overturned] a Biblical reference. Scores of archaeological findings have been made which confirm in clear outline or in exact detail historical statements in the Bible. And, by the same token, proper evaluation of Biblical descriptions has often led to amazing discoveries."[22]

---

[21] Garry Poole and Judson Poling, *How Reliable Is the Bible?* (Grand Rapids, MI: Zondervan, 1998), 38.
[22] Nelson Glueck, *Rivers in the Desert: A History of the Negev* (New York: Farrar, Straus & Cudahy, 1959), 31.

Eyewitness Support

Eyewitnesses were willing to die for the truths contained in the Gospels. Also, because the authors were alive while the letters of the New Testament were in circulation, there was plenty of opportunity for them to answer questions and defend their claims.

Old Testament Prophecies

The Old Testament contains dozens of prophecies about Jesus that were fulfilled in the New Testament. We touched on this in Lesson 2: Who Is Jesus Christ?

Cohesiveness of the Overall Message of the Bible

Considering that the Bible had more than forty authors from every walk of life, was written over fifteen hundred years, was written in three languages (Hebrew, Greek, and Aramaic), and contains many literary styles (poems, histories, prophecies, letters, parables), it is incredible that the overall message remains consistent and cohesive. From beginning to end, it is the story of the Father's unrelenting love for and pursuit of His unfaithful children, His plan to reconcile them to Himself, and His instructions on how to enter into and remain in a relationship with Him.

Unusual Truth Telling

You'd expect a book that's presenting a specific religion as the best choice to put a positive spin on the depictions of its leaders and main characters. In this, the Bible makes it clear that its purpose is to tell the truth, not to hide the dirty laundry. Much of what is written reflects poorly on God's chosen people. It depicts their sins, unfaithfulness, and shortcomings. The divisions within the Church are described. The Bible's focus is reality, not presenting a cleaned-up, winsome version of the story of God's people.

Does anything you read surprise you? Is there an area you would like to research more in order to be reassured of the reliability of the Bible?

4. What do the following verses say in terms of the trustworthiness of God's Word?

Isaiah 40:8

Mark 13:31

Quiet your heart and enjoy His presence. . . . God and His Word are utterly trustworthy.

Jesus:
"Do not think that I have come to abolish the law or the prophets. I have come not to abolish but to fulfill. Amen, I say to you, until heaven and earth pass away, not the smallest letter or the smallest part of a letter will pass from the law, until all things have taken place." (Matthew 5:17–18)

Two men on the road to Emmaus:
"Were not our hearts burning [within us] while [Jesus] spoke to us on the way and opened the scriptures to us?" (Luke 24:32)

Jesus Himself believed in the trustworthiness of the Sacred Scriptures. He came to fulfill them, quoted them often, used them as a weapon in spiritual battle, and always upheld their veracity. He wants you to embrace the Scriptures as truth, as a sure anchor for your soul.

After His Resurrection, Jesus came alongside two men in Luke 24 and "beginning with Moses and all the prophets, he interpreted to them what referred to him in all the scriptures." (Luke 24:27) He longs to do the same for you.

As you read the Bible, invite Jesus on the journey. Ask Him to speak to you through it.

Dear Lord,

I want to read the Bible in a way that transforms me. I long to have the experience that the men on the road to Emmaus had. I know this is totally different from approaching the Bible just as an academic pursuit. I want to read it to know you better. I want to read it to know myself better, and the ways in which I need to be changed. Help me as I look into this book of truth. When I doubt its trustworthiness, please help me believe. Give me the gift of faith, and never leave me alone as I seek to know you better through the pages of your Word. Amen.

Day Two
IT'S WORTH READING BECAUSE IT'S THE KEY TO SPIRITUAL MATURITY

1. In 2 Timothy 3:16–17 is a description of five ways in which Scripture is useful. List them here, then explain what role each could play in your own life.

   A. Scripture is useful for _teaching - Training in righteousness_

   B. Scripture is useful for _sharing God's divine authority_

   C. Scripture is useful for _-inspiration_.

   D. Scripture is useful for _____.

   E. Scripture is useful for _____.

2. Read Hebrews 4:12. When we read that "the word of God is sharper than any two edged sword, penetrating even between soul and spirit, joints and marrow," it may remind us of a dissection experiment in high school. A more helpful way of looking at this passage is to picture a skilled swordsman whose sword finds the precise mark. The purpose of finding that precise mark is not to inflict injury; rather, it serves to pinpoint the place in our heart that needs correction, comfort, or God's grace.

   A. When we read something in the Bible that hits the mark in our hearts, what should be our response?

B. Have you ever experienced this during a reading of Scripture at Mass, or when you're reading the Bible? Record your experience here.

3. There are certain things in our spiritual journeys that only God can do. Only He can soften our hearts so that we long to know Him. Only He can save us through His grace. But because of free will, there are some things that only *we* can do. Only we can choose to ask His forgiveness. Only we can choose to live the way He asks us to. Only we can choose to mature in our faith by reading *and applying* Scripture. He won't do these things for us. He never forces us to choose Him. He holds out the Bible and hopes that we will choose to read it. Whether or not we study it and apply its truths reveals a lot about how serious we are about maturing as Christians. What are the obstacles that get in the way of daily reading the Bible? What can you do to remove them?

Quiet your heart and enjoy His presence. . . . Let's choose maturity and growth.

"Brothers, I could not talk to you as spiritual people, but as fleshly people, as infants in Christ. I fed you milk, not solid food, because you were unable to take it. Indeed, you are still not able, even now, for you are still of the flesh. While there is jealousy and rivalry among you, are you not of the flesh, and behaving in an ordinary human way?" (1 Corinthians 3:1–3)

When Saint Paul wrote this to the Corinthian church, he was longing for them to grow up. It wasn't enough that they had been exposed to truth. They needed to choose to be transformed by it. There was so much "meat" Saint Paul was willing to feed them, but he found he had to keep giving them "milk" over and over.

If we're going to mature, then we need to respond to what we read in the Bible. We can grow as quickly or as slowly as we want to. Some of us have come to Bible study later in life, and we feel like we're late to the party. We think to ourselves, "I've wasted so much time!" "So many people seem to know more than I do!" We wonder if we're ever going to catch up.

Be assured, it doesn't matter when you start. What matters is how you respond to what God is revealing to you at this point. The rate at which you'll grow is up to you.

Dear Lord,

I want to build my relationship with you on a solid foundation. I don't want to skip over any of the basics that are essential to knowing and following you. At the same time, I don't want to hang out in spiritual diapers any longer than is necessary. I want to move upward in maturity! Give me the strength and the desire to put into practice what you reveal to me in the Bible. Help me to resist laziness. May I make growing more like you the highest priority in my life.

Day Three
IT'S WORTH READING BECAUSE IT GIVES DAILY GUIDANCE

"Your word is a lamp for my feet, a light for my path." (Psalm 119:105)

"The Church has always taught that because Christ is God as well as man, all of his words and actions as recorded in the Gospels are not merely edifying events from the past. Christ spoke and lived them with you in mind, so that they are alive and relevant and addressed to you and the circumstances of your life at every moment."[23] —Father John Bartunek, LC

What guidance do the following verses give you in the following situations?

1. When you are feeling afraid (Isaiah 43:1–4)

2. When you are grieving (John 11:25–26 and Psalm 139)

3. When you are facing a major decision (Proverbs 3:5–6)

4. When you are unsure of how best to parent your child (Deuteronomy 6:4–9)

---

[23] Bartunek, *The Better Part*, 10.

Quiet your heart and enjoy His presence. . . . Let His light fall on your path.

We all want our lives to matter. At the end of it all, we'll want to see that our choices were the right ones. So what should we do when we're confused about the right thing to do? We need to go to the source of truth. We need to go to the One who made us, who knows the future, and who knows the hidden pitfalls ahead. It was one of Jesus' greatest heartaches to see people He loved walking down the wrong path. He had this to say to them: "You are misled because you do not know the scriptures or the power of God." (Matthew 22:29) Interestingly, Jesus didn't hold them accountable just for what they did with what they knew. He held them accountable for the things they had been capable of learning. Their choice to not know the Scriptures or the power of God was just that—a choice.

We, too, are held accountable for how we respond to the truth that is available to us. For all our excuses, we have to admit, the Bible is accessible to us all. But we need to pick it up and read it. Good intentions don't mean much if they aren't translated into action.

Dear Lord,

It's just embarrassing when I think that I can find time to read the newspaper or to catch up on Facebook and Pinterest, but I unashamedly say that I don't have time to read the Bible. I realize that I have time for whatever I consider to be most important. Help me to make the most of my time. Help me to carry a Bible with me so that I can turn to you when little pockets of time appear.

Day Four
IT'S MOST EFFECTIVE WHEN IT'S HIDDEN IN OUR HEARTS

"The tempter approached and said to him, 'If you are the Son of God, command that these stones become loaves of bread.' He said in reply, 'It is written: One does not live by bread alone, but by every word that comes forth from the mouth of God.'" (Matthew 4:3–4)

Jesus was able to respond to Satan's temptations because He knew God's truth. When He was under fire, He didn't have time to go find wisdom for the moment. It had to already be in His head. He had memorized Scripture, and found those words to be His most effective weapon in warding off temptation.

Do you ever feel tempted to just give in? To take the easy way when you know the hard way is right? Does discouragement ever nip at your heels and take you to a place of darkness? If you memorize Scripture, the Holy Spirit will be able to bring God's truth to your mind just when you need to fight back.

You may think of memorizing Scripture as an activity for the über-religious, not for the average Christian. A blogger at She Reads Truth (shereadstruth.com) described it this way: "Recalling Scripture isn't for the overachievers; it's for the homesick." It's for those of us who know that earth isn't our home—heaven is. It's for those of us who don't want to be tossed all over the place by our emotions and instead long to be grounded in truth.

But how do we do it? Kids memorize things so easily, but our brains are full of so many other bits of information that we wonder if we're capable of doing it. Never fear. There are easy techniques that can help us to store away God's words in our minds and hearts. Pick a few that work for you. *You can do it!*

1. Learning Through Repetition

Every time you sit down to do the next eight lessons, begin by reading one of the following memory verses. Then begin the remaining eight lessons by reading the other memory verse. The more you read each one, the sooner they will be lodged in your memory. Be sure to read the reference as well; it comes in handy when you want to know where to find the verse in the Bible.

Opening Your Heart Memory Verses:

"For I know the plans I have for you, says the LORD, plans for welfare and not for evil, to give you a future and a hope." (Jeremiah 29:11)

"So whoever is in Christ is a new creation: the old things have passed away; behold, new things have come." (2 Corinthians 5:17)

2. Learning Visually

Write the key verse lightly *in pencil* in the space provided. Read the entire verse, including the reference. Chose one word and erase it well. Reread the entire verse, including the reference. Choose another word, and erase it well. Reread the entire verse, including the reference. Repeat this process until the whole verse has been erased and you are reciting it from memory.

3. Learning Electronically

Go to our website under Courses and save the *Opening Your Heart: The Starting Point* Memory Verse Image to your phone's lock screen so you can read these words throughout the day. Practice it every time you grab your phone.

4. Learning by Writing It Down

Grab a piece of paper and write your verse down twenty times.

5. Learning by Seeing It Everywhere

Write your verse down on index cards and leave them in places you often linger: the bathroom mirror, the car dashboard, the coffeepot, whatever works for you.

6. Learning Together

If you are doing this Walking with Purpose study in a small group, hold each other accountable and recite the memory verse together at the start and end of each lesson. If you are doing the study on your own, consider asking someone to hold you accountable by listening to you say your verse from memory each week.

Quiet your heart and enjoy His presence. . . . Saturate your mind with His truth.

"I have hidden your word in my heart that I might not sin against you." (Psalm 119:11)

"Take the sword of the Spirit, which is the word of God." (Ephesians 6:17)

Memorizing Scripture helps us on multiple levels. On the one hand, the Holy Spirit can bring one of the truths of the Bible to our mind just before we might make a wrong choice. It's like a little whisper reminding us of what we know is true, but there's power in it, because we know they are God's words. For example, in the midst of a conversation in which we aren't listening well, the Holy Spirit can bring to mind Proverbs 18:2: "Fools take no delight in understanding, but only in displaying what they think." This enables us to make a course correction immediately instead of looking back later with regret.

Memorized Scripture can also be used as a weapon in the spiritual life. When negative thoughts and lies run through our minds, we can take a Bible verse and use it as a weapon to kick out the lie and embrace the truth. Verses that speak of God's unconditional love and forgiveness and our new identity in Christ are especially powerful for this kind of battle. When we feel defeated and like we'll never change, when we falsely assume that God must be ready to give up on us, the Holy Spirit can remind us of 2 Corinthians 5:17: "If anyone is in Christ, [she] is a new creation. The old has gone. The new has come!"

Dear Lord,

Please renew my thinking so that I don't get defeated before I even begin, convincing myself that memorizing Scripture is only for the super spiritual. Help me to see myself through your eyes. You know that I am capable of so much more than I give myself credit for. This isn't because you see all my innate untapped abilities. It's because you know the difference it will make if I depend on you and let you do the work through *me. So I come to you, aware of my weaknesses, but assured that "I can do all things through Christ who strengthens me." (Philippians 4:13)*

Day Five
SAINT'S STORY

Saint Irene Keeps the Faith

The Bible is not like any other book. Well, maybe we should say it's not *just* like any other book. It was written by real human authors, who used their own writing style and imagination and wits, but it was written by them under the special inspiration of the Holy Spirit. It is a privileged fount of God's own revelation: "All scripture is inspired by God and useful for refuting error, for guiding people's lives and teaching them to be upright." (2 Timothy 3:16) Saint Thomas Aquinas, one of the most brilliant minds in the history of humanity, used to read the Gospels on his knees. The Church calls the Bible the "soul of theology." God speaks in a unique way through the Scriptures.

Saint Jerome, the great fourth-century scholar who translated the entire Bible into Latin (the language of the street in those days), explained it like this:

> I interpret as I should, following the command of Christ: "Search the Scriptures" (John 5:39), and "Seek and you shall find" (Matthew 7:7). Christ will not say to me what he said to the Jews: "You erred, not knowing the Scriptures and not knowing the power of God" (Matthew 22:29). For if, as Paul says, "Christ is the power of God and the wisdom of God" (1 Corinthians 1:24), and if the man who does not know Scripture does not know the power and wisdom of God, then *ignorance of Scripture is ignorance of Christ.*

That last sentence is actually quoted in Catechism 133.

All the saints have had a deep love for Scripture, even those who couldn't read. Some saints even died because they refused to show disrespect to the Bible by allowing others to desecrate it. Saint Irene was one of these.

In the year AD 303, the misguided Roman emperor Diocletian made it a capital crime to possess even a single page of the Christian Bible. He was trying to wipe out Christianity and reinvigorate the old pagan religions. Three sisters—Agape, Chionia, and Irene, all of whom are now recognized as saints—lived in Greece at the time. They happened to have some biblical texts in their possession, so they hid them away. Soon afterward, God permitted them to be arrested when they refused to eat meat that had been sacrificed to pagan gods. This was a common test used by the authorities to identify Christians. The three sisters were imprisoned and interrogated, but they wouldn't renounce their Christianity. They valiantly defended the faith even as the governor Dulcitius violently tried to make them abandon it. Agape and Chionia were burned at the stake, but Irene was kept in prison. They hoped her resolve would weaken after her sisters' gruesome martyrdom; it didn't.

Meanwhile, a search of their house uncovered the hidden Scriptures, and Irene was called again before the governor. Asked who had ordered her to keep the documents in direct defiance of the emperor's edict, she gave this brave testimony: "Almighty God, who has commanded us to love Him unto death. For that reason, we prefer to be burnt alive rather than give up the Holy Scriptures and betray Him. . . . They were hidden in the house, but we dared not produce them: we were in great trouble because we could no longer read them day and night as we had been accustomed to do." The governor was not exactly pleased with this firm faith, nor by her courageous spunk. He sent her to a house of prostitution to break her down. But even when she was exposed—naked and chained, but praying all the while—to the rough clientele, she miraculously remained unmolested. So the governor simply had her executed.

What love for God's Word those saintly young women showed! Since they loved Christ and they knew that He loved them, they revered and savored His love letters, the inspired books of the Bible.

Saint Irene hid her Bible to protect it. Our Bibles are often hidden, too, but not in order to protect them. More often it's because we know people would think we were weird if we carried them around.

How can the Bible become a greater priority in your life? Dusting off your Bible and keeping it by your side can feel a little risky. But whose opinion of you matters the most?

Conclusion

"Happy are those who do not follow the counsel of the wicked, nor go the way of sinners, nor sit in company with scoffers. Rather, the law of the Lord is their joy; God's law they study day and night. They are like a tree planted near streams of water, that yields its fruit in season; its leaves never wither; whatever they do prospers." (Psalm 1:1–3)

I doubt any of us set out to "follow the counsel of the wicked." But if we don't take the time to learn what is true, and if we don't develop our intellect and educate our conscience, we'll be influenced by whatever seems most convincing. We will be tossed here and there, and we will lack the inner peace that comes from knowing what our Creator wants from us.

One thing we know for sure is that God didn't give us the Bible so that we would become smarter sinners. He gave it to us so that we would apply what we're learning and become more and more like Him. The point is, we don't read the Bible as an academic pursuit, simply accumulating new facts. We read the Bible so that we can put into practice what we are learning. As we read Scripture, we can see ourselves in many of the characters. We recognize that sometimes we act like the people who are opposing Jesus: We want our own way more than His way; we want recognition and to be the favorite instead of wanting someone else to be honored; we value the wrong things. But the good news is that we won't remain in that mind-set. Jesus loves us so much that He won't allow us to stagnate in our spiritual growth. He wants us to grow deeper in Him and to be conformed to His image.

Think about the process you go through when you wake up in the morning. When you drag yourself into the bathroom and look in the mirror, what do you see? Let's just say it's not when we are at our best. So, we set out to make ourselves look better. We shower, brush our teeth, put on makeup, and brush our hair. When you look into the Bible and see yourself, the key is *not* to read it and say, "Hmmm . . . that's interesting!" and then do nothing about what you have read. That's like looking in the mirror in the morning and not bothering to brush your teeth and comb your hair. James 1:22 says, "But be doers of the word, and not just hearers, deceiving yourselves."

But the Bible doesn't just help us become more like Christ. I know of no other writings that give me more *comfort* than the Bible. When I am afraid, feeling misunderstood, grieving, angry, or weary, God speaks to me through His words in the Bible. So often I'll read the Psalms and think, "That's exactly how I feel!" Or I will read Jesus' words to His disciples and be reminded that I am not alone—that someone more powerful is in control, cares about me, and is watching over me. I know that the Bible is living and active. <u>As I read Scripture, I have experienced the kind of peace that only comes from God,</u> filling up my heart and calming me down. What other book can do all that? No other. <u>Only the Bible is a love letter to me</u> (and you!) from the Creator of the universe. What a gift.

My Resolution

Ponder the specific ways you will apply what you have learned in this lesson.

Reflect on the time you spend with God each day. When can you set aside time to read the Bible? Can you schedule this into your daily or weekly routine?

In what specific way will I apply what I have learned in this lesson?

Examples:

1. I will incorporate Scripture reading into my morning prayer time. I will read one Psalm and one Proverb every day. This will correspond to the date: On the fifth day of the month, I'll read Psalm 5 and Proverbs 5. On the sixth day of the month, I'll read Psalm 6 and Proverbs 6, and so on.

2. All week, I will carry an index card with the *Opening Your Heart* memory verse written on it. I'll read it many times a day and have it memorized by the end of the week.

3. I will keep track of the time I spend in one day on e-mail, and match that time the next day reading God's letters to me, the Bible.

My Resolution:

Catechism Clips

CCC 133 The Church "forcefully and specifically exhorts all the Christian faithful . . . to learn 'the surpassing knowledge of Jesus Christ,' by frequent reading of the divine Scriptures. 'Ignorance of the Scriptures is ignorance of Christ.'"

CCC 136 God is the author of Sacred Scripture because he inspired its human authors; he acts in them and by means of them. He thus gives assurance that their writings teach without error his saving truth.

for I KNOW the PLANS I HAVE FOR YOU SAYS THE LORD PLANS FOR WELFARE not evil TO GIVE YOU A HOPE & A FUTURE

JEREMIAH 29:11

NOTES

So whoever is in Christ is a new creation. The old things have passed away. Behold, new things have come.

2 CORINTHIANS 5:17

[25] Full-Color Free Printables available at walkingwithpurpose.com/free-printables

NOTES

Lesson 8

WHAT IS GRACE AND WHAT DIFFERENCE DOES IT MAKE?

Introduction

We use the word *grace* in many different ways. The prayer before dinner is called grace, a woman of elegance and poise has grace, a dignified man with polite manners has grace, and one can grace a party with his or her presence.

We can give grace to our children. A number of years ago, my husband and I received a phone call from our son's school saying that he had been caught cheating on a test and had been suspended as a result. My husband picked our son up at school and brought him to his office. One of the consequences he gave our son was spending the day writing the words "I will never cheat again" five hundred times. He wrote for hours, wisely not complaining. By five o'clock in the evening, it was clear that there weren't enough hours left in the day to finish the writing. My husband decided to give grace, not by saying that the writing didn't need to be done, but by sitting down and writing alongside our son. Together, they finished the five hundred sentences, and drove home.

So what does grace mean in the spiritual sense? The Catechism defines it as follows:

"Grace is favor, the free and undeserved help that God gives to respond to His call to become children of God, adoptive sons [and daughters], partakers of the divine nature and of eternal life." (CCC 1996)

The *Encarta World English Dictionary* defines grace as the infinite love, mercy, favor, and goodwill shown to humankind by God.

The grace my husband gave our son, which is the grace God gives to His children, is free and undeserved help. Both show love and mercy. But God's grace given to us far surpasses anything that we can show to one another. He doesn't just come alongside us, *sharing* the punishment that our sins deserve. He takes on Himself the *entire* punishment due us. After paying that price, He offers us the gift of being His children and spending eternity with Him. The Giver of All Good Things doesn't stop there. He cares about each one of us so personally that He offers us grace each and every day for all of our varied circumstances.

But before we dive in, I've got to warn you . . .

You have to gear up for this lesson, ladies. It plunges you into some theology that at first glance might make you want to yawn or cross your eyes. Stick with it. Don't be put off by vocab that may be new to you. Because hidden within these meaty passages is the stuff that we are longing for.

Day One
THE FIRST WORK OF GRACE

1. According to CCC 1989, what is the first work of the grace of the Holy Spirit? What moves man to turn toward God and away from sin?

Grace's first work is to draw your heart toward God. That first time you felt hungry to learn more about spiritual things? That was grace at work. That sense you get in your gut that what you are doing isn't really in your best interest, that God wants something different and better for you? That is grace at work.

God is always after your heart. But He never blasts through and forces Himself on you. He's gentle, and recognizes that conversion is a gradual process. He'll let you run after the things that you think will satisfy, and He'll wait. When you figure out that you want more, but view Him as an "add-on," as one thing among many that you hope will fill you up, He'll wait patiently. When you come to the point where you recognize He is the only One who can satisfy you, grace will rush in and you'll receive "grace upon grace." (John 1:16)

2. Grace does something else as well—it results in justification. List the descriptions of *justification* found in CCC 1989 and 1990.

In other words . . .

Justification throws our sins as far away from us as the east is from the west. (Psalm 103:12)

Justification renews the inner parts of us—the parts that are wounded and hurting and hidden. (2 Corinthians 4:16)

Justification makes us clean—as white as freshly fallen snow. (Isaiah 1:18)

Justification reconciles us with God. (2 Corinthians 5:19)

Justification gives us what we need to break free from the bondage of habits that destroy us. (Galatians 5:1)

Justification heals us. (1 Peter 2:24)

And it's grace at work in our souls that results in justification. Without grace, we wouldn't be able to experience any of these things.

3. According to Titus 3:4–7, how are we saved? Why did God pour out the Holy Spirit on us?

4. Grace's first work is drawing us to a point of conversion. The effect of conversion is justification. What do we need to do to experience all the benefits of justification? Think about your answer to question 3, and see CCC 1991.

Quiet your heart and enjoy His presence. . . . He wants to give you "grace upon grace."

I don't know about you, but when I read about all the grace that God wants to pour over me through justification, I wonder why the heck I run after so much emptiness. Why do I think that distracting myself, or numbing myself, or losing five pounds is really going to fix the things that aren't working in my life? What I really want is healing. Freedom. A fresh start. And that's what God is offering me—using the word grace to describe it all. Let's reach out and grasp it with both hands.

Dear Lord,

I really want all the grace that you have for me. But I've got some things in my hands that I'm going to have to put down if I'm going to be able to receive it from you. Help me to lay down my self-reliance. Help me to lay down my desire to keep everyone happy—my habit of people pleasing. Help me to lay down my determination to always be comfortable. Sometimes I have to get uncomfortable for a while in order to experience all you have for me. Help me to remember Saint Augustine's words: "God gives where he finds empty hands."

Day Two
THE EXTRAVAGANCE OF GRACE

1. Is the grace of salvation something that we earn? See Romans 11:6 and Ephesians 2:8–9.

2. If we don't merit salvation (justification) because of our good works, does that mean grace is cheap? Does it come at no cost? See CCC 1992.

The grace of our salvation has come to us at an enormous cost: Christ's life. Jesus stepped in and took the punishment that was due each one of us. He didn't do this because our good works make us worth it. He deems us "worth it" simply because He loves us. He asks us to have confidence (faith) in *His* payment for our sins, instead of our own attempts to pay for them. "A person is justified by faith apart from works of the law." (Romans 3:28)

3. What is the source of our merits (our abilities, our achievements, our worth) before God? What role does grace play in this? See CCC 2011. Note: In this context, the word *charity* means "love."

When you think about it, there really is nothing for us to boast about. Even the good things that we do (our "merits") find their source in the love of Christ that He has put in our hearts. We stand before God because of what Christ has done on our behalf, not because of what we have done for ourselves. God pours out extravagant grace, and we are the fortunate recipients.

4. We can't deny that the grace God gives us is free and undeserved. So why do you think we find it so hard to offer grace to others?

Quiet your heart and enjoy His presence. . . . The price has been paid. Rest in His grace.

We've grown up hearing that there's "no such thing as a free lunch." And so we set out to earn our place in the world. We eat our vegetables to earn dessert. We get good grades to earn good college placement. We get the internship to earn the job. We get the gym membership to earn the better body, which we hope will earn us the guy of our dreams. Everything worth having comes at a cost, and we are exhausted trying to get and keep it all.

God speaks into our weariness. He asks us to let go of the "try hard" life. He offers us His grace, and asks us to offer it to others in turn. Spend some time talking to God about what area of your life feels exhausting. Ask Him to help you let go of expectations—those others have for you and those you have for others. Ask Him to replace the expectations with gratitude for the grace He extravagantly pours over you.

Day Three
THE RISK OF GRACE

"But where sin increased, grace overflowed all the more." (Romans 5:20)

When we read of the extravagance of grace, we recognize there's a risk. Won't people take advantage of this? Won't they be tempted to say, "Yes, I know this is wrong. But I'm going to do it anyway and ask for forgiveness later"? As Herod said in W. H. Auden's poem *For the Time Being*, "Every crook will argue: 'I like committing crimes. God likes forgiving them. Really, the world is admirably arranged.'"[26]

Which brings us to the question, "Why be good?" This is exactly the question Saint Paul addresses in the New Testament book of Romans.

1. According to Romans 6:14, why is sin not to have power over us?

2. Read Romans 3:19–20. According to verse 19, why was the law given? What does verse 20 say we become conscious of through the law?

Let's unpack the phrase "under the law." This describes the way God's people lived before Christ's death and Resurrection. God had given them laws to live by. The purpose of these laws was to help them make choices that would keep them healthy, both spiritually and physically. But time and time again, God's people failed to follow the laws. They were unable to live up to those standards.

This is what Saint Paul was talking about in Romans 3:19 when he said that the law was given so that we'd all be silenced. We're silenced because we are aware of how much we fall short of God's standard of holiness. The alternative to being silenced is to justify ourselves by saying, "Look at how good I am! Can you see all the things I've done? I've earned your love, God!" The law acts as a mirror, and when we hold it up to ourselves, our voices fall silent as we see that we haven't been able to obey all that God has asked of us. Living under the law is hard, because we simply don't have what it takes to do it.

---

[26] W. H. Auden, *For the Time Being: A Christmas Oratorio* (Princeton, NJ: Princeton University Press, 2013), 57.

3. Romans 6:14 tells us that as Christians, we don't live under the law. We live under grace. Living under grace is living under a *new* law. According to CCC 1966, what is the new law?

This brings us back to the question, "Why be good?" The answer? *Because we can be.* Because everything is different now that the Holy Spirit dwells in us. What we cannot do for ourselves, the Holy Spirit will do *in us and for us,* if we ask Him. Please don't just speed past these words. Let the truth they contain sink in.

In the words of Father Jacques Philippe, "According to grace, we receive salvation and the love of God freely through Christ, quite apart from our merits, and freely respond to that love by the good works the Holy Spirit enables us to accomplish."[27] The law is not the foundation of our relationship with God; love is. It is love that motivates us to ask the Holy Spirit to help us live in the way that God desires.

4. What is an area of your life where you have been aware of falling short of what God desires to see in you? Have you been trying to "create your own goodness" instead of relying on the Holy Spirit to do the work in and through you? What do you think indicates a person is relying on him- or herself instead of on God to grow in holiness?

Quiet your heart and enjoy His presence. . . . Let Him infuse your heart with the grace to obey.

"What then? Shall we sin because we are not under the law but under grace? Of course not!" (Romans 6:15)

Some people look at grace as the ticket that allows them to live however they want and just ask for forgiveness later. This kind of behavior can result when we look at God's instructions to us as ways He's trying to take away all our fun. But nothing could be further from the truth. Our heavenly Father wants us to be happy and satisfied. The commandments He gives us are there for our protection and to lead us to a place of health and wholeness. Why would we want to sin? It only leads to unhappiness.

---

[27] Jacques Philippe, *Interior Freedom* (New York: Scepter Publishers, 2002), 114.

Take some time to prayerfully think about an area in your life where you find it hard to do things "God's way." Ponder the fact that all He wants is what is best for you. Ask Him to help you to trust that obedience is what will truly make you happy.

Day Four
THE SUFFICIENCY OF GRACE

1. Saint Paul wrote a letter to the church in Corinth, and in it, he talked about a thorn in his flesh that he begged God to get rid of. How did God answer his request? See 2 Corinthians 12:9.

The phrase "is made perfect" means "is given most fully and manifests itself fully."[28] Isn't that amazing? When we are at our weakest, God's power is most fully given and manifests itself most fully. That's a truth to cling to when we're at the end of our resources.

2. When we are in need of grace, we can immediately turn to God in prayer, and He will meet us in our place of weakness. Where else can we go to receive grace? See CCC 1966.

Even when we are struggling with a thorn in our side, God still asks us to love. He doesn't ask us to scrape the bottom of the barrel of our own resources and just do the best we can. He asks us to drink from His endless supply of grace, poured out on us through the sacraments.

Sometimes all we can do is lift up weary, empty hands and ask for the filling of His grace. I can remember a particularly difficult time of my life, when I could barely find the strength to pray. I knew I needed to persevere in loving my family, but the most

---

28 2 Corinthians 12:9 footnote, in New American Bible, Revised Edition (Washington, DC: Confraternity of Christian Doctrine, 2010), 274.

basic things seemed so very hard. My prayer became little more than the outstretching of my empty hands. My words were few, but the physical action meant a lot. It was my way of telling the Lord that I had nothing to offer, and I needed Him to fill me with His grace. I went to daily Mass, and found that simply putting my body in a place where I could receive grace had an enormous impact on my spirit. I believe the Eucharist gave me the strength that I lacked. Bit by bit, I was restored.

3. What "thorn" is in your side right now? I'd guess that you, like Saint Paul, would like God to just take that thorn away. Perhaps He will. Sometimes He does. But other times, He allows the thorn to stay, in order to accomplish His purposes in us. Why was Saint Paul able to deal with his thorn? See 2 Corinthians 12:10.

Quiet your heart and enjoy His presence. . . . "Be strong in the grace that is in Christ Jesus." (2 Timothy 2:1)

"They that hope in the LORD will renew their strength, they will soar on eagles' wings; They will run and not grow weary, walk and not grow faint." (Isaiah 40:31)

Dear Lord,

This is where our hope lies. It lies in you. The renewal and strength that we long for doesn't come from the spa or from perfect circumstances. It shows up when we have nothing to offer, and fills up our empty hands. Thank you for the grace that strengthens and sustains us. Thank you for making it so that at any time and in any place, we can "confidently approach the throne of grace to receive mercy and to find grace for timely help." (Hebrews 4:16)

Day Five
SAINT'S STORY

Saint Josephine Bakhita

Sudan is a land well acquainted with suffering, having been bathed in the blood of genocide and ravaged by slave traders for many years. Josephine Bakhita was born in Olgossa, in the Darfur region of southern Sudan, in 1869. When she was eleven, she was kidnapped and sold into slavery. The trauma of being ripped from her family and sold and resold repeatedly was such that she forgot her own name; in its place, she was given the name Bakhita—ironically, meaning "fortunate."

Josephine Bakhita's life seems anything but fortunate. One of her masters' sons beat her so severely, she could not move from her straw bed for a month. Another master, an Ottoman Army officer, marked her as his property by scarring her body and tattooing her with more than sixty patterns on her breasts, belly, and arms. She was also forcibly converted to Islam.

Different masters took her all over Africa, and eventually to Venice, Italy. God was working through the circumstances of Josephine Bakhita's life, and it was here, through the Canossian Sisters in Venice, that she first heard the words of Jesus: "Come to Me, all you who labor and are heavily burdened, and I will give you rest. Take my yoke upon you and learn from Me, for I am gentle and humble of heart, and you will find rest for yourselves. For my yoke is easy and my burden is light." (Matthew 11:28–30) The heart recognizes the truth in such words of gentleness. By 1890, she was baptized and had taken the Italian Christian name Giuseppina Margarita (Josephine Margaret in English).

A few years later, when her owner wanted to return to Africa, Josephine Bakhita refused to go. The Canossian Sisters and the Patriarch of Venice interceded on her behalf, and guaranteed her the freedom of choice contained in Italian law. Legally in Italy, she was a free woman, the mistress of her own destiny. But in reality, she had become a free woman from the moment of her baptism in 1890. Even in her final years as a slave, she knew that the gift of baptismal grace had already set her free on the inside: "If the Son sets you free, you will be free indeed." (John 8:36) With Christ living inside her by grace, she knew that nothing except sin could ever enslave her again.

With her newfound legal freedom, Josephine Bakhita became a Canossian Sister. In 1893, she entered the convent, and in 1896, she made her profession. A young student once asked her, "What would you do, if you were to meet your captors?"

Showing true grace and understanding, she answered, "If I were to meet those who kidnapped me, and even those who tortured me, I would kneel and kiss their hands. For, if these things had not happened, I would not have been a Christian and a religious today." With this spirit of gratitude and humility, she worked hard doing menial tasks in the convent, often saying, "Be good, love the Lord, and pray for those who do not know Him. What a great grace it is to know God!"

Josephine Bakhita would pray that you, too, would know this great grace and hold it in high esteem. Grace is the gentle Lordship of Jesus Christ. It is His life flowing through our veins, His heart beating inside ours. Grace is what sets us free from slavery and gives us our true dignity. It is what makes us daughters of the King. You are a daughter of the King, and your heart will always be free if you live in His grace.

As you read and reflect on Saint Josephine Bakhita's story, consider how she was able to experience inner freedom despite the outward conditions of slavery that marked the early years of her life. Does this change your appreciation of Christ's grace?

Conclusion

Have you ever felt a heaviness of heart, a sense of despair, or a deep-seated fear that your life will never get better? I remember a period of my life when discouragement and depression nearly blotted out my ability to feel God's grace.

My husband and I had been living in Mexico for a number of years. Something was making me physically ill; whether it was a parasite or emotional unrest, I never knew the cause. I spent a week each month in my bed, unable to keep any food in my system. I longed to go home, as I missed the United States terribly. When we were robbed by someone very close to us, the betrayal felt overwhelming. I felt unsafe, unsettled, and uncared for. Everything made me cry, and each morning when I woke, I longed to pull the covers over my head and escape back into sleep.

All was made more complicated by the fact that I had four children who needed a mother who was strong and loving, and who created a safe environment for them. I realized that my emotional state was not only taking me closer and closer to a dark pit, but it was harming my children.

On one of my lowest days, I read this verse in Psalm 51:14, NAB: "Restore unto me the joy of my salvation." I realized that I had been given such amazing grace when God gave me salvation, but that I wanted *more*. Where was my gratitude? Why could I not appreciate all that He had given me in dying on the cross for my sins? How could I expect more from the person who gave His life for me? I knew God wanted me to experience joy because He had saved me. But how could I drum up feelings I didn't have? It seemed impossible. I was empty.

I sensed Jesus listening to the cries of my heart and saying, "With man this is impossible, but with God all things are possible." (Matthew 19:26) His grace was being offered to me: grace to help me to be grateful for what I had; grace to get up and be the kind of mother my children needed even though I wanted to do nothing but cry and sleep; grace to encourage my husband and smile at him even though I thought it was his fault that we had to live in a place I hated; and grace to quit complaining about all I didn't like because it was only making me feel worse.

I knelt before God that day and said, "God, I know I should feel joy because of my salvation, but I don't. I just feel unhappy. Please, will you do the work of restoring that joy to me? I can't do it myself. I do promise this: I will quit complaining about all that I don't like in Mexico. I'll quit complaining to other people, but also to you. I'll stop asking you to bring me back home. But I only promise because I know that you don't forget anything. You know the desires of my heart. Even if I'm not reminding you, you know. I will try to trust that if you don't change my circumstances, you know what is best for me. But help me. I am so weak."

The progress was slow, but after about three months, I realized I was much better. I didn't cry so much; I could delight in little things; the peace of my heart was returning. And just when I thought, "It's OK. I can live here. I'm all right," my husband quit his job and told me he was taking me home.

I am so grateful that God led me through the valley of despair before giving me what I desired. What I learned along the way was such a gift. God's grace is enough.

"I know indeed how to live in humble circumstances; I know also how to live with abundance. In every circumstance and in all things I have learned the secret of being well fed and of going hungry, of living in abundance and of being in need. I have the strength for everything through him who empowers me." (Philippians 4:12–13)

My Resolution

In what specific way will I apply what I have learned in this lesson?

Examples:

1. I want to experience all the grace that God has for me. I'll grab hold of the opportunity for more of His grace by going to Mass one additional time this week.

2. If I am feeling discouraged about an area in my life where I repeatedly make the same mistakes, I'll increase my prayer about that struggle. Instead of trying harder, I will pray more.

3. I will write 2 Corinthians 12:9 on an index card and carry it with me to remind myself that in my weakness, God is strong.

My Resolution:

Catechism Clips

CCC 1966 The New Law is *the grace of the Holy Spirit* given to the faithful through faith in Christ. It works through charity; it uses the Sermon on the Mount to teach us what must be done and makes use of the sacraments to give us the grace to do it.

CCC 1989 The first work of the grace of the Holy Spirit is *conversion*, effecting justification in accordance with Jesus' proclamation at the beginning of the Gospel: "Repent, for the kingdom of heaven is at hand." Moved by grace, man turns toward God and away from sin, thus accepting forgiveness and righteousness from on high. "Justification is not only the remission of sins, but also the sanctification [growth in holiness] and renewal of the interior man."

CCC 1990 Justification *detaches man from sin* which contradicts the love of God, and purifies his heart of sin. Justification follows upon God's merciful initiative of offering forgiveness. It reconciles man with God. It frees from the enslavement to sin, and it heals.

CCC 1991 Justification is at the same time *the acceptance of God's righteousness* through faith in Jesus Christ. Righteousness (or "justice") here means the rectitude of divine love. With justification, faith, hope, and charity are poured into our hearts, and obedience to the divine will is granted us.

CCC 1992 Justification has been merited for us by the Passion of Christ who offered himself on the cross as a living victim, holy and pleasing to God, and whose blood has become the instrument of atonement for the sins of all men. Justification is conferred in Baptism, the sacrament of faith. It conforms us to the righteousness of God, who makes us inwardly just by the power of his mercy. Its purpose is the glory of God and of Christ, and the gift of eternal life:

> But now the righteousness of God has been manifested apart from law, although the law and the prophets bear witness to it, the righteousness of God through faith in Jesus Christ for all who believe. For there is no distinction: since all have sinned and fall short of the glory of God, they are justified by his grace as a gift, through the redemption which is in Christ Jesus, whom God put forward as an expiation by his blood, to be received by faith. This was to show God's righteousness, because in his divine forbearance he had passed over former sins; it was to prove at the present time that he himself is righteous and that he justifies him who has faith in Jesus.

CCC 2011 *The charity of Christ is the source in us of all our merits* before God. Grace, by uniting us to Christ in active love, ensures the supernatural quality of our acts and consequently their merit before God and before men. The saints have always had a lively awareness that their merits were pure grace.

> After earth's exile, I hope to go and enjoy you in the fatherland, but I do not want to lay up merits for heaven. I want to work for your *love alone* . . . In the evening of this life, I shall appear before you with empty hands, for I do not ask you to count my works. All our justice is blemished in your eyes. I wish, then, to be clothed in your own *justice* and to receive from your *love* the eternal possession of *yourself.* —Saint Thérèse of Lisieux

Lesson 9

WHAT ARE THE LIMITS OF CHRIST'S FORGIVENESS?

Introduction

Have you ever felt that you just weren't good enough for God to love you? When you consider what you've done in the past, do you find you've made mistakes—big mistakes—that you think are too big for God to forgive? Do you think you have to have it all together in order to be acceptable to God?

I remember spending an afternoon with a dear friend who was recovering from a nervous breakdown. She had never wanted to talk with me about spiritual things before, so I was very surprised when she began to ask me about my faith. I talked to her about the many things God wants to give us: unconditional love, forgiveness, strength in our times of weakness. She listened, wistfully. "That's what He does for you," she said. "You haven't done the things I've done." Regardless of what I said, she felt she had surpassed the limits of Christ's forgiveness, and that her weaknesses and failures had disqualified her from receiving His blessings.

How different all our lives would be if we truly understood the heart of our heavenly Father. He longs for an intimate relationship with each one of us. He wants to blanket us with His grace and draw us in close. But all too often, we stand outside the door. Perhaps we feel disqualified. Perhaps we feel underdressed—naked, even—when we think about the fact that He knows everything there is to know about us. We wonder if a "close-up shot" of our shortcomings will cause Him to reject us.

God knows this. He knows what holds us back. So He tells us stories. He comes through the back door and catches us off guard by drawing us into a parable. It's only later that we realize the parable was actually *our story*.

We'll spend this whole lesson on parables that you are probably familiar with. You've likely heard this story before. But this time, let's ask God to help us hear His words in a fresh, new way. Let's turn down the volume of the voices that tell us, "You're not good enough. You've crossed the line. When you made that mistake, you went too far." Let's let Jesus speak for Himself.

Day One
SETTING THE STAGE

Read Luke 15:1–10.

1. While both tax collectors and Pharisees[29] drew near to listen to Jesus, to whom did Jesus address these parables? See verses 1–3.

2. What had upset the Pharisees in verse 2?

To sit down and eat with someone had real significance during Jesus' day. It was more than just sharing a picnic bench. It symbolized acceptance and friendship. When Jesus behaved in this way, it flew in the face of the rules of "separation" and "purity" that the Pharisees followed.

3. What is the common theme in each of the three parables of Luke 15?

---

[29] The Pharisees were members of a religious sect within Judaism during Jesus' day. Pharisees kept the law, studying it and making sure that they checked all the boxes of the moral code. Deeply concerned with keeping the Jewish faith uncontaminated, they not only observed the written law (the Torah), they also held up oral tradition as a key way to prevent violating the law.

4. How do you think Jesus' words in verses 7 and 10 made the Pharisees feel?

Quiet your heart and enjoy His presence. . . . Jesus invites "the poor and the crippled, the blind and the lame." (Luke 14:21)

The way that the Pharisees responded to "sinners" contrasted sharply with Jesus' approach. The Pharisees' message? You are condemned and past the reach of God's mercy. Jesus' message? Come and sit with me—you are welcome at my table.

Some of us have encountered Pharisees on our faith journey, and some of us have acted like them. All of us are in equal need of God's mercy and grace. This will be the focus of our lesson, and I pray it draws us all in equal measure to an awareness of our need for forgiveness.

Take a few moments to ask the Lord to remove any blindness that is keeping you from seeing your need of a savior. He wants to help us see our need for Him if we are making poor moral choices, and just as much if we're steeped in self-righteousness. No matter which category we tend toward, He invites us to sit at the table and draw near.

Day Two
THE YOUNGER SON

Read Luke 15:11–32.

1. What was the younger son communicating to his father when he asked for his share of his Father's estate? Note: At that time, when a father died, the oldest child received double the amount that younger siblings inherited. In a family with two sons, the oldest would receive two-thirds of all that the father had, and the younger son would receive one-third. But this would only occur when the father was dead.

One would expect that the father would be offended by this request, but instead, he did what his son asked. The property was divided and given to both his sons.

2. What was the son willing to do in order to earn his way when he returned home?

3. After the younger son received his inheritance, he went to a distant country and squandered it. Feeling hungry and needy, he decided to return home. His father had every right to refuse to receive him back; the son had paid him the ultimate disrespect. How did the father receive his younger son?

4. What was the significance of the father's actions? He was communicating that his son *was not going to have to earn his way back into his favor.* The father welcomed his son with grace—utterly undeserved favor. This is the way that God welcomes us into His family, too. When we turn toward Him and ask if we can come home, He opens His arms wide. He covers our nakedness with His robe of righteousness. We don't earn that place—it's a free gift. Does this parable challenge the way you have previously thought about how your heavenly Father receives you?

Quiet your heart and enjoy His presence. . . . There are no limits to Christ's forgiveness.

If you are coming up with reasons why what you have done is worse than what the younger son did, stop right now. You are not the exception to this rule. God's grace is more than enough to cover anything that you have done. He offers you His forgiveness and beckons you to come home. He wants you. He longs for you. Can you picture a runner at the beginning of a race, poised and ready for the gun to go off? That's God, poised and ready to come rushing toward you, ready to pounce on you with love and extravagant grace and limitless mercy. But He waits, because He will not force Himself on you. He is a gentleman. Are you ready to come home?

Day Three
THE OLDER SON

When we read the parable of the Prodigal Son, we can be left with the impression that the grace freely given to the younger son didn't have a cost. The truth is, it didn't cost the younger son anything. It didn't actually cost the father, either. Who paid the price? It was the older son.

The father had given all he had to his two sons. In reinstating the younger son, he was asking the older son to share what he had inherited with his wild-child, undeserving little brother.

Reread Luke 15:23–32, putting yourself in the shoes of the elder brother.

1. What was the first emotion the older son had when he heard how his brother was being welcomed? Why did he feel this way? What would an alternative (better) reaction have been? See verse 28.

2. What did the father do when his older son refused to come in? See verse 28.

3. What reason did the older son give for not coming in? See verse 29.

When we look more intently at this story, we see that the two brothers weren't as different as they first appeared. Both of them wanted something from their father. The younger decided to just reach out and grab it. The older felt a better method would be to always follow the rules, so that in the end, he would deserve everything he got. Neither loved the father just for himself. They wanted *what he gave* more than they wanted *him*. Rebellion divided the younger son from his father. Pride divided the older son from his father. Both sons used the father to get what they wanted. Both were in need of forgiveness.

Quiet your heart and enjoy His presence. . . He invites you to come home. When we put the three parables of Luke 15 (the lost sheep, lost coin, and lost son) into context and remember that Jesus was talking to the Pharisees, we are forced to broaden our interpretation of the stories. In the words of theologian Tim Keller, "Jesus is pleading not so much with immoral outsiders as with moral insiders."[30] Moral insiders are the rule keepers. When their behavior is held up to the Ten Commandments, they come out looking shiny and good. But clearly, Jesus is concerned about more than outward behavior.

Through these parables, Jesus redefined what it means to be lost. It wasn't just the sheep, the coin, and the younger brother who needed to be found. The elder brother, the rule keeper, was in equal need of forgiveness.

How can you tell if you're more like the older son? Take some time to prayerfully think about how you feel when things don't go your way. Do you get angry because you feel like you deserve things to go well since you are working so hard to obey God? Deep down, do you feel like God should bless you because of the way that you serve Him? Are you trying to control your life through your performance?

The older son obeyed God to get what he wanted. Why do you obey?

Christ's forgiveness is limitless. The only prerequisite is knowing that you need it.

Day Four
SHEER GRATUITOUS LOVE

1. In the parables of Luke 15, the shepherd didn't stop seeking until he found the one missing sheep, the woman didn't rest until she found her one missing coin, and the father watched the road, waiting hopefully for his son's return. What insight do these parables give into the very personal love God has for each of us?

2. Read CCC 218, 219, and 220. What insight do you gain from the Catechism Clips regarding God's forgiveness?

---

[30] Timothy Keller, *The Prodigal God* (New York: Penguin Group, 2008), 10.

3. The only thing that can limit Christ's forgiveness is our refusal to ask for it. This is why it's so critical that we recognize whether we are more like the younger or the older son. Typically, the "younger son" knows that what he is doing is wrong. He knows he needs forgiveness. The older son, though, can be easily blinded by self-righteousness. We don't just need forgiveness for the bad things we've done. We also need to ask forgiveness for the good things we've done for the wrong reasons. If we do good things in order to earn our salvation, we have put ourselves in Jesus' place. We have made the decision (consciously or not) to be our own savior. We have gotten so busy trying to save ourselves that we have lost sight of our need for rescue. Allow the following questions to sink deep into your heart. Take the time to answer them truthfully. At the end of this reflection, you may feel a need to confess that your self-dependence has kept you from dependence on God. Don't ignore this call from the Holy Spirit. Don't put it off. The time to bring this before the Lord is now. He is waiting for you—He is the father standing in the road, ready to run and blanket you in forgiveness and mercy.

Are you trying to control your life through your performance?

Do you feel that obeying God should result in a smoother road ahead?

Are you motivated to obey God out of a fear of punishment, or out of love for Him?

Do you think you might be trying to earn God's love and salvation?

What is prayer for you? Is it a way to increase the likelihood of getting what you want or is it a time of intimacy with your friend?

Quiet your heart and enjoy His presence. . . . He is longing for you.

How I pray that reflecting on those questions hasn't caused anyone to feel condemned. I know that's a risk. Part of it is because we are so hard on ourselves. We want so badly to get it right, and when we realize that we've been doing something good for the wrong reasons, our anger can turn inward. "How could I? What's wrong with me? Why can't I ever get it right?" Please hear me on this: That voice of condemnation does not come from Jesus. "There is no condemnation for those who are in Christ Jesus." (Romans 8:1) The Holy Spirit convicts us (this is different from condemning us) in order to draw us into a good, healthy, holy relationship with God. He wants to lead you to a place where you obey God out of love for Him—not out of fear of getting punished. God wants to be wanted for

Himself, not for the things He gives. He offers you the gift of limitless forgiveness so that anything between your heart and His can be cleared away. He loves you so very, very much.

Day Five
SAINT'S STORY

Saint Thérèse of Lisieux

Are you worried that Jesus is displeased with your weaknesses, failures, and sins? Put this worry far from your mind; it is your poverty that attracts Him the most. God has so much love and grace to give, and He can't give it when people only present their own strengths and merits. But He can give it when we cry out to Him like a small child who needs His strength, which we do not possess on our own.

Thérèse of Lisieux decided at a young age that when she died, she would take care not to present any of her own merits to God. She would instead present only those of the Lord. She wanted to have nothing, present nothing, and go before the Lord with empty hands. She preferred to let God love her as much as He wanted, not as much as she thought was best to ask for. Her goal in her life was to live as a little child and so enter the kingdom of heaven (Matthew 19:14).

Sometimes during her thanksgivings after Communion, Thérèse would fall asleep while praying. Instead of getting upset and discouraged at her weakness, she reasoned that children please their parents when they are sleeping just as much as when they are awake. She rested in the peace she received from the sacrament, and did not worry that she was displeasing God with this wholehearted trust and comfort in His arms.

We are tempted to think that saints lived their lives to perfection. But this isn't the case. Thérèse was not always faithful, but she never lost courage. Instead, she cast herself into the arms of our Lord. He taught her to draw profit from everything— from the good and from the bad in herself. We have only to surrender ourselves wholly to Him, and to do so without reserve. When we do this, we can be confident in His protection and care.

We can learn from Thérèse not to let our weakness make us unhappy. We must learn again to be little children. Children stumble and fall, even though they love their parents very much, and their parents help them up and keep on loving them all the same. If we are to be as little children, we ought not let our stumbling keep us from the love of God.

If we do fall, an act of love will set everything right. The Lord does not look so much at the greatness of our actions; rather, He sees the love with which we do them. When we live with full trust in His love—what, then, have we to fear?

Thérèse said that even if she had committed all possible crimes, she would still have the same confidence in God's mercy. This is the great trust with which we ought to come to the Lord.

Does the story of Saint Thérèse of Lisieux give you added insight into God's forgiving nature? Saint Thérèse is the patron saint of Walking with Purpose (see Appendix 1).

Conclusion

It's a sobering thought to realize that both sons—the rule-bending youngest and the rule-following eldest—were in equal need of forgiveness. The cross is the great equalizer. We *all* require the mercy that flows from Jesus' sacrifice.

Those of us who recognize ourselves in the older son will struggle with this concept. It doesn't feel right. The sense that we somehow deserve our salvation because we've followed the rules can get rooted pretty deeply in our hearts. The only thing that will pull it out is a deeper understanding of the gospel.

Forgiveness always comes at a cost. In the case of the Prodigal Son, the price was paid by the older son. What about in our case? Is there a cost to our forgiveness? Who paid the price for you and me?

It was a firstborn son who came to our aid. But He didn't sit at home, waiting to see if we'd stop wandering and start the journey back home. He stepped off His throne and came looking for us. When He found us, He didn't just share His inheritance. It cost Him *everything* to bring us home and welcome us back into the family. Even though we were dirty and poor, Jesus was not (and is not) ashamed to call us brothers and sisters (Hebrews 2:11).

Just as the father stood outside the feast and begged his oldest son to come in, God issues an invitation to each of us. He has prepared a banquet and it waits for us in heaven. All those who have received the forgiveness He offers will be welcome at the table.

What will the feast be like? The Old Testament prophet Isaiah described it as "a feast of rich food and choice wines, juicy, rich food and pure, choice wines. On this mountain he will destroy the veil that veils all peoples, the web that is woven over all nations. He will destroy death forever. The Lord God will wipe away the tears from all faces; the reproach of his people he will remove from the whole earth." (Isaiah 25:6–8)

That sounds like my kind of party.

Actually, to call it a party is rather an understatement. We read in the book of Revelation that it's going to be a *wedding feast*. Jesus, the Lamb of God, is the bridegroom, and we are the bride.

> "Let us rejoice and be glad and give him glory! For the wedding day of the Lamb has come, his bride has made herself ready. She was allowed to wear a bright, clean linen garment." (The linen represents the righteous deeds of the holy ones.) Then the angel said to me, "Write this: Blessed are those who have been called to the wedding feast of the Lamb." And he said to me, "These words are true; they come from God." . . . Then I saw the heavens opened, and there was a white horse; its rider was called "Faithful and True." . . . He has a name written on his cloak and on his thigh, "King of kings and Lord of lords." (Revelation 19:7–9, 11, 16)

We have been called to the wedding feast of the Lamb. These are the days when we (the bride) are making ourselves ready. Limitless, freely offered forgiveness will wash us clean and allow us to be presented to our groom with radiance and purity. Let's get ready to feast.

My Resolution

In what specific way will I apply what I have learned in this lesson?

Examples:

1. In order to remind myself of God's love for me, I will read Romans 8:38–39 each morning: "For I am convinced that neither death, nor life, nor angels, nor principalities, nor present things, nor future things, nor powers, nor height nor depth, nor any other creature will be able to separate us from the love of God in Christ Jesus our Lord."

2. If I am struggling to believe that God can really forgive all my sins, I will memorize 1 John 1:9: "If we acknowledge our sins, he is faithful and just and will forgive our sins and cleanse us from every wrongdoing."

3. I'll begin each day by spending five minutes thinking about what it cost Jesus to have me welcomed to the family and invited to the wedding supper of the Lamb. I'll thank Him for being willing to come out and find me when I was lost.

4. If I struggle in the same areas as the older son (in the parable of the Prodigal Son), I will check my heart each day for anger. Am I angry with God because things didn't go my way? Am I angry with myself for not being perfect? I'll ask God for forgiveness if I discover anger in my heart.

My Resolution:

Catechism Clips

CCC 218 In the course of its history, Israel was able to discover that God had only one reason to reveal Himself to them, a single motive for choosing them from among all peoples as His special possession: His sheer gratuitous love. And thanks to the prophets, Israel understood that it was again out of love that God never stopped saving them and pardoning their unfaithfulness and sins.

CCC 219 God's love for Israel is compared to a father's love for his son. His love for His people is stronger than a mother's love for her children. God loves His people more than a bridegroom his beloved; His love will be victorious over even the worst infidelities, and it extends to His most precious gift: "God so loved the world that he gave his only Son" (John 3:16).

CCC 220 God's love is "everlasting" (Isaiah 54:8): "For the mountains may depart and the hills be removed, but my steadfast love shall not depart from you" (Isaiah 54:10). Through Jeremiah, God declares to his people, "I have loved you with an everlasting love; therefore I have continued my faithfulness to you" (Jeremiah 31:3).

Looking for more material? We've got you covered! Walking with Purpose meets women where they are in their spiritual journey. From our Opening Your Heart 22-lesson foundational Bible study to more advanced studies, we have something to help each and every woman grow closer to Christ. Find out more:

www.walkingwithpurpose.com

Lesson 10: Connect Coffee Talk
YOUR HEART – YOU ARE CAPTIVATING

Accompanying DVD can be viewed by disc or please visit our website at walkingwithpurpose.com/videos and select *Opening Your Heart* Bible Study, click through to select Videos.

Key verse:

"Above all else, guard your heart, for it is the wellspring of life." (Proverbs 4:23)

1. **Your Heart's Questions**

   A. Am I _____?

   B. Do I _____?

   C. Am I worth_____?

2. **Your Definition of Self**

   A. Do I define myself based on what I do (pride)?

   B. Do I define myself based on what others think of me (vanity)?

   "Every day, the Christian is tempted . . . In conversations, in behavior, in entertainments, the pressure to conform and the fear of being disdained or rejected strive against the persistent, but gentle, voice of God's will in the conscience. It only takes a little string to keep an eagle tied to the ground; until we are willing to sacrifice the opinions of fickle people in order to please the dependable Lord of the universe, there's no way we'll really learn to fly."[31]

C. Do I define myself based on my possessions or circumstances (sensuality)?

3. Your True Identity: A Beloved Daughter of God

"Captivated" by Vicky Beeching

Your laughter, it echoes, like a joyous thunder.
Your whisper, it warms me like a summer breeze.
Your anger is fiercer than the sun in its splendor.
You're close and yet full of mystery.
Ever since that day, when I saw your face, try as I may,
I cannot look away. I cannot look away.

Captivated by you.
I am captivated by you.
May my life be one unbroken gaze fixed upon the beauty of your face.

Beholding is becoming, so as you fill my gaze, I become more like you and my heart is changed.
Beholding is becoming, so as you fill my view, transform me into the likeness of you.
This is what I ask for all my days—that I may never look away, never look away.

Captivated by you.
I am captivated by you.
May my life be one unbroken gaze, fixed upon your beauty, fixed upon your beauty.

No other could ever be as beautiful. No other could ever steal my heart away . . .
I just can't look away.

I am captivated by you.
I am captivated by you.
May my life be one unbroken gaze fixed upon the beauty of your face.[32]

---

[31] Bartunek, *The Better Part*, 187–88.
[32] Vicky Beeching, "Captivated," *Yesterday, Today and Forever* (Brentwood, TN: Sparrow Records, 2006), compact disc.

QUESTIONS FOR DISCUSSION

1. What are some of the ways that God has shown you His love for you? Think of the memories you cherish and moments that have moved you to tears. They are all gifts sent to you by the One who has been pursuing you since you took your first breath.

2. Have you experienced unconditional love in any of your earthly relationships? When God looks at us, He says, "*Yes!* You are worth fighting for." How does the way in which we have been loved by others affect our ability to truly believe that?

3. God has a place in His heart that you alone can fill. He wants the same thing that you want: to be loved. He wants intimacy with you. What are some ways in which you can love Him back?

   Spend quiet Time each day

NOTES

No program near you? No problem...it's easy to start your own group in your parish or at home and we will walk with you every step of the way. Find out more:

www.walkingwithpurpose.com

Lesson 11

WHAT DOES THE SACRAMENT OF PENANCE HAVE TO DO WITH MY FRIENDSHIP WITH CHRIST?

Introduction

No doubt about it, our view of God will affect how we feel about the sacrament of penance. Some of us think of God as a stern father or an authoritarian dictator. We might picture Him with a face of constant disapproval. We think to ourselves, "Why go to confession and spend time in front of someone who is never going to approve of me, anyway? Why bother? I'll never be good enough."

Some of us think of God as an indulgent father, one who wants us to be happy, and who laughs at our foolish mistakes, never really taking things too seriously. He is our cosmic good buddy—our cheerleader. This image of God, although it contains some truth, is incomplete, and it can cause us not to go to confession because we simply don't take our sins very seriously.

Our feelings about the sacrament of penance aren't impacted just by our view of God. We're also influenced by our culture's sensitivity (or lack thereof) to sin. In the words of philosopher Peter Kreeft, "We usually think we are morally pretty good because we measure ourselves, not against the standards of our Lord, but against the standards of society."[33] And our society excuses quite a lot.

This means we tend to waver between feeling like the sacrament of penance is totally unnecessary because we are basically good people and feeling like it may be necessary,

---

[33] Peter J. Kreeft, *Catholic Christianity: A Complete Catechism of Catholic Church Beliefs Based on the Catechism of the Catholic Church* (San Francisco: Ignatius Press, 2001).

but it's the last place we want to go. Either way, the confessional lines stay pretty short on Saturday afternoons.

The purpose of this lesson is to look at what the sacrament of penance has to do with our friendship with Christ. Make no mistake—**this sacrament is not about condemnation. Its purpose is to heal and reconcile our relationship with our truest, most faithful friend.** This may not be the way it was presented to you in childhood. If that's the case, you may have to let go of some preconceived notions of how God sees and relates to you. I know this isn't easy to do. It's hard to give things a second chance when they've caused us pain in the past.

Many of us have negative memories of confessing our sins to a priest. For those of us who are feeling a little uneasy about this lesson, perhaps the following words from theologian Jean Vanier will offer comfort: "Somewhere along the line in the history of the Church, people have become more centered upon obedience to laws than upon this relationship of love with a person, with Jesus; more centered upon justice than upon love. The heart of our faith is not law, it is a person, Jesus who calls us into the peace and joy of friendship and of love."[34]

My prayer this week is that we will look at the sacrament with fresh eyes and an ever-increasing awareness of God's desire to blanket us with mercy. He doesn't approach His children with the law in one hand and a scowl on His face. He's the father of the Prodigal Son, and He runs toward us with open arms. He never gives up on us. Can you personalize that truth? He hasn't given up on *you*.

Day One
OUR TRUEST FRIEND'S PROMISE

Read the first two pages of Appendix 4, "Confession by the Numbers."

1. What are the 9 Confession Promises described in this article?

2. Which of the 9 Confession Promises do you need the most?

---

[34] Father Paul Farren, *Freedom and Forgiveness: A Fresh Look at the Sacrament of Reconciliation* (Dublin: Columba Press, 2013), x.

3. One of the 9 Confession Promises is a new heart. In the sacrament of penance, we offer God our callused and hardened hearts. In exchange, He gives us hearts that are tender and more sensitive to sin's damaging effects. CCC 1432 says, "God must give man a new heart. . . . It is in discovering the greatness of God's love that our heart is shaken by the horror and weight of our sin," which strengthens us so we can make better choices in the future.

Look up the following verses that speak of the greatness of God's love, then put them in your own words. These are great verses to read and think about before receiving the sacrament of penance because they keep our focus on His steadfast promise of mercy.

Exodus 34:6

Isaiah 49:15

Ephesians 2:4–5

Quiet your heart and enjoy His presence. . . . He offers pardon and peace.

"Let us hold unwaveringly to our confession that gives us hope, for he who made the promise is trustworthy." (Hebrews 10:23)

This is truth we can count on. The One who made the promises we've read about today is trustworthy. He always comes through. He is consistently faithful to His word.

What word does He speak over our mistakes and regrets and failures? Mercy.

Mercy trumps justice. Every time. Justice looks at what is deserved. It demands punishment for all the times we have failed to love others as we should. But God's mercy proves stronger than what is "fair."

No matter how numerous your shortcomings, don't lose hope. God took every one of them into account before you were even born, and made sure that His steadfast mercy would be enough to cover them all.

These are His words for you today:

"Do not be afraid, I have redeemed you. I have called you by name; you are mine. You are precious in my eyes. You are honored and I love you. Do not be afraid. I am with you." (Isaiah 43:1, 4)

Day Two
OUR TRUEST FRIEND KNOWS WHAT'S BEST FOR US

Read the third page of Appendix 4, "Confession by the Numbers." This section is titled "10 Reasons to Confess."

1. According to this section, what are five *human* reasons to go to confession? Note: A "human reason" is something that directs us toward growing into more mature and virtuous humans. It makes us more pleasant to be around. This is different from a spiritual reason, which goes deeper on a soul level.

   A.

   B.

   C.

   D.

   E.

2. Which of the five human reasons resonates most with you?

3. According to the article, what are five *spiritual* reasons to go to confession?

   A.

   B.

   C.

D.

E.

4. Which of the five spiritual reasons resonates most with you?

Quiet your heart and enjoy His presence. . . . He knows us better than we know ourselves.

Our self-perception can get pretty messed up. There are times we go too easy on ourselves, excusing things that God takes seriously. Under other circumstances, we can go to the opposite extreme and hopelessly condemn ourselves. This is why there is enormous benefit in unpacking our sins alongside a priest who can guide us objectively.

In his book Interior Freedom, *Father Jacques Philippe writes about how important it is for us to have a realistic view of ourselves:*

> *One of the most essential conditions for God's grace to act in our lives is saying yes to what we are and to the situations in which we find ourselves. That is because God is "realistic." His grace does not operate on our imaginings, ideals, or dreams. It works on reality . . . The person God loves with the tenderness of a Father, the person he wants to touch and to transform with his love, is not the person we'd have liked to be or ought to be. It's the person we are. God doesn't love "ideal persons" or "virtual beings." He loves actual, real people.*[35]

What we need in confession is an honest, truthful assessment that brings us back to an awareness of who we are and whose we are. We are beloved, and we belong. This message is at the heart of the sacrament of penance. This is the grace God is whispering to our souls.

Father Paul Farren has this to say about God's message to us in the confessional: "When we think about the sacrament of Reconciliation our thoughts most often focus on ourselves and our sinfulness. The role of God in some sense might even appear secondary. However, the sacrament of Reconciliation is primarily that sacred place and moment when God confesses. . . . What does God confess? God confesses his love, his forgiveness, his gratitude, his confidence, his trust and his belief in us."[36]

Spend some time in prayer thanking God for His love, His forgiveness, His gratitude, His confidence, His trust, and His belief in you.

---

[35] Philippe, *Interior Freedom*, 32.
[36] Farren, *Freedom and Forgiveness*, 1.

Day Three
OUR TRUEST FRIEND WANTS AN INTIMATE RELATIONSHIP WITH US

1. According to CCC 1468, what is the "whole power" of the sacrament of penance based on?

2. We read in Genesis that in the beginning, God *walked around* in the Garden of Eden. His relationship with Adam and Eve was intimate, authentic, and face-to-face. There was no sin. There was no shame. There was nothing to separate them. What impact did Adam and Eve's sin have on their relationship with God? See Genesis 3:8–10.

God has never stopped longing for a renewal of that authentic, intimate friendship. This is why He sent Jesus to earth—to provide a means for us to approach Him with the confidence of a child who knows she belongs to her father.

But all too often, what we experience is distance in that relationship. This is not because God has moved away from us. We are the ones who turn away. We do this in all sorts of ways: We hide in fear, hang our heads in shame, or stick up our noses in pride. We'll do anything to avoid making eye contact with God.

It reminds me of times my kids have done something wrong and I'm trying to discipline them. Sometimes they respond with their arms folded, staring at the floor in anger. They are mad that they've been caught. Other times their face is in their hands, and they can't stop crying because they are so upset for messing up. No matter what the heart attitude, what I really want them to do is look me in the eye. I want this for two reasons. One is for them to know that I'm serious about what I'm saying. But I also want them to see the unconditional love in my eyes.

When God invites us to the sacrament of penance, He's asking us to look Him in the eye. He wants to make eye contact with us. In that moment, we can see ourselves from His perspective. Yes, our sin is serious. He isn't saying that it doesn't matter. But it doesn't diminish His love for us. In the confessional, we look the Lord in the eye and experience a moment of deep tenderness as God whispers, "It's OK. Come out of hiding. You're safe here with me."

3. Is there anything that is holding you back from the sacrament of penance?

Quiet your heart and enjoy His presence. . . . "May the eyes of your heart be enlightened, that you may know what is the hope that belongs to his call." (Ephesians 1:18)

Friend, the Lord is calling you. He is inviting you to come and gaze into His eyes of mercy. He's offering you hope for a fresh start. Oh, I pray that the eyes of your heart would be enlightened, and that the darkness of shame would be chased away. Shame keeps your eyes cast down. But God is cupping your face in His hands and calling you to look up.

Dear Lord,

I get so nervous at the thought of looking in your eyes. I don't know if I'm ready to see myself reflected in them. I feel shame over things I've said and done, and I wonder how you could possibly forgive me. But then I look at the cross, and am reminded that while I was still a sinner, you died for me (Romans 5:8). Your love for me isn't dependent on what I do. It depends on what you have done for me. So give me the confidence to approach your throne of grace. I know I am promised that what I will encounter there is mercy. Always. Without exception.

"Who will bring a charge against God's chosen ones? It is God who acquits us. Who will condemn? It is Christ who died, rather, was raised, who also is at the right hand of God, who indeed intercedes for us. What will separate us from the love of Christ? Will anguish, or distress, or persecution, or famine, or nakedness, or peril, or the swords? . . . No, in all these things we conquer overwhelmingly through him who loved us. For I am convinced that neither death, nor life, nor angels, nor principalities, nor present things, nor future things, nor powers, nor height, nor depth, nor any other creature will be able to separate us from the love of God in Christ Jesus our Lord." (Romans 8:33–35, 37–39)

Day Four
OUR TRUEST FRIEND WANTS US TO LIVE IN FREEDOM

1. In John 8:36, we are promised, "If the son sets you free, you will be free indeed." Yet so many Christians don't feel they are experiencing spiritual freedom. One of the reasons for this is described in John 8:34. According to that verse, what gets in the way of our freedom?

Saint Paul addresses this in Galatians 5:1 with the words, "For freedom Christ set us free; so stand firm and do not submit again to the yoke of slavery." All too often, we take our freedom and use it to step right back into the bondage of slavery to sin. We get into bad habits that we don't feel able to break. We harbor bitterness and it keeps our hearts in a vise grip. Our words seem to take on a life of their own and are out of our mouths before we can stop them. We feel dominated by sin, and aren't sure how to get free.

This is where the sacrament of penance comes in. We don't just go to the confessional for forgiveness. There is more.

2. How is the "more" of the sacrament of penance described in the last part of CCC 1496?

Ladies, this is it. This is the secret to growing stronger spiritually. When we receive absolution in the sacrament of penance, we receive supernatural grace to help us go back out into our lives strengthened and fortified in the very areas where we feel the weakest. We get a second wind and find that we are able to keep pursuing the summit. Theologian Scott Hahn describes it this way:

Through confession, we begin to heal. We begin to get our story straight and stop deceiving ourselves. We come home to resume our place in the family of God. We begin to know peace. None of this comes easily. Confession doesn't make change easy, but it does make it possible. It is not a quick fix, but it is a sure cure. We need to go back to the sacrament, and go again, and keep going back, because life is a marathon, not a forty-yard dash. We'll often want to stop, but like a distance runner, we'll need to press on for our second wind, and third, and fourth. In this case, we can count on the wind coming, because it's the "wind" of the Holy Spirit.[37]

3. The "wind" of the Holy Spirit is exactly what we need to persevere in the Christian life. According to 2 Corinthians 3:17, what else does the presence of the Holy Spirit bring us?

Quiet your heart and enjoy His presence. . . . The truth will set you free.

Our truest friend knows how much we need freedom. Father Jacques Philippe writes, "Our freedom is proportionate to the love and childlike trust we have for our heavenly Father."[38] The more we meditate on His character—His mercy, His love, and His forgiving nature—the more our trust in Him will grow.

He is waiting for you. He is longing to fill you with the peace and freedom that comes from hearing that you are beloved. That you belong. That you are forgiven.

"He is lover. He is redeemer. He is father. He is friend. He is our shelter. He is our healer. He is the lifter of our heads."[39] —Meredith Andrews

"The look in his eyes is the purest, truest, tenderest, most loving, and most hope-filled in this world."[40] —Father Jacques Philippe

---

[37] Scott Hahn, *Lord, Have Mercy: The Healing Power of Confession* (New York: Doubleday, 2003), 175.
[38] Philippe, *Interior Freedom*, 15.
[39] Meredith Andrews, "Lift Up Your Head," *The Invitation* (Nashville, TN: Word Entertainment, 2008), compact disc.
[40] Philippe, *Interior Freedom*, 36.

Day Five
SAINT'S STORY

Saint Faustina Reveals God's Mercy

God never gives up on us. This is what we mean when we say that God is merciful. Instead of giving the human race what its sins deserved, He sent His Son to redeem us.

"[H]e predestined us to be adopted as His sons through Jesus Christ, in accordance with His pleasure and will—to the praise of His glorious grace, which He has freely given us in the One He loves. In [Christ] we have redemption through His blood, the forgiveness of sins, in accordance with the riches of God's grace that He lavished on us with all wisdom and understanding." (Ephesians 1:5–8)

Yet, He will not force us to accept the priceless gift of His grace and forgiveness: "O Jerusalem, Jerusalem, you who kill the prophets and stone those sent to you, how often I have longed to gather your children together, as a hen gathers her chicks under her wings, but you were not willing!" (Luke 13:34)

The sacrament of confession proves this: God is always ready to forgive, but He respects our freedom too much to do so unless we really want Him to, and unless we repent. And so He gives us the perfect opportunity to show that we really want His forgiveness: the sacrament of reconciliation. Confession is the "tribunal of mercy," as Jesus Himself described it to Saint Faustina Kowalska.

Saint Faustina died in 1938 in her convent in Krakow, Poland, when she was only thirty-three, her body torn asunder by tuberculosis and a host of other illnesses and suffering. At the time, few guessed what an extraordinary saint she was. But when her diary, *Divine Mercy in My Soul*, was published, word spread fast, and she was recognized as Christ's specially chosen apostle of the Divine Mercy.

She had entered the convent when she was twenty, after an uneventful but pious childhood. For the next thirteen years she would live in four different convents of the same religious congregation, the Sisters of Our Lady of Mercy, and serve as cook, gardener, and doorkeeper—hardly a glamorous résumé. But in those years her intimate union with Christ deepened steadily under the subtle action of grace, and she was granted visions, revelations, hidden stigmata, participation in the Lord's Passion, bilocation, the ability to read souls, the gift of prophecy, and the privilege of mystical engagement and marriage.

All these gifts were directed toward helping Saint Faustina fulfill her threefold mission of reminding the world of God's powerful, loving mercy, sparking a new devotion to that mercy, and founding the Apostolic Movement of the Divine Mercy. All three were successfully carried out in her brief but intense life.

In her famous diary, she recorded many things that our Lord spoke to her. One of His favorite topics was the sacrament of reconciliation. From His comments, it is clear that He has a special love for that sacrament as a unique and powerful place of encounter between a soul who recognizes its need for grace, and Himself, who is so eager to meet that need. Here are some of our Lord's words to Saint Faustina:

> [Today the Lord said to me,] Daughter, when you go to confession, to this fountain of My mercy, the Blood and Water which came forth from My Heart always flows down upon your soul and ennobles it. Every time you go to confession, immerse yourself entirely in My mercy, with great trust, so that I may pour the bounty of My grace upon your soul. When you approach the confessional, know this: that I Myself am waiting there for you. I am only hidden by the priest, but I Myself act in your soul. Here the misery of the soul meets the God of mercy.[41] (Diary entry 1602)

> Write, speak of My mercy. Tell souls where they are to look for solace; that is, in the Tribunal of Mercy [the sacrament of reconciliation]. There the greatest miracles take place [and] are incessantly repeated. To avail oneself of this miracle, it is not necessary to go on a great pilgrimage or to carry out some external ceremony; it suffices to come with faith to the feet of My representative and to reveal to him one's misery, and the miracle of Divine Mercy will be fully demonstrated. Were a soul like a decaying corpse so that from a human standpoint, there would be no [hope of] restoration and everything would already be lost, it is not so with God. The miracle of Divine Mercy restores that soul in full. Oh, how miserable are those who do not take advantage of the miracle of God's mercy! You will call out in vain, but it will be too late.[42] (Diary entry 1448)

How does Saint Faustina's description of God's mercy affect your feelings toward the sacrament of penance?

What can you take away from her life that might strengthen your faith?

---

[41] Saint Maria Faustina Kowalska, *Diary of Saint Maria Faustina Kowalska: Divine Mercy in My Soul* (Stockbridge, MA: Marian Press, 2005), 352–53.
[42] Ibid., 319.

Conclusion

There is a song I haven't been able to get out of my head as I've written this lesson. It's my current favorite, and because of the truth of the words, I think I'm going to love this song forever. To me, it summarizes perfectly what God is inviting us to through the sacrament of penance. I leave you with its lyrics, and am praying that you'll be able to listen to the actual song and to close your eyes as you play it. If I were with you, I'd have you sit down and would put headphones on your ears. It doesn't matter how many times I hear it; it gets me every time. Ladies, we are so crazy loved by our God. If we could just grasp how much, we would be utterly changed.

May God call to your heart through these words.

"Out of Hiding" (from the album *The Undoing*, by Steffany Gretzinger)

Come out of hiding, you're safe here with me
There's no need to cover what I already see
You've got your reasons but I hold your peace
You've been on lockdown and I hold the key

'Cause I loved you before you knew it was love
And I saw it all, still I chose the cross
And you were the one that I was thinking of when I rose from the grave
Now rid of the shackles my victory's yours
I tore the veil so you could come close
There's no reason to stand at a distance anymore
You're not far from home

I'll be your lighthouse when you're lost at sea
And I will illuminate everything
No need to be frightened of intimacy
No, just throw off your fear and come running to me
And oh, as you run, what hindered love will only become part of the story
You're almost home now . . . please don't quit now . . . you're almost home to me.[43]

---

[43] Steffany Gretzinger, "Out of Hiding," *The Undoing* (Redding, CA: Bethel Music, 2014), compact disc.

My Resolution

In what specific way will I apply what I have learned in this lesson?

Examples:

1. It's been a while since I've received the sacrament of penance and I'm nervous that I won't know what to do. I'll prepare by reading the section of Appendix 4 titled "7 Things Expected from You in Confession."

2. I'll receive the sacrament of penance this week, using the sections of Appendix 4 titled "6 Ways to Examine Your Conscience" and "10 Commandments" to help me prepare.

3. If shame and fear are keeping me from receiving all the promises and benefits of the sacrament of penance, I will take time each day this week to meditate on God's unchanging love for me. I'll do this by meditating on Romans 8:33–39.

My Resolution:

Catechism Clips

CCC 1468 "The whole power of the sacrament of Penance consists in restoring us to God's grace and joining us with him in an intimate friendship." Reconciliation with God is thus the purpose and effect of this sacrament. For those who receive the sacrament of Penance with contrite heart and religious disposition, reconciliation "is usually followed by peace and serenity of conscience with strong spiritual consolation." Indeed the sacrament of Reconciliation with God brings about a true "spiritual resurrection," restoration of the dignity and blessings of the life of the children of God, of which the most precious is friendship with God.

CCC 1496 The spiritual effects of the sacrament of Penance are:
-Reconciliation with God by which the penitent recovers grace;
-Reconciliation with the Church;
-Remission of the eternal punishment incurred by mortal sins;

-Remission, at least in part, of temporal punishments resulting from sin;
-Peace and serenity of conscience, and spiritual consolation;
-An increase of spiritual strength for the Christian battle.

Lesson 12

WHAT DOES THE EUCHARIST HAVE TO DO WITH MY FRIENDSHIP WITH CHRIST?

Introduction

Even though I didn't convert to Catholicism until I was an adult, I've enjoyed a close friendship with Christ since childhood. I knew He loved and cared about me personally. Turning to Him in prayer with my concerns and my joys was easy. I can't remember a time when I didn't love the Bible, when reading it daily wasn't just my habit, but my source of peace.

The sacraments are the normal means by which we receive God's grace, but the Catechism teaches us that God *can* and *does* work outside the sacraments. I know this to be true. My experience of God as a Protestant was real, and I felt satisfied. I was not longing for more. In truth, I had no idea there was anything more to long for, spiritually speaking. I had my Bible and my personal relationship with Jesus. It felt like enough.

I became Catholic in my early twenties, not because of a love for the sacraments, but because I was in love with a handsome Brit who happened to be Catholic. I wanted spiritual unity in our marriage, so I was willing to convert. Due to my ignorance (and a less than stellar RCIA experience), before my conversion the sacraments seemed like choices in the grocery store: If I wanted to take advantage of them, they were there. But if I felt satisfied with what I had, they could sit on the shelf. For years, that is where I left the Eucharist.

My journey toward discovering the riches of the sacraments began with a long period of frustration. I was trying so hard to figure everything out, reading book after book. I found I could be convinced by any number of different perspectives. "Which one is true?" I would ask God.

Through studying the Bible passages in which Jesus gives Peter the authority to lead the Church, I began to learn that God didn't want me to be confused about important matters of faith. He had entrusted the Catholic Church with the job of interpreting Scripture and teaching Christ's followers. In the words of Peter Kreeft, "Scripture itself calls the Church 'the pillar and ground of the truth.' (1 Tim. 3:15) Scripture was the Church's textbook, but the Church was the living teacher who taught and interpreted that textbook."[44]

I could trust what the Church taught. This was groundbreaking information for me. I had never thought about Scripture in that way. But when I considered that the earliest Christians didn't have Bibles (they had to rely on the oral tradition of the Catholic Church), I had to let go of some previously held assumptions.

That being said, I still found it hard to believe in Christ's real presence in the Eucharist. I didn't understand it. I couldn't prove it. I couldn't explain it.

Hebrews 11:1 made a real impact on me at this time. It says, "Faith is the realization of what is hoped for and the evidence of things not seen." I grasped the fact that I was going to have to take a leap of faith. Until I stepped out and decided to believe that Christ was truly present in the Eucharist, I wasn't going to receive the benefits that He was offering. "Lord, I believe; help my disbelief," became my prayer. And this is a prayer He *loves* to answer.

I find it difficult to describe the difference this has made in my life. How can I put words to such intimacy, such depth of friendship, such a source of inner peace? When I receive Christ in the Eucharist, I receive strength and grace. Practically, this means that I can get things done for my family and for Christ that I wasn't previously able to do. I have experienced exponential growth, a supernatural stretching of my resources that leaves me amazed.

There are times people ask me how I "get it all done." They wonder how I can find enough time to develop and run the ministry of Walking with Purpose while meeting the needs of my husband and seven children.

It's the *real presence* of Jesus. I am like a glove, sitting lifeless on a table. But when He fills me, He can do all sorts of things in spite of my limitations. I don't feel worthy of His presence within me, but I am so grateful that He makes Himself so available. He waits for me every day in the Eucharist. What a waste it would be if I left Him on the shelf. Today, I embrace Him whenever possible.

---

[44] Peter Kreeft, *Jesus Shock* (Singer Island, FL: Beacon Publishing, 2008), 113.

Day One
THIS ISN'T SOME NEW IDEA

The *Compendium of the Catechism of the Catholic Church* 282 states: "Jesus Christ is present in the Eucharist in a unique and incomparable way. He is present in a true, real, and substantial way, with his Body and his Blood, with his Soul and his Divinity. In the Eucharist, therefore, there is present in a sacramental way, that is, under the Eucharistic species of bread and wine, Christ whole and entire, God and Man."

Some of us read that and think to ourselves, "I know. This is what I've always been taught since I was a kid." Maybe you can even recite a memorized version of that truth.

Others read the very same thing and think, "*What?* Where did that come from?" They might not say it out loud, but it's what they are thinking. I know. It was my first reaction many years ago. When you haven't grown up being taught something, it's hard to let go of old beliefs and embrace a teaching that says bread and wine actually become Jesus—His body, blood, soul, and divinity. So for the sake of those of us who need a little background, let's head back to the Old Testament. God started dropping hints about the Eucharist to His people pretty early on.

For hundreds of years, God's people (the Israelites) had been enslaved by the Egyptians. God chose a man named Moses to be His mouthpiece and to lead His people to freedom. To convince Pharaoh that freeing the Israelites would be in his best interest, God sent ten plagues on Egypt. The final plague was the worst: Every firstborn—human and animal—would be killed. The Israelites would be protected from this plague as long as they followed God's instructions.

1. A. What instructions did God give the Israelites in order for them to escape the tenth plague? Read Exodus 12:3–8.

If the Israelites wanted to live, their doors needed to be covered by the blood of the lamb, and the Passover lamb needed to be eaten. This was called the Passover Ritual. God told the Israelites to remember that day forever and continue to celebrate it once every year.

B. How did John the Baptist refer to Jesus in John 1:29?

C. The last Passover Jesus celebrated with His disciples (commonly called the Lord's Supper) is described in Matthew 26:26–28. What did He give the disciples to eat at that meal, and what did He tell them it was?

2. After the tenth plague, Pharaoh freed the Israelites, and their journey to the Promised Land of Israel began. What did they eat during this time? See Exodus 16:4 and 31.

According to CCC 1094, the manna in the desert prefigured the Eucharist, "the true bread from heaven." Interestingly, the manna was to be collected every single morning. If the Israelites tried to gather extra to save for the next day, they woke up in the morning to find that it stank and was full of worms. This supernatural food was to be gathered as a part of a daily discipline. Throughout the journey to the Promised Land, God was teaching His people how to depend on Him moment by moment, day by day.

3. The eating of the Passover lamb and the manna in the desert both pointed to the Eucharist. You can imagine a New Testament Jew putting it all together, nodding his head and saying, "Yeah . . . I get it! I see the connection!" But there was some Old Testament teaching going on that actually made it harder for New Testament Jews to believe in the Eucharist. In Leviticus 3:17, God forbade the Israelites to consume any blood. Father John Bartunek sheds interesting light on this in the following commentary:

> The Mosaic and Levitical Law prohibited Jews from drinking the blood of their sacrifices, or even eating any meat with the blood still in it. In blood, they believed, was life, and all life belonged to God—it's off-limits for men . . . Pagan religions had no prohibition against the consumption of blood. Pagans were accustomed to consuming bloody meat and bloody sacrifices. Just as they worshiped idols (creatures that were considered divine), they believed they could enter into communion with the divine

through the consumption of those creatures' blood. But the Jews were protected from such practices.[45]

If the Jews were forbidden to consume blood, what might the disciples have thought when Jesus told them to drink His blood?

The only way the Jewish people would have believed that somehow things had changed and it was now OK to drink Jesus' blood would be if they trusted His authority to the same degree that they trusted God the Father's. Jesus ushered in change that could only be received by people who believed He was far more than a prophet, a teacher, or a revolutionary. They needed to believe that He was divine, with authority to bring change to the old way of communing with God.

Quiet your heart and enjoy His presence. . . . Let the Old Testament shed light on the New.

The Passover commemorated the rescue of God's people. The sacrifice of a lamb—its blood on the door, its flesh eaten by the family—brought about that rescue.

The manna in the wilderness was the bread of life to the hungry Israelites, teaching them to depend on God for sustenance every single day.

The Israelites were taught from the very beginning that there was something significant about blood— it contained life, power.

Put it all together:

Jesus, our rescuer, was the final Passover lamb. Today He asks us to consume His body and blood. Jesus invites us to receive the daily spiritual bread of the Eucharist, far more supernatural than manna.

---

[45] Bartunek, *The Better Part*, 304.

Jesus invites us to drink His blood in the Eucharist, and in doing so, to share in His divine life. He wants His blood to flow through our veins, giving us the supernatural power to live in freedom.

Spend some time talking to God about what you've studied today. Does it strengthen your faith? Thank Him for that. Do you still have questions? Ask Him. Does it make you long for His presence? He is longing for you, too.

Day Two
HE MEANT WHAT HE SAID

Our reading for today takes place the day after Jesus' miracle of the multiplication of the loaves and fishes. A boy had five barley loaves and two fish, and Jesus multiplied them to feed about five thousand men (plus women and children), with twelve baskets of bread and fish left over. It was a picture of superabundance—another prefiguring of the Eucharist.

Read John 6:22–69 with that miracle in the back of your mind. It's a long reading, I know. But it's just too loaded with good truth to skip bits of it.

As you look at verses 22–34, do you sense the people's hunger? Not just physical hunger, but a yearning for something deeply satisfying? Jesus responds to the hunger with a cryptic comment: "The bread of God is that which comes down from heaven and gives life to the world." And they respond by saying that they want this bread; they are desperate to be filled.

I wonder if Jesus paused at that point. Did He look in their faces, trying to gauge if they were ready for His next words? Were His eyes pleading, hopeful that these people would be able to take the leap of faith that would allow them to embrace what He was going to offer? Jesus saw their emptiness. He knew (and knows!) that only He could satisfy.

1. What did Jesus claim in John 6:35? How did the people react? See John 6:41–42.

2. Instead of backing down because of their critical response to Him, Jesus spoke even more strongly. How did He describe Himself in John 6:48–51? How did the people respond? See John 6:52.

3. Clearly, Jesus' words weren't winning Him any popularity contests. He could have downplayed what He had previously said, or changed the subject. But that's not how He responded. What did He say in verses 53–58?

Some of the deeper meaning of the word *eat* gets lost in translation. Two Greek words, *trogein* and *phagein*, are translated as "eat" in English. At the beginning of the discourse, Jesus used the word *phagein*, which is used to describe a human eating. As He continued speaking, He intensified His word choice and used the word *trogein* instead. *Trogein* is chosen to describe the way an animal eats—more of a gnawing. He had opportunity after opportunity to clarify, correct, or back down. Instead, Jesus' words just got more and more intense.

4. What happened as a result of Jesus' words? See John 6:66.

Many of His followers left and no longer accompanied Him. Make no mistake, Jesus didn't watch with indifference as they walked away. He came to seek and save the lost. His love for each of those retreating souls was so immense that He was soon to die for them. If they had simply misunderstood Him, don't you think He would have chased them down the road to clarify? But if He had meant what He said, simply telling them the truth, the truth He had been waiting throughout the Old Testament to reveal, then He would have had to let them respond as they chose. He never has been one to force Himself on anyone.

Quiet your heart and enjoy His presence. . . . How Jesus longs to satisfy your emptiness.

"Jesus then said to the twelve, 'Do you also want to leave?' Simon Peter answered him, 'Master, to whom shall we go? You have the words of eternal life.'" (John 6:67–68)

So how will we respond? Will we turn away? Or will we take the leap of faith and believe? Will we ask to be filled by the One born in Bethlehem (which means "house of bread")? Will we look for the "food that endures for eternal life" (John 6:27)? The choice is ours. Will we turn away or bow down in worship?

To help bring your heart to a place of worship, listen to Matt Maher's song "Adoration," from his album All the People Said Amen. *It's a contemporary take on the following medieval Latin hymn by Saint Thomas Aquinas.*

"Tantum Ergo"

Down in adoration falling,
This great sacrament we hail
Over ancient forms departing
Newer rites of grace prevail;
Faith for all defects supplying,
Where the feeble senses fail.

To the everlasting Father,
And the Son who reigns on high
With the Spirit blest, proceeding
Forth from each eternally
Be salvation, honor, blessing
Might and endless majesty

Pour upon us, Lord of mercy
Spirit of Thy selfless love
Make of us one true heart yearning
For the glory of thy Son
Jesus, fire of justice blazing
Gladdening light forevermore!

Day Three
JUST KEEPING THE FAITH

I love the way Peter Kreeft describes the Catholic Church. In one of his talks, he compared the Church to a mail carrier: She doesn't write what's delivered or change anything about it; she just delivers it safely. For all that people might not like about the Catholic Church, history proves that she hasn't changed what was originally taught about the Eucharist, regardless of how unpopular or hard to believe it might be. Even Martin Luther didn't deny the real presence of Christ in the Eucharist.[46] This belief went unquestioned for the first thousand years of the Church. That's a pretty long time. In the words of Peter Kreeft:

> The center of all Christian worship until the Reformation was always the Eucharist, not the sermon, as it is for Protestants. The Eucharist was never omitted, as it usually is for Protestants. Any pre-Reformation Christian would see a church service without the Eucharist as something like a marriage without sex. Now comes the supreme irony. What is it that the Eucharist provides? The very thing Protestant Evangelicals cherish the most: the Real Presence of Christ and our real union with Christ, "accepting the Lord Jesus Christ as your personal Savior" in the most real, total, complete, personal, concrete, and intimate way![47]

1. Read CCC 1345 and note the ways in which the Eucharistic celebration has remained consistent throughout the centuries.

2. The earliest written account of the institution of the Lord's Supper in the New Testament is 1 Corinthians 11:23–29. In this passage, Saint Paul describes "handing on what he received from the Lord." What does it mean to eat and drink without "discerning the body"?

---

[46] Luther wrote the following in his *Smalcald Articles*: "Of the Sacrament of the Altar we hold that bread and wine in the Supper are the true body and blood of Christ, and are given and received not only by the godly but also by wicked Christians." He departed from Catholic Church teaching regarding transubstantiation, but never let go of the belief that Christ was present in the Eucharist.

[47] Kreeft, *Jesus Shock*, 107.

3. "From the beginning, the Church has been faithful to the Lord's command." (CCC 1342) Hippolytus of Rome wrote *The Apostolic Tradition* around AD 215. In it, he wrote of the liturgical teachings that had been handed down from the apostles. Here is a section that lays out a script for the ordination of priests:

PRIEST: The Lord be with you.
CONGREGATION: And with your spirit.
PRIEST: Let us lift up our hearts.
CONGREGATION: We lift them up to the Lord.
PRIEST: Let us give thanks to the Lord.
CONGREGATION: It is right and just.[48]

How does reading this impact the way you feel about the celebration of Mass?

Quiet your heart and enjoy His presence. . . . He is unchanging and ever near.

"Behold, I stand at the door and knock; if anyone hears my voice and opens the door, I will come in to him and eat with him, and he with me." (Revelation 3:20)

As we discuss and debate and doubt whether or not He is really present in the Eucharist, Jesus stands at the door of our hearts and knocks. He wants to intimately enter the deepest part of who we are to give us His divine life. Many of us don't open the door because we don't realize who is on the other side. He's been faithfully doing this for centuries, never giving up, because His love for us is never failing. Whether we recognize Him in this hidden form doesn't change reality. He is there. He waits.

He longs for true intimacy with you—for a connection that is soul deep and personal. Open the door of your heart and never be lonely again.

---

[48] Scott Hahn, *The Lamb's Supper: The Mass as Heaven on Earth* (New York: Random House, 1999), 37–38.

Day Four
THE KEY TO SAINTHOOD: A FIRE HOSE OF GRACE

Before I could even look at the benefits of the Eucharist, I had to understand where it came from. Just telling me to believe wasn't enough. A wonderful priest was kind enough to teach me the very things we've explored in Days One to Three. Once I understood that this wasn't some new teaching, that if I interpreted John 6 literally this was the only possible conclusion, and recognized that for a thousand years this was the unchallenged teaching of the Church, my heart settled and got incredibly excited. There was *more* for me to discover about Christ. I could get closer to Jesus than I previously had.

Do you want to become a saint? I'm not talking about wanting recognition for your holiness. A saint is simply someone who has been radically transformed by Christ. She has pursued Jesus wholeheartedly, and in that pursuit has been changed for the better.

This is what I long for and one of the reasons I find it such a privilege to be Catholic. Two of the most effective ways to become a saint are through Eucharistic adoration and receiving Christ in the Eucharist. This isn't because doing these things checks a box or makes us poster-child Catholics. It's because Jesus is a saint maker. And wherever He is, He is at work. His presence burns away the things that don't resemble Him, and fans into flame the love that allows us to live as He did.

1. What is the principal fruit of receiving the Eucharist? See CCC 1391.

The principal fruit of the Eucharist isn't some*thing* Jesus gives us; it's some*one*. It's the gift of *Himself*. All too often, we are overwhelmed by our problems and underwhelmed by our humble Savior, who waits to be invited in. Yet He is the answer to all our deepest longings and the fulfillment of our greatest needs.

2. What is strengthened and what is wiped away when we receive the Eucharist? See CCC 1394.

3. You may wonder if everyone who receives the Eucharist has the same experience. The answer is no. Peter Kreeft (yet again) nails it with this explanation: "Sacraments are like hoses. They are the channels of the living water of God's grace. Our faith is like opening the faucet. We can open it a lot, a little, or not at all. When the faucet handle is turned off, no water flows to us, even though the water is still objectively present. When it is 'turned on' by faith, the water flows out and into us and we get wet."[49]

No, not everyone has the same experience at Communion, but it's up to us how open we want to be. If you are Catholic, how do you typically receive the sacrament of the Eucharist? Do you open the faucet a lot or a little? What do you think might help you to turn the faucet on full blast?

Quiet your heart and enjoy His presence. . . . His fire hose of grace is pointed at your heart at every Mass.

Jesus,

You are the bread of life. You are what I am hungering for. I may run after all sorts of things that will never satisfy me, yet you never give up on me. What other response can I give you than to draw as close to you as humanly possible, and then bow before you? Oh . . . shower me with your grace! Not just a trickle, but a waterfall! Cleanse me; change me; make me more like you.

Forgive me for all the times I've received you with indifference or disbelief. Thank you for your patience with me. Light a fire within me that only intensifies over time. Save me from living numb or short of all you have prepared for me. You promise an abundant life, a feast prepared in the presence of my enemies (Psalm 23:5). May I never content myself with junk food again. Satisfy my deepest yearnings with your real presence!

---

[49] Kreeft, *Jesus Shock*, 117.

Day Five
SAINT'S STORY

Saint Clare

In the mid-thirteenth century, Saracen mercenaries were storming the city of Assisi, in Italy. They had entered the monastery of San Damiano, intending to raid and loot the convent, and had penetrated the inner cloister, where the sisters trembled and cried out in fear.

Clare, daughter of a wealthy Italian family, who was inspired to give her life in service to Christ when she heard the teachings of Francis of Assisi, knew she had to act to try to save her sisters. She rose and went to the chapel. She took the silver and gold monstrance to the window overlooking the enemy. The soldiers were a dark mass of movement down below; their weapons gleamed in the moonlight and their crude shouts echoed in the courtyard. She placed the monstrance with the Host on the windowsill in sight of the men, and she prostrated herself in prayer like Queen Esther before her king. In tears, she begged, "Behold, my Lord, is it possible that you want to deliver your defenseless handmaids, whom I have taught out of love for you, into the hands of pagans?" She begged Him to protect them, since she was powerless to protect them herself. Then, a voice like that of a child echoed in her ears: "I will always protect you!"

Clare also prayed for the city, and the voice answered, "It will have to undergo trials, but it will be defended by My protection." At these words, she lifted her face from the stones and told the sisters, "I assure you, daughters, that you will suffer no evil. Only have faith in Christ." Shortly after, the Saracens took flight, scaling the walls in their haste to depart.

Jesus had spoken, and He had acted from the Eucharist, where He is truly present. It is not only in the past that He has acted. It is today, now, with you. Do you believe that all of your enemies—the problems that plague you, the stresses that take away your peace of heart, the sins you cannot seem to conquer, the sins of others that weigh on your heart and bring suffering into your home—can be vanquished from your place of prayer before the Eucharist?

The sacrament on the altar is not a thing; it is a person. It is He, Jesus, who waits for us there. It is He, alive. He listens, He understands, He speaks. And when we are distant, He gently calls our name. He brings us home again. Jesus in the Eucharist is always at work in a gentle, powerful, but often hidden way. But there are times when

He allows us to see His hand so that we can praise Him and "remember the works of the Lord." (Psalm 77:11)

Prayer, do not forget, is a conversation with your best friend, with the One who will never, ever abandon you. How much more powerful, then, is your conversation with this friend *in the flesh*, in the Blessed Sacrament, where He is really present! It is there that His eyes look upon you with so much love, His hands reach out to console you, His words penetrate your heart like a river of peace, and His soul embraces you and draws you into Him. You may not see it; you may not feel it; but He is there, and He is acting in your life.

Jesus said, "A man can have no greater love than to lay down his life for a friend." (John 15:13) He laid Himself down for Clare and the sisters that day when the Saracens were invading. Like a good shepherd, He placed His body between them and the enemy. But He also lays Himself down for you every day in every tabernacle in the world. He waits for you there, the great friend who understands all of your problems, who accepts you as you are, and who wants to heal and save you.
This great friend has come from heaven to be with you. Will you not go to Him?

What does Saint Clare's story reveal to you about the role the Eucharist plays in our friendship with Jesus?

Conclusion

Jesus has made a way for all of us to enter into a life-changing relationship with Him, but He is a gentleman; He waits to be invited in. Will you do that now? Will you invite Him to intersect your life with power and authority? Are you ready to stop trying to control it all yourself? Are you ready for freedom?

Do you long for more?

Oh, friends. There is more. It's just that we've settled for less than what God is holding out to us. Aren't you ready to let the religiosity, pride, cynicism, and hopelessness go, and instead step out in faith?

Ask the Lord for eyes to see. Is the Eucharist any more unbelievable than the Incarnation? Both are mind-boggling. Both require recognizing God in a hidden form—one is a wafer; the other is a human body. To wrap your mind around either of those miracles is a pretty tall order. That's why we need faith. Faith is believing without seeing (2 Corinthians 5:7). And the beautiful thing is that we don't need to conjure up faith when we lack it. We can ask God to give it to us. Ask God to give you the gift of faith, and then follow the example of Saint Augustine, who said, "I believe so that I may understand."

Jesus will always refuse to fit into a box. He won't conform to our definitions. He won't be controlled. He won't be molded into some version of a deity that pleases us. He approaches us as He chooses, and as wild as it may seem to us, the Eucharist is how He has chosen to draw near. He is beyond our ability to comprehend. "The foolishness of God is wiser than human wisdom, and the weakness of God is stronger than human strength." (1 Corinthians 1:25) Our minds can't wrap around or contain Him.

One last thing: When you receive Christ in the Eucharist, lack of feelings is *not* proof that nothing is happening. It's a reminder that God doesn't want us to be "experience junkies," relying on our emotions. What is it that pleases Him most of all? Faith.

~A faith that says, "Regardless of what I've done, I know that Jesus' sacrifice purchased my forgiveness and it is enough."

~A faith that says, "As crazy as it seems, the God of the universe has made Himself small and *wants me.*"

~A faith that says, "I'm not worshipping a dead Savior. He is alive. And active. And even though I can't see Him, I know that wherever He is, He is at work."

He's issued you the invitation. Will you draw near?

My Resolution

In what specific way will I apply what I have learned in this lesson?

Examples:

1. *I want more of Jesus!* Because of this, I'm going to go to Mass more frequently this week. I'll go on _____ in addition to Sunday.

2. I will spend time with the Lord in adoration on _____, asking Him to shower me with His love and grace.

3. Before I receive the Eucharist, I'll spend some time in prayer telling God that I am turning the faucet *all the way on* because I want everything He has for me.

My Resolution:

Catechism Clips

CCC 1094 It is on this harmony of the two Testaments that the Paschal catechesis of the Lord is built, and then, that of the Apostles and the Fathers of the Church. This catechesis unveils what lay hidden under the letter of the Old Testament: the mystery of Christ. It is called "typological" because it reveals the newness of Christ on the basis of the "figures" (types) which announce him in the deeds, words, and symbols of the first covenant. By this re-reading in the Spirit of Truth, starting from Christ, the figures are unveiled. Thus the flood and Noah's ark prefigured salvation by Baptism, as did the cloud and the crossing of the Red Sea. Water from the rock was the figure of the Spiritual gifts of Christ, and manna in the desert prefigured the Eucharist, "the true bread from heaven."

CCC 1345 As early as the second century we have the witness of St. Justin Martyr for the basic lines of the order of the Eucharistic celebration. They have stayed the same until our own day for all the great liturgical families. St. Justin wrote to the pagan emperor Antonius Pius (138–161) around the year 155, explaining what Christians did:

On the day we call the day of the sun, all who dwell in the city or country gather in the same place.

The memoirs of the apostles and the writings of the prophets are read, as much as time permits.

When the reader has finished, he who presides over those gathered admonishes and challenges them to imitate these beautiful things.

Then we all rise together and offer prayers for ourselves . . . and for all others, wherever they may be, so that we may be found righteous by our life and actions, and faithful to the commandments, so as to obtain eternal salvation.

When the prayers are concluded we exchange the kiss.

Then someone brings bread and a cup of water and wine mixed together to him who presides over the brethren.

He takes them and offers praise and glory to the Father of the universe, through the name of the Son and of the Holy Spirit and for a considerable time he gives thanks (in Greek: *eucharistian*) that we have been judged worthy of these gifts.

When he has concluded the prayers and thanksgivings, all present give voice to an acclamation by saying: 'Amen.'

When he who presides has given thanks and the people have responded, those whom we call deacons give to those present the "eucharisted" bread, wine and water and take them to those who are absent.

CCC 1391 Holy Communion augments our union with Christ. The principal fruit of receiving the Eucharist in Holy Communion is an intimate union with Christ Jesus. Indeed, the Lord said: "He who eats my flesh and drinks my blood abides in me, and I in him." Life in Christ has its foundation in the Eucharistic banquet: "As the living Father sent me, and I live because of the Father, so he who eats me will live because of me."

On the feasts of the Lord, when the faithful receive the Body of the Son, they proclaim to one another the Good News that the first fruits of life have been given, as when the angel said to Mary Magdalene, "Christ is risen!" Now too are life and resurrection conferred on whoever receives Christ.

CCC 1394 As bodily nourishment restores lost strength, so the Eucharist strengthens our charity, which tends to be weakened in daily life; and this living charity wipes away venial sins. By giving himself to us Christ revives our love and enables us to break our disordered attachments to creatures and root ourselves in him:

Since Christ died for us out of love, when we celebrate the memorial of his death at the moment of sacrifice we ask that love may be granted to us by the coming of the Holy Spirit. We humbly pray that in the strength of this love by which Christ willed to die for us, we, by receiving the gift of the Holy Spirit, may be able to consider the world as crucified for us, and to be ourselves as crucified to the world. Having received the gift of love, let us die to sin and live for God.

Lesson 13

HOW CAN I CONQUER MY FEARS?

Introduction

The storms of the rainy season in Guadalajara, Mexico, were powerful and breathtakingly intense. The kids loved it when we'd take our Suburban out in the midst of a storm. They'd scream with excitement as the water broke over the hood of the car and splashed on their windows, climbing up the sides of the car. Smaller cars would start to float around the roads, out of control. The sensible thing would have been to stay home, but we loved the thrill of being out in the middle of it all, and we had (somewhat groundless) confidence in our Suburban's ability to stay steady no matter what. Our kids liked the rain and the sense of adventure that the storms would bring.

At least that was the case until one particularly crazy storm. We were all at home, enjoying the afternoon, when the rains began. Five-year-old Amy was playing in her bedroom and I was reading in the living room. Bedrooms were on one side of the house, the kitchen on the other, and the two-story, open living room was in the middle with skylights covering most of the ceiling. The rain started calmly enough, but all of a sudden, noises began to explode as hail pelted the skylights. There was a crack, and as I looked up to see the skylights shattering and raining down shards of glass everywhere, Amy appeared at the doorway of her bedroom. Terrified, she began to run through the flying glass to get to me.

And I froze.

I froze. What kind of a mother *freezes* at a time like that? The same mother who knows the Heimlich maneuver yet froze when her three-year-old was choking on a marble. Thank heavens someone with a cool head was nearby to help. I don't know why on earth that has been my reaction not once, but twice, and thank the Lord our brave babysitter was in the kitchen and ran through the glass to rescue Amy. But fear can do that. It can be utterly paralyzing at the absolute worst times imaginable.

Not surprisingly, Amy wasn't so fond of rain after that. And like clockwork, we could count on a daily storm during the rainy season. My response was to comfort her and hold her, to play music loudly during the storms to drown out the sound of the rain. Her daddy's approach was a little different. When the storm would start, he would scoop her up and take her outside. He'd ask her to look at his face, and then he'd smile and talk about how much he loved the rain. He'd stomp in the puddles and make it all a game. Little by little, as she'd watch his lack of fear and total comfort in the storm, she got to the point where she would stomp in the puddles herself. Fear didn't get the last word.

Jesus desires that peace rule in each of our hearts. Yet many people live paralyzed by fear. Panic attacks are on the rise; in any given year, about one-third of American adults have at least one. Sometimes one can see the effects of fear in people in the form of phobias or fearful behavior. But more often, we hide our fears in our hearts. Sometimes even our best friends don't know our secret fears, but they are there, robbing us of the joy that Jesus wants each of us to experience every day. During this lesson, we'll explore ways we can conquer our fears, allowing them to come under the control of God's loving hand.

Day One
AFRAID OF THE STORM

The emotion of fear is a gift insofar as it alerts us to danger. Our senses become heightened, and we look for a way out. Fear lets us know the storm is coming or has hit, but it's not enough to get us *through* the storm. We need something more than that.

Read Matthew 14:22–33.

1. What shift in focus caused Peter to start sinking in the waves? How was he saved from drowning?

2. What kind of a spirit has God given us? See 2 Timothy 1:7.

A spirit of fear will alert us to danger and sharpen our senses, but it will never provide us with what we need to navigate the storms of life. To make it through those circumstances, we need supernatural power, God's unconditional love, and the self-control that helps us choose to dwell on certain things and not others. The good news is, this is exactly what the indwelling Holy Spirit provides. If we replace our spirit of fear with the Spirit of power, love, and self-control, we can conquer our fears.

3. In what ways have you seen God's power in your life? When have you experienced His unconditional love? Has He ever strengthened you by helping you to have self-control in an area of weakness? Share your experiences here and let God's track record of faithfulness increase your confidence in Him. Whatever you face, His presence within you will make all the difference.

Quiet your heart and enjoy His presence. . . . Allow God to dispel your fear.

Fear is unavoidable, but what we choose to do with it is up to us. In the very moment that we feel afraid, we can remind ourselves, "God has not given us a spirit of cowardice but rather of power and love and self-control." (2 Timothy 1:7) That *is what is inside us.*

When panic hits, grab hold of Jesus' hand. Lock your eyes on the truth that you are not alone, that He is present, and that His presence makes all the difference. Ask Him to dispel your fear.

"You who dwell in the shelter of the Most High, who abide in the shade of the Almighty, say to the Lord, 'My refuge and fortress, my God in whom I trust.'" (Psalm 91:1–2)

"I learned that courage was not the absence of fear but the triumph over it. The brave man is not he that doesn't feel afraid, but he who conquers that fear." —Nelson Mandela

Day Two
AFRAID OF WALKING ALONE AT NIGHT

A survey conducted by Chapman University, in California, discovered that one of Americans' greatest fears is walking alone at night.[50] When people answered the survey, they were probably thinking of the dark alley, the dimly lit parking lot—that sort of thing. I understand this fear. Once the sun goes down, I imagine someone is hiding under my car in the mall parking lot, just waiting to slash my ankles. I start to regret that my hair is always in a ponytail because that's easy for some ne'er-do-well to grab. I walk with my finger over the alarm button on my key fob because you just never know. So I get being freaked out at night.

Night can mean all that—or it can be a metaphor for a general darkness in our circumstances or a darkness in our souls. And we are very afraid of walking through those times alone. That's when walking with your hair down and the key fob in hand just doesn't offer much comfort. So what does Scripture have to say to that fear? Let's dive in. There are lots of verses to look up today, friends. But hang with me. You might end up discovering a couple that you'll carry with you from now on.

1. Did Jesus promise that if we follow Him, He'll remove all challenges from our lives? See John 16:33.

2. What did Saint Teresa of Ávila learn from her experience of trusting God in every circumstance? See CCC 227.

3. Look up the following verses. What does each teach you about walking through darkness?

   A. Deuteronomy 31:6

---

[50] Jolie Lee, "Biggest American Fear? Walking Alone at Night, Survey Finds," *USA Today*, October 22, 2014, http://www.usatoday.com/story/news/nation-now/2014/10/22/fear-study-chapman-university/17663861/.

B. Psalm 27:1 and John 8:12

C. Isaiah 41:10

D. Romans 8:28

4. Which of these verses helps you the most in dealing with your fears? Write it down on an index card and carry it with you.

Quiet your heart and enjoy His presence. . . . God does His finest work in the darkness.

"God has to work in the soul in secret and in darkness because if we fully knew what was happening and what Mystery, transformation, God and Grace will eventually ask of us, we would either try to take charge or stop the whole process." —Saint John of the Cross

The deepest soul work is done in the darkness, and it isn't a group exercise. There are times when God allows us to go to places that we wouldn't choose to go, because it is only there that we will be transformed in the most beautiful of ways. But we shouldn't be afraid of this, because God accompanies us there. We never walk in darkness alone. True, we may feel *alone. But our feelings don't define reality. God does. And He promises never to leave us. He is there in the secret places in a way that our minds don't really comprehend.*

Take the verse you chose for question 4 and personalize it. Turn it into a prayer of thanksgiving. For example, using Isaiah 41:10, you could pray:

Dear Lord,

Thank you for making it so that I do not need to be afraid, because you are with me. I don't need to be anxious, because you are my God. Thank you for strengthening me. Thank you for helping me. Thank you for upholding me with your victorious right hand. Thank you for grasping hold of me and never letting me go.

Day Three
AFRAID OF REJECTION

We don't always recognize this as a personal struggle because we don't connect the fear of rejection with its fruits. This fear manifests itself as people pleasing, approval seeking, a heightened sensitivity to criticism, feelings of worthlessness, and a rejection of others so that we turn away before they do. We need to get to the root of this fear if we want to walk in freedom.

1. How does Proverbs 29:25 describe "fear of man" or "fear of others"? Note: The phrase used in the Bible to describe being a people pleaser or caring too much what others think of us is "fear of man."

A snare is a trap that typically has a noose of wire or a cord. Caring too much what others think is a snare that strangles our freedom. It causes us to crave approval and fear rejection, and puts people in a place meant for God alone.

2. We all experience rejection at some point in our lives. It's unavoidable. But being afraid of it or totally train wrecked by it is actually optional. It all boils down to what our identity is based on. If the way our worth is defined is through people's acceptance of us, then fear of rejection will always be a noose around our necks. But if we can totally embrace the truth that **people's opinions do not determine our worth or identity, that our worth is determined by God and our identity is rooted in being His beloved daughter**, then freedom can be ours.

God's approval is the only one that ultimately matters, and He *adores you*. Yes, *you*. You are not an exception to the rule, no matter what you've done or what you're struggling with today.

What insight do the following verses give as we seek to please God and find our identity in Him?

Romans 8:31

Galatians 1:10

Colossians 3:23

3. Do you struggle with a fear of rejection? If so, in what specific way? (Typical manifestations of this fear are people pleasing, approval seeking, sensitivity to criticism, feelings of worthlessness, tendency to reject others.)

Quiet your heart and enjoy His presence. . . . Do you want to see God show up in your life in a powerful way? Are you tired of the status quo and ready for more? Would you like to see God, in all His glory, intersect your circumstances?

God wants us to experience His glory. He wants to pour out His power on us and to see us living freed, transformed lives. This has always been His desire. When Jesus walked the earth, there was nothing He wanted more—for the people to see His glory and to be changed as a result. But so many of them missed it. Why? The reason is found in the Gospel of John: "For they preferred human praise to the glory of God." (John 12:43) They wanted something more than God's power and glory. They wanted human praise.

Jesus is turning to you now and asking, "What do you want?" How will you answer Him?

Day Four
AFRAID TO LEAN IN TO JOY

"What if I fall?
Oh, my darling, what if you fly?"[51]

1. Jesus came to set us free from the fears that hold us back from soaring as God's beloved daughters. How is the life He desires for us described in the following verses?

John 10:10

1 Timothy 6:17 (the second part of the verse)

Isaiah 30:18

These verses paint a picture of God wanting us to live deeply satisfying, meaningful, joy-filled lives. These are God's own words, so we can count on them as truth.

But how often do we believe the lies instead? All too often, we don't see God as a gracious, generous father. We believe the lie that He's going to hold out on us (this, of course, was the thought that got things spiraling out of control in the Garden of Eden). Some of us believe the lie that God is a disinterested father. Disaster might be just around the corner, but He's too busy with other things to do anything about it.

Believing lies about God really messes with our ability to embrace and live the life we were created for.

Have you ever realized that your life is going pretty well, and instead of resting in the joy of that moment and thanking God for all He's given, you think, "Oh, no! The other shoe is about to drop"? In her vulnerability research, Dr. Brené Brown has found that the most terrifying, difficult emotion we experience is *joy*. We're afraid to

---

[51] Erin Hanson, "Just My Poems," The Poetic Underground,
   http://thepoeticunderground.com/post/87639964775/the-talent-of-all-of-you-astounds-me-this-a-quote.

lean in to joy, because the thought of it being taken away is so scary. She describes our mental response as "dress-rehearsing tragedy":

> Dress rehearsing tragedy, she explains, is imagining something bad is going to happen when in reality, nothing is wrong. "How many of you have ever stood over your child while they're sleeping and thought, 'Oh . . . I love you'—and then pictured something horrific happening?" Brown asks. "Or woke up in the morning and thought, 'Oh my gosh, job's going great. Parents are good. This can't last.'"[52]

This isn't how God wants us to live. He wants us to lean in to joy and soar! So how do we do that? How can we break free of our tendency to pull back in fear and miss our lives because we are living in the gray?

2. We spent Lesson 12 learning about the Eucharist. Hidden in its meaning is one of the ways we can lean in to the joy we were created for. *Eucharist* means "thanksgiving." Practicing gratitude is one of the best ways to live a life of joy.

   List an area of life where you fear something that is currently wonderful going awry. What are you afraid of specifically?

   Practice gratitude by listing all the things you are grateful for about that very area of life.

It's up to you. You decide which of those lists you are going to dwell on. One will leave you paralyzed by the fear of "what if." The other will lead you to joy.

3. Underneath our reluctance to really embrace joy is the fear that we will fall. And consciously or not, we figure that the higher the place we're falling from, the more it will hurt. So we climb down from the peak of joy and sit in the middle ground of low expectations because it feels safer. And life passes us by.

---

[52] "Brené Brown: 'Joy Is the Most Vulnerable Emotion We Can Experience,'" *Huffington Post*, October 27, 2013, http://www.huffingtonpost.com/2013/10/18/brene-brown-joy-numbing-oprah_n_4116520.html.

I can't promise you that you will never fall or that life will never bring you pain. But God makes us promises in Scripture that should make an enormous difference in the way we live. In Deuteronomy 33:27, He promises, "The eternal God is your refuge, and underneath are the everlasting arms." Write that verse below. Think about it. Why does this truth matter? What difference does it make to you personally?

Quiet your heart and enjoy His presence. . . . The Lord is your refuge.

Have you whispered these questions?

"What if I fall?"
"What if I fall because of disappointment?"
"What if I fall because of tragedy?"
"What if I fall because I'm just not good enough?"

Lean in and listen, my friend. If you fall, God will catch you. It's as simple as that. He promises that underneath you, no matter what height you are falling from, He will catch you in His everlasting arms. What do we find at the end of our resources, the end of our dreams, the end of our hopes? We find God's mercy. We find God's graciousness. We find shelter from the storm.

That shelter is available to you right now. "He will shelter you with his pinions, and under his wings you may take refuge." (Psalm 91:4) Come under His wings in prayer. Rest in safety.

"Because he clings to me I will deliver him; because he knows my name I will set him on high. He will call upon me and I will answer, I will be with him in distress; I will deliver him and give him honor. With length of days I will satisfy him, and fill him with my saving power." (Psalm 91:14–16)

Rest in these promises.

Don't miss your life.

Day Five
SAINT'S STORY

Blessed Anne of Saint Bartholomew, Saint Frances Xavier Cabrini, and Saint Joan of Arc

What God is asking of us—to cast our fears aside and follow Him, and to become saints and bring His message of hope to everyone around us through word, deed, and example—is too much for us. The funny thing is that He knows we can't do this without His help. He said it a long time ago: "I am the vine, you are the branches. Whoever remains in me, with me in him, bears fruit in plenty; for *cut off from me you can do nothing.*" (John 15:5) When we experience fear in our pursuit of God's purpose for our life, it's because we are forgetting about that. Almost always, our fears are the result of depending too much on ourselves and not trusting enough in God, who is so powerful that He can turn even the most bitter failures (Christ's death on the cross) into the most glorious victories (Easter Sunday). Jesus put it concisely: "For men, it is impossible, but not for God, because everything is possible for God." The more we think about God's omnipotence and love, the more we fill our imagination with His goodness and the wonders He has done in so many lives throughout history, the more easily we will be able to overcome our fears and undertake the Christian adventure in which "the Spirit comes to the aid of our weakness." (Romans 8:26)

This was an especially difficult lesson for Blessed Anne of Saint Bartholomew. She came from a poor shepherding family in sixteenth-century Spain. As a Carmelite nun, Blessed Anne was sent to Belgium and France to start Carmelite convents, and to be prioress in some of them. She would often complain to our Lord that she was too ignorant and shy to be given such important responsibilities. In fact, she complained so much that finally He had to appear to her to calm her down. She had just tried to convince Him that He should choose someone else to do the work she was being asked to do, someone more intelligent, better educated, and more outgoing. So our Lord appeared to her and said, "It is with straw that I start my fires." He didn't comfort her by telling her how great she was. He simply wanted to do things in and through her, if she would let Him.

Saint Frances Xavier Cabrini, America's first canonized saint, illustrates this truth in a more down-to-earth way. She was born in Northern Italy in the 1800s. Early on, she experienced a strong desire to become a missionary, but no religious order would accept her because she had unstable health. So she gathered a group of companions and started her own religious order under the protection of her bishop. Soon she received approval from the pope and began her tireless apostolate with the poor Italian immigrants throughout the Americas. Her work required extensive travel between Europe and America. She ended up crossing the Atlantic more than thirty times on those clunky, uncomfortable, old-fashioned ocean liners. To do so, she had to overcome a mortal fear of water that she acquired after falling into a river and almost drowning when she was just a girl. That fear never left her; God never took it away. Even after years of sea travel, she declined an invitation from her sisters to go for a leisurely boat ride one day because she was afraid of the water! She told them: "I admit my weakness: I am afraid of the sea, and if there is no very holy motive in view, I have no courage to go where I fear danger."

Perhaps the most remarkable example of how trusting in God enables us to overcome fear is found in the truly amazing person of Saint Joan of Arc. A teenage girl, illiterate, of peasant stock, unable to ride horses, and unschooled in war, she received a call from God to liberate a divided and corrupt France from the overpowering and almost complete English invasion toward the end of the Hundred Years' War in the 1300s. No wonder she at first resisted the imprecations of the voices she heard (i.e. the saints whom God sent to her as His messengers)! They continually brought her God's message for four years before she finally obeyed when she was eighteen years old. It was only when they told her, "It is God who commands it," that she complied, entrusting herself completely to God's power. And the world has never been the same. She led armies, outfoxed evil courtiers, emboldened a cowardly king, revived an entire nation, and befuddled the most learned clerics and lawyers of her day. This illiterate teenager single-handedly reversed the fortunes of France and altered the history of Europe while enduring moral, physical, and psychological tortures of the cruelest kind. Through it all, she suffered profoundly, including confusion, exhaustion, and betrayal, ultimately being burned at the stake, dying with Jesus' name on her virgin lips.

And why? "It is God who commands it." She was able to do it because she *hoped in God*. She knew that serving God was her only true occupation, and that He would always be faithful to those who serve Him truly. Saint Joan of Arc left us a message: "Hope in God. Put your trust in Him, and He will deliver you from your enemies [fears]." Indeed, only God will never disappoint us; only He is worthy of our unbridled hope. When we feel helpless or fearful of all that Christ is asking of us, that's what we need to remember.

What fears are you facing in your life right now? How can Blessed Anne, Saint Frances, and Saint Joan of Arc inspire you to deal with them?

Conclusion

Most of my fears have to do with my children. Fear of becoming seriously ill can get the better of me, too. I always want to avoid suffering. What I often forget is that it may be the very thing I need to experience in order to become the woman God wants me to be. Whenever I begin to think, "Surely, I shouldn't have to suffer since I try to do the right thing and live the way God wants me to," I think of the cross. It seems like the worst thing that could happen to anyone—defeat, humiliation, pain—but it was the ultimate victory and the accomplishment of our salvation.

So how do I conquer my fears? It's a journey. Sometimes it feels like two steps forward and one step back. But even then, progress is being made.

Because I'm so prone to fall back into fear, I frequently have to remind myself of the lessons contained in the points that follow. When fear starts to get the better of me, I go back to these lessons to readjust my thinking *and* my feelings:

1. Develop a mature view of suffering.

Because I live in a fallen world, I am quickly influenced by the world's view of the relationship between suffering and joy. We're told that they are polar opposites, but the truth is, there can be joy in suffering. When we meet God in the dark places and He gets us through, we can feel the joy of His presence. We can also feel joy when we realize that we are progressing spiritually as we face our fears, even when doing so is hard. A mature woman realizes that suffering can't be avoided, and if we never encountered it, there would be a lot of life lessons missed.

2. Grow in faith and trust.

Faith and trust are the antidotes to fear. I'm so glad that we can ask God to give us more faith when we feel we are lacking. When we stay close to the Lord and exercise the little faith we do have, He waters that seed of faith and makes it grow. When I focus on how God has been faithful to me in the past, I grow in trust.
It's been helpful for me to keep a prayer journal so that I can go back and see the ways God has rescued me and given me what I have needed countless times. When I read the Bible, I get to know God better, which helps me see that He is worthy of my trust. I won't trust someone I don't know. If we want to grow in trust, we have to take the time to get to know God personally.

3. Remember that I am never alone.

This comforts me most of all. Jesus has suffered more than I ever will, so He knows how I am feeling. The Bible promises that no matter what happens to me, God has made sure I can endure it (1 Corinthians 10:13). But He doesn't say I'll be able to handle anything in my own strength. I will have to cling to Him in order to receive the strength I need, just as a small branch clings to the main vine.

What is it that you most fear? Can you write it here?

Then write a prayer asking for God's help. You might want to affirm your trust in God's goodness and His control over all things, and thank Him for His wise plan for your life.

Dear God,

My Resolution

In what specific way will I apply what I have learned in this lesson?

1. When my fears are getting the better of me, I will make a Trust List. This is a list of ways in which I know I can trust God. It can contain words describing His character, or descriptions of times when He has proven to be faithful in the midst of my struggles. I'll reread this list (or make a new one) whenever I need a reminder.

2. I'll memorize one of the verses from this week's lesson. This will allow the Holy Spirit to bring it to my mind when I most need it.

3. I'll experience the shelter and safety of God's presence by spending some time this week at adoration.

My Resolution:

Catechism Clips

CCC 227 [The implications of Faith in One God:] It means trusting God in every circumstance, even in adversity. A prayer of St. Teresa of Jesus wonderfully expresses this trust:

Let nothing trouble you/Let nothing frighten you
Everything passes/God never changes
Patience/Obtains all
Whoever has God/Wants for nothing
God alone is enough.

NOTES

Walking with Purpose is a community of women growing in faith – together! This is where women are gathering. Join us!

www.walkingwithpurpose.com

Lesson 14: Connect Coffee Talk

MARRIAGE – TRANSFORMED BY GRACE

Accompanying DVD can be viewed by disc or please visit our website at walkingwithpurpose.com/videos and select *Opening Your Heart* Bible Study, click through to select Videos.

1. The Foundation: A Personal Relationship with Jesus Christ

Author Ruth Bell Graham wisely wrote, "It is a foolish woman who expects her husband to be to her that which only Jesus Christ Himself can be: always ready to forgive, totally understanding, unendingly patient, invariably tender and loving, unfailing in every area, anticipating every need, and making more than adequate provision. Such expectations put a man under an impossible strain."[53]

We are created with a _____ that only God can fill.

He who had no sin *became sin* for us. He paid the price so that we would not have to. Through Jesus Christ, man was offered reunion with God.

Romans 6:23 says, "For the wage paid by sin is death; the present given by God is eternal life in Christ Jesus our Lord."

Author Mike Mason wrote:

> One of the most profound ways in which the Lord touches us and teaches us about Himself and His own essential otherness is through the very limits He has placed upon our relationships with one another. It is an enormous source of human frustration that our need for intimacy far outstrips its

---

[53] Debra Evans, *Blessing Your Husband: Understanding and Affirming Your Man* (Carol Stream, IL: Tyndale House, 2003), 30.

capacity to be met in other people. Primarily what keeps us separate is our sin, but there is also another factor, and that is that in each one of us the holiest and neediest and most sensitive place of all has been made and is reserved for God alone, so that only He can enter there. No one else can love us as He does, and no one can be the sort of friend to us that He is.[54]

2. The Enemy: Root Sins in Marriage

A. Sensuality

B. Vanity

"Whoever wants to become great among you must be your servant, and whoever wants to be first must be your slave—just as the Son of Man did not come to be served, but to serve, and to give his life as a ransom for many." (Matthew 20:26–28)

"Do nothing out of selfish ambition or vain conceit, but in humility consider others better than yourselves." (Philippians 2:3)

C. Pride

Questions for Discussion

1. What quality do you think is most important in marriage?

   1. Respect
   2. Love

2. Let's take a moment to reconsider the quote by Ruth Bell Graham mentioned earlier in this talk: "It is a foolish woman who expects her husband to be to her that which only Jesus Christ Himself can be: always ready to forgive, totally understanding, unendingly patient, invariably tender and loving, unfailing in every area, anticipating every need, and making more than adequate provision." Which of those attributes are you most likely to expect from your husband?

---

[54] Cynthia Heald, *Loving Your Husband: Building an Intimate Marriage in a Fallen World* (Colorado Springs: NavPress, 1989), 17.

3. Have you ever experienced a difficult circumstance in your marriage that drew you closer to Christ? In what way did He help you through the trial?

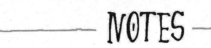

NOTES

Lesson 15

WHAT IS THE ROLE OF SUFFERING IN MY LIFE?

Introduction

I have stood beside a beloved friend when she was in the midst of unthinkable suffering, and I don't know when I have ever felt more helpless. My words couldn't bring healing. I could hold her but I couldn't prevent her from falling into despair. I felt the howl of her soul but could do nothing to lessen the pain.

I've felt the weight of suffering myself, and have wondered if I would come out the other side whole, or if I would be crushed underneath it all.

Saint Teresa of Ávila's words, "Dear Lord, if this is how you treat your friends, it is no wonder you have so few," have resonated with me.

As we step into this lesson on suffering, I must acknowledge that I don't know your story. I don't know the pain you've endured in the past, or the suffering you might be experiencing in this very moment. And I recognize that when we come to this subject, we are treading on sacred ground. This is the place where people quoting Bible verses often inflict pain more than they bring comfort. I don't know about you, but when I am in the vise grip of suffering, I don't really want to hear someone whose life looks a heck of a lot easier than mine quoting Romans 8:28: "We know that all things work for good for those who love God, who are called according to his purpose."

But I don't want to drown in my pain, either. And if there is comfort and hope to be had in the midst of it all, I want it. Oh, how I long for that.

The Lord draws near to us in our pain, and whispers in our ears, "I am close to the brokenhearted and save those who are crushed in spirit." (Psalm 34:19 NAB)

He is true to His word. He never fails to keep His promises. But notice what He *doesn't* promise. Nowhere in Scripture does He promise to be our genie or errand boy. He isn't our servant.

When we encounter suffering, nothing robs us of peace like expectations. During this lesson, we're going to focus on four of those expectations and see if we can come to a deeper understanding of the role of suffering in our lives.

Day One
EXPECTATION 1: WE EXPECT TO UNDERSTAND GOD

We have questions. Suffering intersects our lives and our hearts cry out to know *why*. Some of us are angry, and we want God to give an explanation of what He has allowed or even caused. Some of us aren't angry, but we are deeply disillusioned. We just can't bear the senselessness of it all. The unanswered questions feel intolerable. Life around us feels chaotic sometimes, and we silently question, "How can a loving God be *in charge* if this is what it all feels like?"

1. What insight do the following verses shed on our expectation that we will understand God and His plans?

   Isaiah 55:8–9

   Heavens are higher - Thoughts are higher Our thoughts & ways are not the same.

   Proverbs 3:5

   Trust with all your Heart

2. When will we fully understand "the ways of God's providence"? See CCC 314.

   Only in heaven.

3. In his work as a licensed psychologist and a marriage, family, and child counselor, Dr. James Dobson has witnessed the impact of suffering on people's faith. He has this to say about what causes the most difficulty during crushing circumstances:

> It is an incorrect view of Scripture to say that we will always comprehend what God is doing and how our suffering and disappointment fit into His plan. Sooner or later, most of us will come to a point where it appears that God has lost control—or interest—in the affairs of people. It is only an illusion, but one with dangerous implications for spiritual and mental health. **Interestingly enough, pain and suffering do not cause the greatest damage. Confusion is the factor that shreds one's faith . . .** The human spirit is capable of withstanding enormous discomfort, including the prospect of death, *if the circumstances make sense.*[55]

Do you agree or disagree with Dr. Dobson's observation? Have you experienced this in your own life?

I agree
I haven't experienced this kind of pain

4. According to Psalm 9:11 NAB, how are the people who trust in God described?

Those who know your name, Trust in you, Lord,

"Knowing God's name" signifies knowing something about who God is. A name has great significance in the Bible; it goes beyond being something that sounds nice or has some sentimental value. In the Bible, a name represents the worth, character, and authority of a person. When someone knows God's name, it means that he or she has taken the time to know Him intimately. When we *know* Him, we can base our trust on His character, instead of on our ability to understand our suffering.

Quiet your heart and enjoy His presence. . . . He is so great that it's impossible for us to wrap our minds around Him, yet He stoops low and draws near.

---

[55] Dr. James Dobson, *When God Doesn't Make Sense* (Wheaton, IL: Tyndale House, 1993), 13.

The essence of who God is can be grasped in a small yet faith-building way by studying the names of God. As you read these Hebrew names, focus on God's character and ask the Lord to help your trust in Him grow.

El Shaddai (Lord God Almighty)
El Elyon (The Most High God)
Jehovah-Raah (The Lord My Shepherd)
Jehovah-Rapha (The Lord That Heals)
Jehovah Shammah (The Lord Is There)
Jehovah Mekoddishkem (The Lord Who Makes You Holy)
Jehovah Jireh (The Lord Will Provide)
Jehovah Shalom (The Lord Is Peace)

✯ *God doesn't promise us an answer to our whys, but He promises something better:* His presence.

"He will stand and shepherd his flock
in the strength of the lord,
in the majesty of the name of the lord his God.
And they will live securely, for then his greatness
will reach to the ends of the earth.
And he will be our peace." (Micah 5:3–4 NAB)

Day Two
EXPECTATION 2: WE EXPECT GOD'S DEFINITION OF HAPPINESS TO BE THE SAME AS OURS

It seems so straightforward to us. We know that good relationships, health, financial security, and blessings on our loved ones will make us happy. We read over that list and assume that since none of those things are bad, they must be the very things that God considers good sources of happiness. And when things go wrong, we feel perplexed. We wonder if God cares if we are happy or not. We start to question His goodness and whether or not He truly wants what is best for us. As a result, our trust in God starts to take a beating, and our hearts grow cold and disillusioned. We blame God, because if He's all-powerful, then He is able to give us any and all of these things. Yet He holds back just what we are certain would make things all right again.

We become convinced that the problem lies in having something we don't want or wanting something we don't have. But open your mind to another possibility—could it be that the real problem lies in our understanding of what true happiness is?

1. *The Merriam-Webster Dictionary* defines happiness as "a state of well-being and contentment: joy." Read the following verses and record what Scripture says will bring us joy.

Psalm 16:11

Joy in Your Presence

James 1:2

The Law of the Lord is Joy

1 Peter 1:8–9

As you attain the goal of your life the salvation of your soul

2. It has been said that joy comes from obedience. When we understand how God wants us to live and then we obey Him no matter the cost, we experience the joy of pleasing God. He knows what will bring us to "a state of well-being and contentment." As hard as it is to accept, He knows better than we do. What we think will bring us happiness today might be the very thing that will keep us from experiencing happiness in eternity. Because of this, we are called to obey even when we don't understand why. Is there an area of your life where God has asked you to obey Him and you're finding it hard to do? Share the struggle here. Then read Hebrews 12:2. What helped Jesus to obediently go to the cross even though it meant abject suffering?

He endured knowing he'd have His eternal reward.

The world says happiness is found through pleasure. God says happiness is found through obedience.

3. If we make the source of our happiness the temporal things of this world, at any given point we can be made unhappy, because those things can be taken away from us. God wants us to experience a deeper kind of happiness, a joy that can't be taken away. What did Jesus promise about joy in John 16:22?

I will see you again & no one will take away your joy!

The promise Jesus made to His disciples in John 16:22 is also true for us today. He rose from the dead, and because of this, we are assured of His presence here on earth. He will never leave us. We're also promised joy in heaven—eternal joy—where Jesus "will wipe every tear from [our] eyes, and there shall be no more death or mourning, wailing or pain." (Revelation 21:4)

Quiet your heart and enjoy His presence. . . . "Many say, 'May we see better times! LORD, show us the light of your face!' But you have given my heart more joy than they have when grain and wine abound. In peace I will lie down and fall asleep, for you alone, LORD, make me secure." (Psalm 4:7–9, NAB)

True happiness comes from more than "grain and wine abounding." It's found in God's presence. Our security and joy lie in Him, not in our circumstances. Whether our relationships are peaceful or full of conflict, whether our finances are in great shape or not, whether our loved ones are suffering or experiencing smooth sailing, we are safe and secure in Christ.

"What has happened to all your joy?" (Galatians 4:15)

Could it be that you've been looking for it in the wrong place?

You would have torn out your eyes & given them to me.

Day Three
EXPECTATION 3: WE EXPECT GOD'S LOVE TO ALWAYS FEEL GOOD

Nothing feels better than a police officer giving me grace when I deserve a speeding ticket. My family thinks I have perfected the art of crying under duress. I just think the police officer is caught off guard when I say, "You were so right to pull me over. I totally deserve a ticket." You are free to borrow this technique in your own hour of need.

Each and every time I've been pulled over, the officer has checked my record, seen a clean slate, and let me go with a warning. He of course has no idea how many warnings I've received. Bless. *And I am grateful.* That being said, do you know what I probably *need*? I probably need a whopping ticket to teach me that there is no reason to speed and that we have speed limits for our protection. Getting away with speeding feels good in the moment, but it doesn't really help me to slow down.

(And I hope that there aren't any police officers living near me reading this. Because even when I know what is best for me, I don't really want it if it doesn't feel good. So just in case you thought I was writing about these things from a high and lofty place of holiness, be assured, I'm right smack in the middle of the mess with you.)

What happens when we expect God's love to always feel good? Suffering, which was meant to help us and teach us something, ends up making us bitter. That root of bitterness goes down deep into our hearts, and we start to question God's character. That's not all. We get stuck there. Instead of growing up in our faith, we become perpetual teenagers. Who wants that? Let's take a look at what God's love feels like when He is in the process of making His beloved daughters more closely resemble His Son.

1. Read Hebrews 12:5–11 and answer the following questions.

   A. Whom does the Lord discipline? (see verse 6)

   Those he loves - every Son

   B. Why does the Lord discipline us? (see verse 10)

   For our benefit so we can share his holiness

   C. Discipline will bring "the peaceful fruit of righteousness" to whom? (see verse 11)

   To those who are trained by it.

We don't all experience "the peaceful fruit of righteousness"; it doesn't automatically accompany discipline and suffering. Some women who've been through a lot wear their suffering as a badge. We notice it, and there is always a certain amount of respect we give to someone who has endured something terribly difficult. But the holiness we're after isn't the same thing as wearing a badge of suffering. We need to be refined by what we experience. It's not *that* you've suffered; it's *how* you've suffered that really matters.

2. Left to our own devices, all too often we will choose temporary comfort over what will ultimately benefit us most. C. S. Lewis points this out in the following excerpt from his book *The Problem of Pain*:

> Everyone has noticed how hard it is to turn our thoughts to God when everything is going well with us. "We have all we want" is a terrible saying when "all" does not include God. We find God an interruption. As St. Augustine says somewhere, "God wants to give us something, but cannot, because our hands are full—there's nowhere for Him to put it." Or as a friend of mine said, "We regard God as an airman regards his parachute; it's there for emergencies but he hopes he'll never have to use it." Now God, who has made us, knows what we are and that our happiness lies in Him. Yet we will not seek it in Him as long as He leaves us any other resort where it can even plausibly be looked for. While what we call 'our own life' remains agreeable we will not surrender it to Him. What then can God do in our interests but make our own life less agreeable to us, and take away the plausible source of false happiness? It is just here, where God's providence seems at first to be most cruel, that the Divine humility, the stepping down of the Highest, most deserves praise.[56]

Underline any phrases from the excerpt that resonate with you. Do C. S. Lewis' words give you any insight into why your loving God has allowed suffering in your life?

3. Even though I know that a speeding ticket would help me to slow down, I don't want the correction. This is a common human tendency that it seems I share with C. S. Lewis (and unfortunately that's about where our similarities end). In *The Problem of Pain*, he writes of the way in which suffering has grabbed his attention. Suffering causes him to realize that his greatest treasure is Christ and that there is nothing more important than being utterly dependent on Him. But as soon as his suffering lifts, Lewis observes that he goes right back to trying to fill himself up with life's little pleasures. He continues with the following words:

> Thus the terrible necessity of tribulation is only too clear. God has had me for but forty-eight hours and then only by dint of taking everything else

---

[56] C. S. Lewis, *The Problem of Pain* (New York: Harper Collins, 2001), 94.

away from me. Let Him but sheathe that sword for a moment and I behave like a puppy when the hated bath is over—I shake myself as dry as I can and race off to reacquire my comfortable dirtiness, if not in the nearest manure heap, at least in the nearest flower bed. And that is why tribulations cannot cease until God either sees us remade or sees that our remaking is now hopeless.[57]

Do you relate to this? Can you see this tendency in yourself to return to the "comfortable dirtiness" of old habits?

Quiet your heart and enjoy His presence. . . . His discipline is proof not that you are bad, but that you are beloved.

"My [daughter], do not despise the LORD's discipline or be weary of his reproof, for the LORD reproves [her] whom he loves, as a father the [daughter] in whom he delights." (Proverbs 3:11–12)

God loves you so very, very much. You are His beloved daughter, and He wants you to resemble your brother Jesus. He knows that the more you are like Jesus, not just in outward actions but deep in your heart, the more happy and fulfilled you will be. He knows that this refining process is absolutely essential if you are going to walk in the freedom you were created for. Have you resisted the discipline of your heavenly Father? Let today be the start of a new attitude toward the difficulties He allows to come your way. Instead of responding to them with the words, "Why me, Lord?" change the response to, "Father, what are you trying to teach me?"

Day Four
EXPECTATION 4: WE EXPECT TO SEE CLEAR EVIDENCE OF GOD WHEN WE NEED HIM

The rug is pulled out from under us and we need God like never before. We want to *see* Him. Yet He remains invisible, and we start to wonder, all this time that we've been loving, worshipping, and serving Him, is our God actually distant, uncaring, and

---

[57] Ibid.

silent? Doubts seep in like smoke, clouding our vision and causing us to wonder if we have any faith at all.

What do we do with these doubts? Are they signs that we don't have any faith? What do we do when we desperately want evidence that God is real, that God is there? Are we alone in this struggle?

1. Read Job 23:2–9 and underline every phrase that expresses Job's frustration over the hiddenness of God.

> Today especially my complaint is bitter, his hand is heavy upon me in my groanings. Would that I knew how to find him, that I might come to his dwelling! I would set out my case before him, fill my mouth with arguments; I would learn the words he would answer me, understand what he would say to me. Would he contend against me with his great power? No, he himself would heed me! There an upright man might argue with him, and I would once and for all be delivered from my judge. But if I go east, he is not there; or west, I cannot perceive him; the north enfolds him, and I cannot catch sight of him; the south hides him, and I cannot see him.

2. Read Psalm 13:2 and write it below. Have you ever felt like this? Record the experience here.

How long, Lord? Will you utterly forget me? How long will you hide your face from me?

You are not alone in your struggle to see evidence of God in the midst of your suffering. You are not the only one who doubts. Struggling with doubt doesn't mean that you don't have faith. It can simply mean that you are in the midst of the process in which bit by bit you are learning to accept this:

God's greatness means that there will be times when you don't understand what He is doing, and you don't get to demand an explanation from Him. You are asked to trust, even when you can't see.

Are you wrestling with this? That's OK. It's totally different from giving up on God and closing off your heart to Him. Staying in the struggle is evidence of faith.

3. When we are having trouble seeing evidence of God in the midst of our suffering, we need to refocus on what we already know of Him. Record your thoughts on

the following verses. Underline them in your Bible. Go back and reread these verses when doubts begin to creep into your heart.

Psalm 100:5

Good indeed is the Lord.

Romans 8:31–32

He did not spare His own Son. How will he not give us everything else.

2 Peter 3:9

The Lord is patient...... that all should come to repentance

Quiet your heart and enjoy His presence. . . . He is real. He is here.

"Faith doesn't erase doubt, insecurity, or fear, it just overcomes them." —Jen Hatmaker

"In all these things, we conquer overwhelmingly through him who loved us. For I am convinced that neither death nor life, nor angels, nor principalities, nor present things, nor future things, nor powers, nor height, nor depth, nor any other creature will be able to separate us from the love of God in Christ Jesus our Lord." (Romans 8:37–39)

We can overcome doubt, insecurity, and fear. Inside each of us is God's very own Spirit. It's not a spirit of fear, but one of power and love (2 Timothy 1:7). The Spirit within us testifies that we are God's beloved daughters (Romans 8:16). Not only does the Lord go before and behind us, He is within us. God within us can do all things. Nothing is impossible. There is nothing He holds back from His daughters that is for their good.

God is for you. When all around you is shifting and misty and unclear, grab hold of that truth. When you're in the fire of suffering, shout into the flames that they are not going to overpower you, because God is in you and with you.

How do you arm wrestle? You grab hold of the other person's hand and you don't let go.
How do you wrestle with God? Grab hold of His hand. Don't let go. I promise you, He won't let go of you.

"For I am the LORD, *your God, who grasp your right hand; It is I who say to you, Do not fear, I will help you." (Isaiah 41:13)*

Day Five
SAINT'S STORY

Saint Rita of Cascia Fights the Good Fight

Following Christ is neither a hobby nor a game; it's an adventure. And every adventure worth the name is fraught with challenges, setbacks, threats, and enemies. This adventure is no exception. Christ needs us to grow in love so that His grace can take its full effect, both in our short life here on earth and in heaven for all eternity. But growth in love means perseverance through trials. Saint Paul assures us that God will never let us be tested beyond our strength: "You can trust that God will not let you be put to the test beyond your strength, but with any trial will also provide a way out by enabling you to put up with it." (1 Corinthians 10:13) But Saint Peter assures us that we will indeed be tested: "For a short time yet you must bear all sorts of trials." (1 Peter 1:6) And Saint James sums up the reason why: "My brothers, consider it a great joy when trials of many kinds come upon you, for you well know that the testing of your faith produces perseverance, and perseverance must complete its work so that you will become fully developed, complete, not deficient in any way." (James 1:2–4) Saint Rita had an especially grueling series of trials, which God used to turn her into a particularly remarkable and inspiring model of Christian womanhood.

Rita grew up in a little town in Central Italy during the early Renaissance. As all Italian towns were experiencing at the time, hers was torn by civil and political strife. Adverse conditions didn't impede the seed of faith from putting down deep roots in her soul, though, and early on she discovered her vocation to the religious life. Her parents, however, disagreed, and betrothed her to an abusive, violent, cantankerous man named Paolo, whom she married when she was twelve. For eighteen years she loved and served him faithfully, in spite of his infidelity and abuse. She bore him two sons, who spent their youth learning their father's ways.

These conditions tried her faith, and in the end strengthened it, as she saw that God had sent her this family so that she could pray and sacrifice for their salvation. Just before Paolo died (after being stabbed in an alley), he repented and begged his wife's forgiveness. And when the two sons vowed vengeance on their father's assassins, Rita prayed that they might die rather than commit murder. They fell ill (See how powerful prayer is?), and as their mother tended them, their hearts softened, and they, too, died in peace with God and man.

Because of the deaths of her husband and sons before she was even thirty-six years of age, Rita was able to pursue her heart's desire of dedicating her whole life to God. She applied various times for entrance into the local Augustinian convent. She was denied on multiple grounds (the order only admitted virgins; some members of the convent were relatives of the men who had killed Paolo), but she never gave up hope. In fact, she took action. She resolved the most salient family feuds in the town, achieving sufficient peace that it was considered safe to have her join the sisterhood, wherein she lived pursuing (and reaching) holiness for the next forty years.

Rita's love for Christ led her to a deep desire to share our Lord's suffering even more than she already had. He granted this desire in a rather unique way. One day in prayer, she was contemplating His Passion when she felt one of the thorns from His crown of thorns pierce her forehead. The wound turned out to be real. It bled and festered for the last sixteen years of her life, so much so that she had to live in seclusion in order to avoid revolting the other sisters. But during her final, bedridden years, the younger ones often stayed at her side to learn from her wisdom.

After her death, miracles abounded through her intercession, and to this day, she remains a patron saint for abuse victims, desperate causes, and difficult marriages. Her story reminds us that Christians, together with Christ, reach the joys of Easter Sunday only through the purifying struggles of Good Friday.

When you read Saint Rita's story, does a part of you feel mortified at the thought that this mother prayed that her sons would die rather than commit murder to avenge their father's death? Our response to Saint Rita's prayer reveals something about what we consider most important in life. We are tempted to live for the here and now instead of keeping our eyes fixed on heaven. The time we will spend on earth is such a tiny amount compared to eternity. We should live our lives (and pray that our children live their lives) in such a way that we can spend eternity with God. When we develop an eternal perspective, we take a different approach toward suffering. Even though the death of her sons would bring her suffering, Saint Rita trusted that God would bring a great good from that pain. Could it be that our struggle with the age-old question, "How can a good, loving God permit evil?" has a great deal to do with our lack of trust in God?

How does Saint Rita of Cascia's story add to your understanding of the suffering you have endured in your life?

Conclusion

No matter how faithfully we buckle our seat belts and lock our doors at night, we'll never be able to prevent suffering from intersecting our lives. How I wish I could promise you that if you love Jesus with all your heart, that heart will never break. But even the strongest faith and the presence of our Savior don't shield us from the effects of sin and evil in the world. Suffering comes into our lives, uninvited. So how will we be shaped by it? Will it form us into bitter, unforgiving, hardened women? Or will we be refined and come out the other side stronger, wiser, and more like Christ? The choice is ours. Even in the most horrific circumstances, the choice is still ours. No one says it better than WWII concentration camp survivor Viktor Frankl: "Everything can be taken from a man but one thing: the last of human freedoms—to choose one's attitude in any given set of circumstances, to choose one's own way." No matter what you face, hold on to hope. Hold on to the promises of the God who loves you so much and will never let you go. Cling to these truths:

1. God is **present** even when we feel that He isn't.
2. God's timing is **perfect**.
3. We are known and we are **precious** to Him.
4. **Prayer** makes a difference.
5. There is always a **purpose**.

That purpose is directly tied to God's greatest desire—to spend eternity with each person He lovingly created. Our life on earth is simply our journey toward that destination. And along the way, suffering is unquestionably one of the ways we are prepared to meet Him face-to-face. In the words of author Philip Yancey:

> The Bible consistently changes the questions we bring to the problem of pain. It rarely, or ambiguously, answers the backward-looking question "Why?" Instead, it raises the very different, forward-looking question, "To what end?" We are not put on earth merely to satisfy our desires, to pursue life, liberty, and happiness. We are here to be changed, to be made more like God in order to prepare us for a lifetime with Him. And that process may be served by the mysterious pattern of all creation: Pleasure sometimes emerges against a background of pain, evil may be transformed into good, and suffering may produce something of value.[58]

Let's live with our eyes fixed on eternity. Grasping hold of the moments of joy, let's see them as tastes of the utter fulfillment we'll experience in heaven. Let's check our

---

[58] Philip Yancey, *Where Is God When It Hurts?* (Grand Rapids, MI: Zondervan, 1997), 88.

expectations. Are we expecting life to be on earth what God promised us only in heaven?

"Therefore, since we are surrounded by so great a cloud of witnesses, let us rid ourselves of every burden and sin that clings to us and persevere in running the race that lies before us . . . strengthen your dropping hands and your weak knees." (Hebrews 12:1, 12)

Run for that finish line with all you've got. And remember, it's not a sprint. It's a marathon. Stay steady and faithful, and press on through the pain. There is glory on the other side.

My Resolution

In what specific way will I apply what I have learned in this lesson?

1. I will think of one struggle in my life, and instead of asking God why, I will turn my question into a prayer: "God, how do you want me to respond when I struggle with this?" My prayer could sound something like this: "I am struggling in my relationship with my husband. While things could be worse, it feels like suffering. I want to ask you why we are going through this difficult time, but instead I'm asking you to show me how I should respond."

2. If I am struggling to believe that God is really *for me*, I will take time every morning to read Romans 8:31–32. I'll spend time really thinking about the significance of verse 32. How can I ever think that God is holding out on me when He didn't hold back His Son, and allowed Him to suffer for me?

My Resolution:

Catechism Clips

CCC 314 We firmly believe that God is master of the world and of its history. But the ways of His providence are often unknown to us. Only at the end, when our partial knowledge ceases, when we see God "face to face" (1 Corinthians 13:12), will we fully know the ways by which—even through the dramas of evil and sin—God has guided His creation to that definitive Sabbath rest for which He created heaven and earth.

Lesson 16

WHAT DOES MARY HAVE TO DO WITH MY RELATIONSHIP WITH CHRIST?

Introduction

Technology today has made it so that we can communicate with people at an unprecedented rate. Americans alone are sending 6.1 billion texts per day—that's almost 70,000 every second![59] Social media sites such as Twitter and Facebook give us even more opportunities to connect, with users sending 600 tweets per second (think 50 million tweets per day)[60] and the 500 million worldwide Facebook users spending 700 billion minutes on the site a month.[61] It makes me picture millions of hearts yearning to be known, to be understood—to be seen. Although stats like these make it clear that we are reaching out, current research also shows that 25 percent of Americans say they don't have anyone they can talk to about their personal troubles.[62]

The truth is, we are growing increasingly socially isolated while online social networks are exploding. We are seeking connection, but so many of our connections aren't satisfying. Too many of our relationships feel superficial, artificial, one step removed from the real thing. This isolation can be soul deadening.

We long for a soft place to land, a place characterized by unconditional love made more powerful and healing through gentle truth telling.

---

[59] "Infographic: Americans Send 69,000 Texts Every Second," CTIA, November 25, 2013, http://www.ctia.org/resource-library/facts-and-infographics/archive/americans-texts-2012-infographic.

[60] Ben Parr, "Twitter Hits 50 Million Tweets Per Day," Mashable, February 22, 2010, http://mashable.com/2010/02/22/twitter-50-million-tweets/.

[61] Doug Gross, "Who in the World Isn't on Facebook?" CNN, July 22, 2010, http://www.cnn.com/2010/TECH/social.media/07/22/facebook.500million/.

[62] Johannah Cornblatt, "Lonely Planet: Isolation Increases in the US," *Newsweek*, August 20, 2009, http://www.newsweek.com/lonely-planet-isolation-increases-us-78647.

We are craving a family.

In John 14:18, Jesus promised, "I will not leave you as orphans." God has given us a spiritual family—a heavenly Father, a heavenly mother, and the best older brother imaginable. We are children of God, adopted into a family. We belong. This is where we are cherished and protected. We discover a safe haven in the context of these relationships.

The Catholic Church has always believed that when Jesus hung on the cross in John 19, His final words to the apostle John and His mother, Mary, had meaning for the entire Church. When Jesus said to Mary, "Woman, behold, your son," and to John, "Behold your mother," Mary was being given the role of mother of all Christians. "Mary had only one Son, Jesus, but in Him, her spiritual motherhood extends to all whom He came to save." (*Compendium of the Catechism of the Catholic Church* 100)

In his book *Hail, Holy Queen*, Scott Hahn writes, "Every family needs a mother; only Christ could choose His own, and He chose providentially for His entire covenant family . . . For a family is incomplete without a loving mother. The breakaway Christian churches that diminish Mary's role inevitably end up feeling like a bachelor's apartment: masculine to a fault; orderly but not homey; functional and productive—but with little sense of beauty and poetry."[63]

Mary invites us home and longs to mother each of her children in a very personal way. Father Michael Gaitley unpacks this truth in his book *33 Days to Morning Glory: A Do-It-Yourself Retreat in Preparation for Marian Consecration*:

> Mary's new motherhood is not some vague or abstract sort of thing. It's concrete and personal. And even though it's universal, it's also intensely particular. Mary is your mother. She is my mother. In this light, Saint John Paul II thinks it's significant that Mary's new motherhood on Calvary is expressed in the singular, "Behold, your son" not "Behold, your billions of spiritual children." The Pope gets to the heart of it when he says, "Even when the same woman is the mother of many children, her personal relationship with each one of them is of the very essence of motherhood." In short: Mary is uniquely, particularly, personally your mother and my mother, and she doesn't lose us in the crowd.[64]

---

[63] Scott Hahn, *Hail, Holy Queen: The Mother of God in the Word of God* (New York: Doubleday) 27–28.

[64] Michael E. Gaitley, *33 Days to Morning Glory: A Do-It-Yourself Retreat in Preparation for Marian Consecration* (Stockbridge, MA: Marian Press, 2011), 99.

What does Mary have to do with our relationship with Christ? As our heavenly mother, she wants what is best for us. She knows that so many of our attempts to connect and be known by people around us will fill the hours, but never the heart. Because of this, she never stops pointing us toward the only One who will truly satisfy our inner longing for belonging, safety, and love. She always leads us home to her Son.

Day One
MARY: FULL OF GRACE

We don't just want to have a friendship with Christ; we want to grow more and more like Him. We want to be changed. In our efforts to follow Christ and more closely resemble Him, no greater example exists than the Blessed Mother. From the first moment we meet her in Scripture, she stands out as the supreme model of a woman so full of God that there's no room for selfishness, fear, or bitterness. There's only grace.

Read Luke 1:26–38.

1. A. What does the angel Gabriel call Mary in Luke 1:28?

    "Favored One"

The word translated "favored one" is *kecharitōmenē* in the original Greek language, and means "to endow with grace" or to be "full of grace." In his book *Walking with Mary*, Dr. Edward Sri observes, "In Luke 1:28, [kecharitōmenē] appears in the passive tense, which underscores how Mary's special favor is based on God's activity in her life. Mary is the recipient of this unique grace."[65] It's God's gift to her.

   B. Some of us are motivated by Mary's holiness, and others feel that emulating her is impossible because she's just too good. It's interesting that the root word used in Luke 1:28 is also used in Ephesians 1:5–8. Read that passage and note what is lavished on God's children—on *us*.

   Grace
   Redemption – Forgiveness

---

[65] Edward Sri, *Walking with Mary: A Biblical Journey from Nazareth to the Cross* (New York: Crown Publishing Group, 2013), 42.

Yes, God filled Mary with divine grace from the very beginning—from her conception. True, she didn't start life with original sin the way we do. Nevertheless, God has given us everything we need today to make the right choices, to reflect Mary's character in all we do and say.

2. The angel Gabriel knew that the shock of his arrival and the news he was about to give Mary was terrifying. What words did he use to comfort her? See Luke 1:28 and 30.

Hail! Favored One!

3. What was Mary's response to the angel's shocking revelation? See Luke 1:38.

Hail, I am a Handmaid of the Lord. May it be done to me according to your Word.

4. We will all encounter times when God intersects our plans with one of His own. Just like Mary, we'll have to choose between following God and insisting on our own way. More often than not, His plan will seem cloaked in shadows—we won't clearly see exactly how it's all going to roll out. In the midst of the uncertainty, God makes us the same promise He made to Mary: "I will be with you." Is there an area of your life where God is asking you to follow Him into the unknown? How can Mary's example help you to obey without fear?

To live alone in the World and to completely Trust in God.

Quiet your heart and enjoy His presence. . . . He doesn't promise to reveal every detail of His plan for you, but He promises never to leave your side.

Not only does God promise never to leave us, He has given us a mother who is attentive to our every need. We can entrust ourselves to her care because there is nothing she wants more than to draw us to Jesus and to see us become more and more like Him.

Draw close to Jesus through Mary. . . .

Mary, I want to love and follow the Lord the way you did. Please intercede on my behalf. While I do all I can to remain like putty in the Lord's hands, please ask your Son to give me the grace I need to obey Him.

Hail Mary, full of grace; the Lord is with thee; blessed art thou among women, and blessed is the fruit of thy womb, Jesus. Holy Mary, Mother of God, pray for us sinners, now and at the hour of our death. Amen.

Day Two
MARY: PILLAR OF FAITH

"Now faith is the assurance of things hoped for, the conviction of things not seen." (Hebrews 11:1, RSV)

"The coming of faith first occurs in the Virgin's heart and then fruitfulness comes to the Mother's womb." —Saint Augustine

1. How did Elizabeth describe Mary in Luke 1:45?

   She believed

2. A. Hebrews 11:1 tells us that faith is believing in what we cannot see. In John 11:40, what is promised to us if we believe?

   We will see the Glory of God

   B. In what way did the promise of John 11:40 come true for Mary?

   When he arose from the dead

3. According to James 1:3, what does the testing of our faith produce?

   Perseverance.

4. Throughout her life, Mary persevered on her pilgrimage of faith. Each step of the way, she had to choose to trust God with the unknown. Edward Sri beautifully describes the culmination of this journey at the foot of the cross:

   At this crucial moment, however, no human crutch can support Mary. The only thing Mary can cling to is faith—faith that this is indeed the Son of

God, who will reign forever; faith that she really is "the mother of my Lord" as Elizabeth told her; faith that this "sword" is truly part of God's plan as Simeon prophesied long ago, and that her son once again is doing his "Father's business." When Mary is found "standing by the cross of Jesus," she is, doubtless, experiencing great sorrow. But as a faithful disciple to the end, Mary also stands by the cross in great faith, trusting in God's plan for her son and clinging to what the Lord has revealed to her through angels, shepherds, prophets and Jesus himself.[66]

We all reach a point in life when all we can cling to is faith. We're at the bottom of our resources. We can't get ourselves out of whatever situation we are in. All we can do is trust that God will get us through. In what area of life do you need to trust God today? Write a prayer to Him, asking Him to increase your faith in His ability and willingness to take care of this concern. Ask Mary to intercede for you, to pray that you will persevere in faith so you can see God glorified in your circumstances.

Quiet your heart and enjoy His presence. . . . You will be blessed if you believe.

The fundamental attitude in the life of the Mother of God was one of faith. Mary trusted in God's Providence. As Elizabeth said of her: "Blessed is she who believed that there would be a fulfillment of what was spoken to her from the Lord" (Luke 1:45). I pray that your lives will likewise be marked by a deep faith in the providence of God. Then, with trusting surrender to the Lord's will in all things, you will be hope-filled witnesses of Christ in the world. May Mary obtain this grace for you. And may her divine Son bless you with his peace. —Saint John Paul II, Address to Marists, Rome, September 27, 1985

What has the Lord spoken to you? What has He promised? He has promised His presence. He has promised there is always a purpose in whatever you face. He has promised that He is in control. Can you surrender to Him? Can you release your grip on your plans? Can you trust that His way is the best one, even if it seems to be a crooked path to follow? Ask Him for the gift of faith—for the belief in His power when you can't see it and His presence when you can't feel it.

---

[66] Ibid., 142.

Day Three
MARY: OUR LADY OF SORROWS

1. When Elizabeth greeted Mary and praised her faith (Luke 1:42–45), Mary responded with a psalm of praise. What were the first words of her song? See Luke 1:46–47.

   My soul proclaims the greatness of the Lord. My spirit rejoices in God my Savior.

2. After Jesus' birth, Mary and Joseph brought Him to the temple to present Him to the Lord. There they encountered Simeon, a prophet. What did he tell Mary her future held? See Luke 2:34–35.

   Behold this child is destined for the fall & rise of many in Israel. And to be a sign that will be contradicted.

3. When was Mary's heart "pierced with a sword"? See John 19:25.

   Standing at the foot of the cross

4. Mary's soul magnified the Lord through her suffering, when her heart was pierced at the foot of the cross. Edward Sri issues us a challenge as we meditate on her suffering: "If we desire to magnify God in our souls, we too must be willing to draw near to Christ's cross and be pierced by the sword."[67] Do you agree? In what way have you seen God increase in importance in your life when you have drawn near to Him in suffering?

Quiet your heart and enjoy His presence. . . . Bring your suffering to the foot of the cross.

"Prayer to Our Lady of Lourdes"

O Holy Virgin, in the midst of your days of glory, do not forget the sorrows of this earth. Cast a merciful glance upon those who are suffering, struggling against difficulties, with their lips constantly pressed against life's bitter cup.

---

[67] Ibid., 103.

❧ *Have pity on those who love each other and are separated.*
❧ *Have pity on our rebellious hearts.*
❧ *Have pity on our weak faith.*
❧ *Have pity on those we love.*
❧ *Have pity on those who weep, on those who pray, on those who fear.*
Grant hope and peace to all.
Amen. —*Abbé Perreyve*

Day Four
MARY: MOTHER OF MERCY

Saint John Paul II beautifully explains why we call Mary the Mother of Mercy in his encyclical titled *Rich in Mercy*:

> *No one has experienced, to the same degree as the Mother of the crucified One,* the mystery of the cross, the overwhelming encounter of divine transcendent justice with love: that "kiss" given by mercy to justice. No one has received into his heart, as much as Mary did, that mystery, that truly divine dimension of the Redemption effected on Calvary by means of the death of the Son, together with the sacrifice of her maternal heart, together with her definitive *"fiat."* Mary, then, is the one who *has the deepest knowledge of the mystery of God's mercy.* She knows its price, she knows how great it is. In this sense, we call her the *Mother of mercy,* our Lady of mercy, or Mother of divine mercy.[68]

1. How did the cross exemplify "justice with love: that 'kiss' given by mercy to justice"? Read the following verses and summarize.

Romans 3:23-24

Romans 6:23

---

[68] John Paul II, *Dives in Misericordia* (Rome: Libreria Editrice Vaticana, 1980), section 9, http://w2.vatican.va/content/john-paul-ii/en/encyclicals/documents/hf_jp-ii_enc_30111980_dives-in-misericordia.html.

Romans 5:8

2 Corinthians 5:21

Summarize what you learned from these verses: *We are all sinners but God let Jesus die for us to save us*

2. Read CCC 725. How are we described in this Catechism passage? According to this passage, what does the Holy Spirit do through Mary? Who does this passage say are the first to accept Christ?

The Humble

3. Why is humility the precursor to accepting Christ? See Titus 3:4–5.

God saved us because of his mercy. By bath of the Holy Spirit

Quiet your heart and enjoy His presence. . . . Accept His kiss of mercy.

O Mary,
Mother of Mercy,
watch over all people,
that the cross of Christ
may not be emptied
of its power,
that man might not stray from
the path of the good
or become blind to sin,
but may put his hope
ever more fully in God,
who is "rich in mercy"
(Eph. 2:4).

may he carry out
the good works prepared
by God beforehand
(cf. Eph. 2:10)
and so live completely
"for the praise
of his glory"
(Eph. 1:12).
Veritatis Splendor, 120

Day Five
SAINT'S STORY

Saint Bernadette Soubirous

Bernadette was born in France in 1844 into a loving, successful family. During her early childhood, her family's fortunes turned, plunging them into dire poverty. Bernadette suffered from chronic illness, and due to her family's circumstances, she was not well educated. Her biography leaves nothing to suggest that she would become a great saint. But even as she lived in poverty, the Lord was close to her and working in her life.

When she was fourteen years old, Bernadette received her first vision of the Blessed Virgin Mary, whom she knew as "a beautiful lady." She would go on to receive eighteen such visions in a grotto on the outskirts of Lourdes, France. Her visions were widely doubted, and Bernadette paid dearly for the privilege of seeing Mary. The people mocked her, accused her, and made a great display of her.

But Bernadette learned from Mary that her heaven was within. She learned that even if she walked through a desert of scorn and misunderstanding, deep inside her was a well of joy, a river of healing that did not come from her but flowed through her—just like the healing stream that sprang up under her fingers at the grotto.

Through these visions, Bernadette also learned that God is good. He is not a faraway Father; He is Abba, Daddy, Papa: close at hand and full of tenderness. She saw the face of God shining through Mary's gentle eyes. She learned that God is not to be feared, but to be loved and trusted. In these visions, Mary taught her that prayer is an experience of being loved to the very roots of her being; she learned to approach God with all the confidence of a child who knows that she is loved, and whose Father will provide for her. God is beautiful, and He is the author of everything true, lovely, and good.

Bernadette never sought fame for her visions or with the knowledge she learned. But she did become a bit of a national spectacle, with people traveling to Lourdes to hear from her.

She eventually entered the convent at Nevers in 1866 to live a quiet life. Here, Bernadette (called Sister Marie Bernarde) lived simply, eschewing the fame of the world. She continued to suffer ill health for the next thirteen years, in addition to the skepticism of her superiors at the convent. Still, she never lost faith, and lived her life in devotion and service to the Lord and the Blessed Virgin. She let the lessons she learned completely take over her heart and fill her with holy love and service to others.

Most of all, she learned from her visions that God sees each one of us, no matter how insignificant we may be. We all have an important part in His plan. Bernadette was chosen to be His instrument at Lourdes, and she lived her life echoing the words of the Blessed Virgin: "He who is mighty has done great things for me, and holy is his name." (Luke 1:49)

True prayer is this constant gazing, this looking upon, this being with, this faithful contemplation of God's beauty and goodness. That is what Bernadette experienced. Saint Bernadette learned great lessons from Mary, which helped her during struggles in her life. Which of Mary's lessons would help you right now?

Conclusion

In Mary, we have a mother who will never leave us, one who is totally dedicated to our well-being. She knows that nothing will bring us greater fulfillment and satisfaction than being close to her Son. She "continues to intercede for her children, to be a model of faith and charity for all, and to exercise over [us] a salutary influence deriving from the superabundant merits of Christ." (*Compendium of the Catechism of the Catholic Church* 197)

Jesus, who held nothing back from us, offers us His mother. She is one of His most precious gifts, and He longs for us to know her, admire her, and become more like her. There's a love that only a mother can give, and He wants us to experience that love at its best.

Her "fiat," her yes, changed the world. Her life quietly reminds us that sacrificial love is the only love that really makes a difference. Loving with abandon can involve risk, the loss of reputation, and the letting go of a comfortable life. It isn't a safe love, but it's the kind that brings light to the darkness around us.

As Saint John Paul II said, "She, more than any creature, shows us that the perfection of love is the only goal that matters, that it alone is the measure of holiness and the way to perfect communion with the Father, the Son, and Holy Spirit."[69]

Nestle into your place in the family. Let Mother Mary love you, pray for you, and challenge you to love radically, sacrificially, and wholeheartedly. You are not an orphan. You belong; you are cherished. This family is the safe place to land, refuel, and then launch into a world that needs your yes. May your time "at home" give you the strength to hold nothing back, and to echo Mary's words, "May it be done to me according to your Word." (Luke 1:38)

My Resolution

In what specific way will I apply what I have learned in this lesson?

1. I'll increase my devotion to Mary by praying a decade of the Rosary every night.

2. To help me follow Mary's example, I'll take time this week to read the following words from Saint John Paul II and pray about areas where I need to improve: "In light of Mary, the Church sees in the face of women the reflection of a beauty which mirrors the loftiest sentiments of which the human heart is capable: the self-offering totality of love; the strength that is capable of bearing the greatest sorrows; limitless fidelity and tireless devotion to work; the ability to combine penetrating intuition with words of support and encouragement."[70]

3. When I hear God asking me to step out into unknown territory, I'll remember Mary's example as she responded to the angel, and I'll follow that example by saying yes to what He asks.

---

[69] Margaret R. Bunson, *Pope John Paul II's Book of Mary* (Huntington, IN: Our Sunday Visitor, 1996), 17.

[70] Pope John Paul II, *The Mother of the Redeemer: Redemptoris Mater* (Washington, DC: United States Conference of Catholic Bishops, 1987), 51.

4. I'll take time this week to go to adoration, and when I'm there, I'll meditate on how the cross was the "kiss given by mercy to justice."

My Resolution:

Catechism Clips

CCC 725 Finally, through Mary, the Holy Spirit begins to bring men, the objects of God's merciful love, *into communion* with Christ. And the humble are always the first to accept him: shepherds, magi, Simeon and Anna, the bride and groom at Cana, and the first disciples.

Compendium of the Catechism of the Catholic Church 100
In what way is the spiritual motherhood of Mary universal?
Mary had only one Son, Jesus, but in Him, her spiritual motherhood extends to all whom He came to save. Obediently standing at the side of the new Adam, Jesus Christ, the Virgin is the new Eve, the true mother of all the living, who with a mother's love cooperates in their birth and their formation in the order of grace. Virgin and Mother, Mary is the figure of the Church, its most perfect realization.

Compendium of the Catechism of the Catholic Church 197
How does the Virgin Mary help the Church?
After the Ascension of her Son, the Virgin Mary aided the beginnings of the Church with her prayers. Even after her Assumption into heaven, she continues to intercede for her children, to be a model of faith and charity for all, and to exercise over them a salutary influence deriving from the superabundant merits of Christ. The faithful see in Mary an image and an anticipation of the resurrection that awaits them, and they invoke her as an advocate, helper, benefactress, and mediatrix.

NOTES

Looking for more material? We've got you covered!
Walking with Purpose meets women where they are in
their spiritual journey. From our Opening Your Heart
22-lesson foundational Bible study to more advanced
studies, we have something to help each and every
woman grow closer to Christ. Find out more:

www.walkingwithpurpose.com

Lesson 17

CAN GOD REALLY CHANGE ME OR IS THAT JUST WISHFUL THINKING?

Introduction

"I can't kick that habit. It's just too ingrained in me."
"Worrying is in my nature. It's how I process things."
"I know I drink more than I should, but I need it to take the edge off."
"I can't help the way I fly off the handle."
"I can never lose weight."
"I can't change. This is how God made me."

It probably wouldn't take us very long to make a list of things we'd like to change about ourselves. I sure would love to break free of my fear of failure and the fact that my default coping mechanism is perfectionism and performance. That would be so fantastic. The weight of the world just might lift off my shoulders. But when I'm asked if I believe it's possible for these changes to occur, I can quickly feel discouraged. I hear other people's success stories, but all too often I doubt that this level of radical transformation could happen to me.

Can you relate? Perhaps you've prayed for God to help you, but you're still stuck in the same rut. Has it caused you to wonder if God cares? Do your spirits lift at the thought that God's unconditional love means you're OK just as you are, but then deflate at the thought of never being free from the habits that keep you in bondage?

While it's true that God loves us unconditionally, He loves us too much to leave us as we are. He knows that the sins that disfigure us are keeping us from the abundant life He created us for. And He knows that Christians walking around looking no different than people who don't have Christ in their lives is not the way it's supposed to be. We are promised in 2 Corinthians 5:17, "If anyone is in Christ he is a new creation. The old is gone, the new has come." A *new creation* is a picture of freedom—a beautiful butterfly that has emerged from a cocoon after metamorphosis.

When we feel stuck, we are forgetting the secret of the Christian life. The truth is: **The same power that conquered the grave lives in you!** This means that there is *always* hope for change.

In 1 Corinthians 3:16, Saint Paul asks, "Do you not know that you are the temple of God, and that the Spirit of God dwells in you?"

Then in Romans 8:11, Saint Paul writes about the difference the indwelling Holy Spirit makes: "If the Spirit of the one who raised Jesus from the dead dwells in you, the one who raised Christ from the dead will give life to your mortal bodies also, through his Spirit that dwells in you."

This means that the Holy Spirit *in you* wants to bring new life to places you have long felt were dead. He wants to radically change you from the inside out. And He's got the power to do it. This week we're going to look at four steps that'll help us to move toward becoming the women we long to be.

Day One
ADMIT THAT THERE'S A PROBLEM

Step 1 is admitting that the area where you want to change is actually a problem. It's not a "thorn in the flesh" that you're expected to live with forever, and it's not a quirky part of your personality. This is something that God wants you to be free of.

1. List an area of your life where you would like to see transformation. Is this something friends and family believe you have a problem with? Is it impacting your relationships with others? Do you try to hide this problem from people? Can you go without engaging in this behavior for a week? Do you arrange parts of your life (your schedule, your spending) around it? Answering these questions can give an indication of how strong a hold the problem has on you. Be honest with yourself; you're the only one reading this.

2. A. What does Romans 6:14 tell us about the power of sin?

Sin is not to have any power over you because you are not under the law but under grace.

B. According to this passage, if we're no longer under the law, what are we under?

Under Grace

When the Bible says that we are "not under law but under grace," it's referring to our position as daughters of God—as Christians. This position is described in the footnotes of the Ignatius Catholic Study Bible as follows:

> *under grace:* The new position of the believer, who can master the urges of sin with the assistance of God. This inward strength to suppress our fallen inclinations was a grace not yet available to Israel living under the yoke of the Law.

Because we are under grace, we can master the urge to sin. We can be changed. The law had the power to point out the way people were to live, but it totally lacked the power to help people to actually obey. Everything radically changed when Jesus was raised from the dead, breaking the chains of death.

We talk a lot about what the cross accomplished. Jesus' sacrifice allowed us to be totally forgiven; He paid the price for our sin in full. But the Resurrection—that's where our freedom was really won. That's when Jesus broke through all the things that keep us dead, bound, and defeated. He was victorious over it all—He *was* and *is* stronger than it all—and He wants us to walk in the freedom He won for us.

3. What has set us free from the law of sin and death? See Romans 8:2.

The "law of the Spirit" is the power of grace at work in our lives.

God knows we feel a continual pull toward sin—it's the pull to take the easy way out, to value the wrong things, to make the selfish choice. Knowing that's the human condition, He steps in and pours divine love into our hearts so we can resist temptation. He places His very own Spirit, the Holy Spirit, into our hearts so that we have power within to slay the dragons that seek to keep us in bondage.

Quiet your heart and enjoy His presence. . . . You'll find grace and mercy—not condemnation.

I believe it's easier to face our problems—to call them what they really are: sins, addictions, idols—when we believe that freedom from them is possible. So lean in close and listen: God does not want you to stay in this place. He is just waiting to help you experience freedom and victory. But it has to start with you. It has to begin with you acknowledging that your behavior is hurting you—and probably people close to you. It has to begin with you admitting that this ingrained habit isn't something that you can control in your own strength. You are at a crossroads. You can choose to face the need to change or you can ignore it. But hasn't it been heavy to carry this load? Aren't you tired of the price you pay? God wants to lift this burden from you. He lovingly waits to be invited into the struggle.

Write a prayer to the Lord in the space provided, telling Him that you want to be free. Name the problem and ask Him for His help. Trust that as you spill out your struggle in His presence, He is whispering over you, "I love you. I love you. I love you."

My dear Lord Jesus I Thank you for the countless Blessings you bestow on me each day! I know you are always present at my beckon call. I need you dear Lord to give me awareness of the needs around me. Help me to push aside my selfishness and to do something kind for those around me who are in need.

Day Two
ASK FOR GOD'S HELP

Really coming to terms with our need to change—naming a problem that requires a solution—is the first step toward freedom. The next is to invite God into the process. As good as this sounds in theory, it isn't our typical response. Most of us begin to address a problem by getting to work and searching for solutions. This is trying to change in our own strength, and all too often, we'll fail to see real transformation. We are promised in Mark 10:27 that "with man, this is impossible—but not with God; all things are possible with God." We aren't promised that all things are possible in *our own* strength. In fact, in John 15:5, we are told, "apart from [God] we can do nothing."

There's a big difference between saying we're going to pray about something and then actually doing it. Hopefully the verses we study today will motivate us to live out Colossians 1:29: "To this end I labor, struggling with all *his* energy, which so powerfully works in me." (emphasis added)

Read 2 Corinthians 10:3–5.

1. This passage talks about a battle. As we battle toward freedom from sin, God gives us weapons to help us fight. How are they described in 2 Corinthians 10:3–4?

2. The weapons of our battle are capable of destroying three specific things mentioned in this passage. What are they?

3. In the original Greek, the word *fortress* describes the place a person goes to seek shelter (a safe place) or to escape reality. When we think of battling to break free of habits and sins that have a grip on us, it's helpful to consider them fortresses that need to be destroyed. Why do we continue to do these things that we know ultimately harm us and those we love? Sometimes we're trying to escape reality. Sometimes we fool ourselves into thinking that these behaviors or coping mechanisms are helping us to be more in control of things. Whatever our reason, the very thing we think will bring us greater control ends up having control over us. On our own, we can't get out from under them. But with the weapons God gives us, freedom can be won.

Do you recognize this pattern in your own life? As you identify the area where you desire to change—to experience freedom—has it been a place where you have gone to escape? Or has it been something that has caused you to feel more in control?

4. The weapons of our battle also equip us to destroy "arguments and every pretension raising itself against the knowledge of God." This is referring to the outward reasoning and inward pride that convince us that we don't need God—that we can solve our problems on our own. This isn't just a battle "out there" in our messed-up world. This is a problem that goes on within us. Do you recognize this tendency in yourself? Have you experienced this pull toward self-sufficiency?

Quiet your heart and enjoy His presence. . . . You need Him; an earnest desire to change is not all it takes.

We have got to get rid of the illusion that we have it within us to break down the fortresses that keep us from freedom. We have got to let go of our pride that says it's all up to us. When we're talking about deep-seated issues, long-held patterns of behavior, and addictions, we have got to have weapons that are powerful enough for the battle. The weapons God gives us allow us to fight in the spiritual dimension. It adds supernatural power to our resolve, self-discipline, and determination.

Spend some time talking to God about your need for His help. Invite Him into the struggle. Ask His forgiveness for running to fortresses instead of running to Him. Ask Him to forgive you for any pride that has caused you to rely on yourself instead of Him. Ask Him to break through any barriers that are keeping you away from a life of freedom.

Note: In no way am I suggesting that professional help is unnecessary as we battle addictions. I am making the point that pursuing freedom apart from God means that we miss out on supernatural power that can make all the difference in the world. Going to God first does not mean that we don't take advantage of other resources available.

Day Three
PUT ON YOUR ARMOR AND PICK UP YOUR WEAPONS

What provisions does God give us for the spiritual battle? In Ephesians 6, we read about both the defensive armor and the offensive weapons at our disposal. As we engage in the battle to experience true freedom, we're to draw our "strength from the Lord and from his mighty power." (Ephesians 6:10) We do this by putting on the armor of God, picking up our weapons, and using them.

1. A. Describe the armor of God from Ephesians 6:13–17.

The Belt of Truth: When God's truth surrounds us, we are protected from lies that keep us from living as beloved daughters of God. The lies say, "I can't. I'll never change." The Truth says, "With God, all things are possible." (Mark 10:27)

The Breastplate of Righteousness: Greek historian Polybius described the breastplate that covered the soldier from the neck to the thigh as "the heart protector." A holy life protects the most vital part of us: the soul. Self-discipline is like a muscle—the more it gets exercised, the stronger it becomes. There is protection in obedience.

Feet Fitted with the Gospel: A soldier's shoes had nails or spikes in the sole to help him stand firmly and keep his balance. In that same way, the gospel gives us something solid to stand on. We don't stand on the foundation of our own perfection. We stand on the truth of Christ's perfect sacrifice having paid the price for our sins. He makes up for where we are lacking.

The Shield of Faith: We put up the shield of faith to protect ourselves from the fiery darts of doubt, fear, discouragement, and condemnation. Our prayer becomes, "I believe; help my disbelief!" (Mark 9:24) God faithfully strengthens our faith when we ask Him to.

The Helmet of Salvation: The helmet protects the brain. When we focus on the gift of salvation, our minds are protected from thoughts of worthlessness and hopelessness. We remember that we are worth *everything* to Jesus.

The Sword of the Spirit: The sword of the Spirit is an offensive weapon. This is Scripture, and the more we know it, the more we can use it to gain ground spiritually instead of just treading water and staying in the same place. As we learned in Lesson 7, when we have memorized Scripture, the Holy Spirit can bring God's truth to our minds just when we need to fight temptation or negative thoughts.

B. Do you wear this armor? Are there some pieces that you forget to put on each day?

2. The sword of the Spirit (Scripture) is the first offensive weapon mentioned in this passage. What is the second offensive weapon? See Ephesians 6:18.

Prayer ensures that we have a constant supply of the grace and help we need to resist temptation. It calls down the help of heaven and makes all the difference in the world. Prayer should never be our last resort, because battles are won when we fight on our knees.

3. The sacraments are essential weapons that allow us to battle the constant pull toward mediocrity and compromise. Read each of the following quotes or passages, and record your thoughts regarding how God uses the sacraments to help you change and live as "a new creation" (2 Corinthians 5:17) in Christ. Do you take advantage of all that the sacraments offer you?

A. **CCC 1266** The Most Holy Trinity gives the baptized sanctifying grace, the grace of justification:

-enabling them to believe in God, to hope in him, and to love him through the theological virtues;
-giving them the power to live and act under the prompting of the Holy Spirit through the gifts of the Holy Spirit;
-allowing them to grow in goodness through the moral virtues.

Thus the whole organism of the Christian's supernatural life has its roots in **Baptism**.

B. **CCC 1394** As bodily nourishment restores lost strength, so **the Eucharist** strengthens our charity, which tends to be weakened in daily life; and this living charity wipes away venial sins. By giving himself to us Christ revives our love and enables us to break our disordered attachments to creatures and root ourselves in him.

C. "Satan tempts us to deny responsibility for our sins. Our only defense is to take responsibility for them. The only weapon that can defeat the Prince of Darkness is light. That is the purpose of the **Sacrament of Penance**. The priest in the confessional is a more formidable foe to the devil than an exorcist."[71] —Peter Kreeft

Quiet your heart and enjoy His presence. . . . He is waiting to outfit you for battle.

Dear Lord,

Please cover me with the armor of God.

Buckle the **belt of truth** *around my waist. You are truth, so wrap yourself around me and help me to dwell on what is true.*

I take the **breastplate of righteousness** *from your hand and thank you for giving me your righteousness. Help me to stay protected by your grace by making the right choices today.*

Place the **helmet of salvation** *on my head and protect my mind.*

May my **feet be shod by the gospel**. *Everywhere I go today, may I spread that message.*

Oil my **shield of faith** *with the Holy Spirit so that all the fiery darts flung at me will be extinguished.*

I take up the **sword of the Spirit**. *Let me be ready to fight back any lies with the truth found in Scripture.*

Amen.

---

[71] Peter Kreeft, *Catholic Christianity: A Complete Catechism of Catholic Beliefs Based on the Catechism of the Catholic Church* (San Francisco: Ignatius Press, 2001).

Day Four
WALK AWAY FROM THE QUICKSAND

There's no question that God gives us everything we need to resist temptation. While He certainly equips us for battle, there are some battles He wants us to just walk away from. These are the battles on top of quicksand, and the only way to win is to avoid the area completely. This is essentially the message of Romans 6: You are free from the grip of sin, *so walk away from it.*

1. Read 1 Corinthians 15:33 and reflect on your choice of friends. Do some of your friends encourage you to live the way God wants you to? Do others consistently draw you into behavior that you later regret? Is God asking you to change where you are spending your time?

We are wise to be discerning in choosing our friends, because as it says in Proverbs 13:20, "He who walks with the wise grows wise, but a companion of fools suffers harm." No matter how strong our personality or how well we know ourselves, we are always influenced by our friends. Even Jesus gave careful thought to choosing His friends. He spent all night in prayer before selecting His twelve disciples, asking God to help Him discern whom He should surround Himself with.

2. According to Colossians 3:1–10, what are we to be seeking and setting our mind on? What should we be "putting to death" within us? Which of these behaviors is like quicksand for you? What do you need to walk away from?

3. How is "the way of perfection" described in CCC 2015?

You're Blessed when you're at the end of your rope!

Quiet your heart and enjoy His presence. . . . Walk away from the quicksand and run toward the One who gives you life.

There's no growth in holiness without battling temptation and walking away from situations that are sure to take us down. It involves a thousand little deaths. It's hard, and requires grit and sacrifice. Through it all, we're called to persevere. As Saint Gregory of Nyssa said, "He who climbs never stops going." The journey isn't easy, but the destination makes it all worth it.

Dear Lord,

This is where the rubber meets the road. As long as I don't feel equipped to change, I feel like I don't have to. I have an excuse. In John 5:6, you asked the man lying by the pool in Bethesda, "Do you want to be well?" The man replied with an excuse. He was so used to being crippled that all he could think of were the reasons he'd never get better. And there you stood, with all the power imaginable at your disposal, ready to help. You looked at the man and said, "Rise, take up your mat, and walk."

I know that you ask me the same question. "Do you really want to be well?" It's time for me to stop making excuses and to grasp hold of your promise from Philippians 4:13: "I can do all things through Christ who strengthens me." It's time for me to pick up my mat and walk—to walk toward freedom. No more excuses. I want to be well.

Day Five
SAINT'S STORY

Saint Monica Outlasts the Devil

Two of the most difficult Christian virtues are patience and perseverance. Having patience means elegantly putting up with persistent difficulties—especially one's own personality flaws and selfish tendencies. Having perseverance means maintaining the struggle to overcome obstacles (especially those same flaws and tendencies) no matter how long it takes or how hard it gets. At times we are tempted to get discouraged because we don't see results right away. But discouragement never comes from God. What seems a long time to us is only a heartbeat to Him, and what seems like slow or no progress to us may be yielding abundant fruit in ways we cannot see. "But do not ignore this one fact, beloved, that with the Lord one day is like a thousand years and a thousand years like one day. The Lord does not delay his promise, as some regard 'delay,' but he is patient with you, not wishing that any should perish but that all should come to repentance." (2 Peter 3:8–9) God hears every prayer and values every effort, as Saint Monica can attest. She is a model of Christ's own love coursing through our hearts—the reason why true Christians can find the strength to be heroically patient and persevere amazingly. And Christ's love never, ever gives up. It dies on the cross instead, and then rises again.

Monica spent almost twenty years pleading with God through tears and entreaties to bring her wayward son into the Christian fold. At times she spent entire nights in prayer. More often than not, when she allowed herself a few hours of rest, she cried herself to sleep. She had grown up a Christian in northern Africa in the 400s, but had married a pagan. Her husband tolerated her faith, although his temper and dissolute living (as well as his mother, who was a most disagreeable person and resided with them) caused her constant grief and difficulty. Eventually, however, her prayers and Christian example won both her husband and her mother-in-law over to the faith a year before her husband's death. At about that time, their eldest son was finishing his elite education and notified his mother that he had embraced Manichaeism (a heresy). Nothing could have pained her more. She spared no effort to save him, arranging meetings for him with eminent churchmen, arguing with him herself, disciplining him by taking away family privileges, and always, day after day, year after year, praying for him. Only after she had pursued him to Rome and Milan, where the rebellious Augustine (who had meanwhile taken up residence with a mistress and fathered an illegitimate child) finally met his match in Saint Ambrose, was her prayer answered. Augustine, the future Bishop of Hippo, saint, and Doctor of the Church, was baptized while she looked on, her eyes overflowing with tears and her heart overflowing with gratitude.

She stuck it out. Why? Because she loved. Love simply can't give up. When we truly love Christ, we keep going, knowing that since He truly loves us, all our efforts will eventually bear wonderful fruit for us and for those around us. One of the many lessons that Saint Monica taught her son was precisely that: unlimited confidence in the transforming power of God's love. When Augustine left North Africa (after abandoning his Christian faith), he did so in secret so that his mother wouldn't go with him (she actually wanted him to stay because she feared he would drift further away from the truth if he traveled to Italy).

Here is Saint Augustine's later reflection on that incident:

> Why I left the one country and went to the other, you knew, O God, but you did not tell either me or my mother. She indeed was in dreadful grief at my going and followed me right to the seacoast. . . . That night I stole away without her; she remained praying and weeping. And what was she praying for, O my God, with all those tears but that you should not allow me to sail! But you saw deeper and granted the essential part of her prayer: you did not do

what she was at that moment asking, that you might do the thing she was always asking.

As you read Saint Monica's story, consider how she embodied the virtues of patience and perseverance as she prayed for her son to experience spiritual transformation. What lessons have you learned this week to help you persevere in your journey toward holiness?

Conclusion

"When Christians stop being different from the world and instead fall back into their old habits, it is as tragic as finding a royal prince sleeping out on the streets in a gutter, having forgotten he belongs in the palace."[72] —Adrian Warnock

You are God's beloved daughter, a child of the King of Kings. He doesn't want you lying on a mat, crippled by sin. He offers you His hand, invites you to get up and walk with Him toward the freedom of holiness.

Holiness is within reach. It isn't beyond you. This isn't a call to live in a constant state of fear, afraid of disappointing God or making Him angry. It's an invitation from your heavenly Father, who is *good*, who is *for you*, and who gives you the power of the Holy Spirit. This power breaks the chains of addiction, destructive habits, and behaviors that hurt us.

As it says in The Message version of Matthew 5:3, "You're blessed when you're at the end of your rope. With less of you there is more of God." You can't change in your own power. If you feel overwhelmed at the thought of breaking free of sins that have long held you in their grasp, then turn to the One who is bigger than all things. He will be strong in your weakness.

God has given you everything you need in order to live your life the way He desires. He's given you His very presence in your soul. The Holy Spirit fills you with love, joy, peace, patience, kindness, goodness, faithfulness, gentleness, and self-control. If those are the things you need, you can't say you don't have them. It's just that we often don't tap into the power that is within us. God has given us the sacraments to fill us with His grace, which is exactly what we need for whatever we face.

---

[72] Adrian Warnock, *Raised with Christ: How the Resurrection Changes Everything* (Wheaton, IL: Crossway Books, 2010), 143.

"Do not be afraid to be holy! Have the courage and humility to present yourselves to the world determined to be holy, since full, true freedom is born from holiness."
— Saint John Paul II

My Resolution

In what specific way will I apply what I have learned in this lesson?

Examples:

1. If I need professional help with an addiction, I will make an appointment to talk with someone this week.

2. I will receive the sacrament of penance this week, recognizing that when I do this, God deals a blow to the sin that has been gripping me. I'm not only forgiven; I receive power to resist temptation in the future.

3. I've recognized that some of my friendships are not leading me in the right direction. I'll make a concerted effort to build a relationship with a woman whose character is the type I would like to reflect.

My Resolution:

Catechism Clips

CCC 1394 As bodily nourishment restores lost strength, so the Eucharist strengthens our charity, which tends to be weakened in daily life; and this living charity wipes away venial sins. By giving himself to us Christ revives our love and enables us to break our disordered attachments to creatures and root ourselves in him.

Since Christ died for us out of love, when we celebrate the memorial of his death at the moment of sacrifice we ask that love may be granted to us by the coming of the Holy Spirit. We humbly pray that in the strength of this love by which Christ willed to die for us, we by receiving the gift of the Holy Spirit, may be able to consider the world as crucified for us, and to be ourselves as crucified to the world. . . . Having received the gift of love, let us die to sin and live for God.

CCC 1266 The Most Holy Trinity gives the baptized sanctifying grace, the grace of justification:

-enabling them to believe in God, to hope in him, and to love him through the theological virtues;
-giving them the power to live and act under the prompting of the Holy Spirit through the gifts of the Holy Spirit;
-allowing them to grow in goodness through the moral virtues.

Thus the whole organism of the Christian's supernatural life has its roots in Baptism.

CCC 2015 The way of perfection passes by way of the Cross. There is no holiness without renunciation and spiritual battle. Spiritual progress entails the ascesis and mortification that gradually leads to living in the peace and joy of the Beatitudes: "He who climbs never stops going from beginning to beginning, through beginnings that have no end. He never stops desiring what he already knows." (Saint Gregory of Nyssa)

NOTES

No program near you? No problem...it's easy to start your own group in your parish or at home and we will walk with you every step of the way. Find out more:

www.walkingwithpurpose.com

Lesson 18: Connect Coffee Talk

CHILDREN – REACHING YOUR CHILD'S HEART

Accompanying DVD can be viewed by disc or please visit our website at walkingwithpurpose.com/videos and select *Opening Your Heart* Bible Study, click through to select Videos.

Key verse:

"Hear, O Israel: The Lord our God, the Lord is one. Love the Lord your God with all your heart and with all your soul and with all your strength. These commandments that I give you today are to be upon your hearts. Impress them on your children. Talk about them when you sit at home and when you walk along the road, when you lie down and when you get up. Tie them as symbols on your hands and bind them on your foreheads. Write them on the doorframes of your houses and on your gates." (Deuteronomy 6:4–9)

You can reach your child's heart by:

1. Training the "Control Center"

Ginger Plowman writes in *Don't Make Me Count to Three!*:

The heart is the control center of life. Behavior is simply what alerts you to your child's need for correction. But don't make the mistake that so many parents make and allow your desire for changed behavior to replace your desire for a changed heart. If you can reach the heart, the behavior will take care of itself. . . . We are tools used by God to whittle away the calluses of the heart, keeping the heart tender and inclined to obedience. When we call our children to obey us we are preparing them to obey Jesus, which is our ultimate goal.[73]

Tedd Tripp states in *Shepherding a Child's Heart*, "A change in behavior that does not stem from a change in heart is not commendable; it is condemnable. Is it not the same hypocrisy that Jesus condemned in the Pharisees? In Matthew 15, Jesus denounces the Pharisees who honored Him with their lips while their hearts were far from Him. Jesus censures them as people who wash the outside of the cup while the inside is still unclean."[74]

2. Teaching Key Spiritual Truths

Fill your child with hope by teaching:

A. God is the same yesterday, today, and forever.

B. God keeps His promises.

C. Your child is unconditionally loved by God.

D. Your child is weak, but He is strong.

Questions for Discussion

1. Have you experienced the difference between disciplining children for outward behavior and disciplining to reach the heart? Do you think the second is more effective or unnecessary?

2. What are some ways that we can continue to reach our children spiritually when they are at the age when their peers are their greatest influence?

---

[73] Ginger Plowman, *Don't Make Me Count to Three!* (Wapwallopen, PA: Shepherd Press, 2003), 33, 75.
[74] Tedd Tripp, *Shepherding a Child's Heart* (Wapwallopen, PA: Shepherd Press, 1995), 20–21.

3. Are you involved in any activities or commitments that are keeping you from giving your children spiritual guidance and nurturing? Are there any things in your family life that need to be removed or scaled back?

Monthly Prayer List for Our Children

January: I pray that my children will never be without godly friends and role models. I pray they will be discerning in choosing both friends and lifestyle, caring as much about inner beauty as outward beauty and achievement.

February: I pray that they will understand they have been created by God, and that they will be content and confident in the way they were made—spiritually, emotionally, and physically.

March: I pray that they will be protected from people and activities that could influence them negatively, and that they will maintain a passion for living the way Christ desires.

April: I pray that they will recognize hate and run away from evil and sin. I pray they will resist temptation through Christ's power.

May: I pray that they will love to give and serve, and will be glad, grateful, and generous givers to the world, not just takers.

June: I pray that early in life they will learn and love to pray, and that they will develop intimacy with God and become true worshippers of Him.

July: I pray that they will treat people with godly kindness in a meek and gentle spirit, without losing the ability to take a stand for what is right.

August: I pray that they will readily seek forgiveness when they sin and be quick to forgive others.

September: I pray that they will grow spiritually as quickly as they do physically and mentally.

October: I pray that they will understand who Jesus is and love Him with all their hearts throughout their lives.

November: I pray that they will enjoy Bible stories now, and make and keep a commitment to study the Bible every day of their lives.

December: I pray that they will speak about Christ with boldness and become leaders for the cause of Christ.

Lesson 19

WHAT CHALLENGES WILL I FACE IN MY EFFORTS TO FOLLOW JESUS MORE CLOSELY?

Introduction

"I didn't go to religion to make me happy. I always knew a bottle of Port would do that. If you want a religion to make you feel really comfortable, I certainly don't recommend Christianity."
—C. S. Lewis

There's nothing I'm more passionate about than seeing women come to know Jesus in a personal, life-changing way. Our time on earth is so short, and there's no more important decision than whether or not we'll follow Christ. The thought of women spending their whole lives looking in the wrong places for the only love and relationship that will *truly satisfy* totally wrecks me. Knowing that true freedom, fulfillment, and peace are available to them through Christ, and knowing that so many women have never heard the gospel explained in a way that they really understand . . . Well, sometimes I think I just can't bear it.

Because I desperately want women to just give faith in Christ a *try*, it can be really tempting to "sell" Jesus—to tell a would-be follower of Christ of all the perks of faith, leaving out any bits that might be off-putting. "He'll fill your emptiness! He'll give you peace in circumstances that you would never have thought you could endure! He'll restore what's broken! He'll never leave you!" Before you panic and think I'm going to make the point that all those things are false advertising, let me assure you, they are all *true*. They are promises that we can count on. But they aren't the whole story. And only talking about the sweet truths and never the more difficult ones is a bit like expecting a child to grow strong while only eating cake. Ultimately that would be a disservice. In order to grow strong, we need the "meat."

As we study Jesus in the Gospels, it's clear that there was nothing He wanted more than for people to follow Him. But at no point did He attempt to draw them closer by just giving them the comforting truths. In fact, when a large crowd gathered around Him, over and over again He would say the very things that caused people to walk away. Why? If He cared about their souls, wouldn't He have done anything to get them to stay?

Jesus let them choose. He never compromised or watered down truth to win them over. He didn't try to talk them into joining His club.

What was true then is true now. Jesus isn't interested in us giving Him a nod of approval, or just attending His weekly get-togethers, or wearing a label that has no bearing on our hearts. He wants us to be *all in*. He wants a wholehearted commitment from us. He wants to be the game changer that turns our world upside down. Because of this, following Christ can be hard. It's always costly. It involves challenges that aren't for the fainthearted.

This week, we're not going to be gorging on sweets. We're going to serve up some meat. We're going to be taking a good and honest look at the level of commitment Jesus is asking from us. We're going to focus on the challenges instead of the perks. Why? Because when life gets hard (which it inevitably will or might even be in this very moment), I don't want you to feel sideswiped or to wonder if your tough circumstances mean that God doesn't love you. Following Christ means entering into a battle that requires courage and perseverance. It isn't easy. But it is so very worth it.

Day One
THE CHALLENGE TO DENY YOURSELF

1. What condition did Jesus give for following Him in Luke 9:23?

2. The alternative to denying yourself and following Christ is saying, "I'll follow Jesus when it's comfortable. But this area of my life is off-limits. When it comes to [blank], I'm doing it my way." Is there an area of your life where what Jesus is asking of you just seems too much? Where are you feeling tempted to take the easy way out?

3. Picking up a cross and carrying it is always painful. It involves accepting a load that God has asked you to carry, and *walking forward*. This is different from sitting down with the weight of the cross on your back, a pool of pity in the tears at your feet. Picking up a cross is accepting circumstances that you are powerless to change, and determining to allow them to refine you, to sharpen you, to make you more spiritually fit. What cross has God asked you to pick up and carry forward?

4. What do we gain if we are willing to "lose our lives" for the sake of Christ? See Luke 9:24.

Quiet your heart and enjoy His presence. . . . Are you willing to lose your life for His sake?

". . . he must deny himself and take up his cross daily . . ." (Luke 9:23)

Daily. As in, day after day. It's one thing to gear up for one really tough challenge and to give it all you've got. Childbirth comes to mind. You know it's going to be really painful, but you also know it won't last forever and there will be a reward at the end. But the self-sacrifice that Jesus asks of us is the kind that feels especially hard because there is no guarantee that the end is in sight. We are to make a daily decision to deny ourselves, pick up our cross, and follow Jesus. "For whoever wishes to save his life will lose it, but whoever loses his life for [Jesus'] sake will save it." (Luke 9:24) Let's never forget the second part of that verse. The end of the story is not misery. The end of the story is life—a life well lived; a life with meaning; a life with depth. A life with empathy because you know—you understand. A life in which you have loved Jesus for who He is, not what He gives you. A life in which the message of Calvary has become your story: After death comes the promised resurrection.

Day Two
THE CHALLENGE TO ACCEPT HEALTHY CONFLICT

Read Matthew 10:34–39.

1. Did Jesus promise that following Him would make all our relationships peaceful and conflict-free? Have you experienced conflict in relationships as your values, morals, and goals have changed as a result of following Christ?

2. Did Jesus say in Matthew 10:37 that we aren't supposed to love our parents and children? What important distinction is made in this verse regarding our love for others and our love for Christ?

We are called to be committed to our families and to love them as Christ loves us. But when we have to make a choice between pleasing God and pleasing the people in our lives (even those who are closest to us), we are to choose God. While Jesus did say, "blessed are the peacemakers," (Matthew 5:9) He never advocated the kind of peace that ignores or avoids hard discussions just for the sake of artificial harmony.

3. When we have chosen to follow Christ and people close to us are following a different path, conflict inevitably arises. Most people respond in one of two ways. They either avoid uncomfortable discussions or situations, and if that involves compromise at times, so be it. Or they are always willing to engage, but feedback from others would suggest that they are coming off as judgmental. *So what exactly are we supposed to do?* Oh, if only there was a manual to follow with a perfect response for every situation we might face. The Bible doesn't give us a concise answer to every sticky position we might find ourselves in, but it does provide principles that we can apply to a variety of circumstances. Read the following verses from Ephesians 4, noting the principles that we are to follow when we experience conflict with others because of our faith.

Ephesians 4:2

Ephesians 4:26

Ephesians 4:29

Ephesians 4:32

Quiet your heart and enjoy His presence. . . . He heals the brokenhearted and binds up their wounds. (Psalm 147:3)

As Christians, we are called to be "imitators of God." (Ephesians 5:1) As we seek to reflect Him to a world that finds Him repugnant and divisive, there will be times when conflict arises. When it does, we aren't to shrink back and compromise. We aren't to deny what we know to be true. But as we communicate, we should be doing it in a way that makes it clear it's all about Him, not all about us. And perhaps that's where a lot of our difficulties lie. We take things personally. We get our feelings hurt. We feel devalued, alone, dismissed. These are genuine hurts, and the Lord does not take lightly the fact that you are suffering for Him. But He asks that you bring that hurt back to Him instead of responding in bitterness, rage, and anger. Those feelings have got to go somewhere. We can bury them, we can hurl them back at the people we disagree with, or we can take them to Jesus and ask Him to absorb them in His limitless love. Have you been hurt by people who don't respect or embrace your decision to follow Christ? Go to God with your pain. He listens and cares. He is waiting to bind up your wounds and kiss your tears.

Day Three
THE CHALLENGE TO STAND FIRM

1. What do Luke 22:31 and 1 Peter 5:8 reveal about the source of some of our challenges?

2. How is the whole of man's history described in CCC 409? Where do we find ourselves in the midst of this description?

3. As we engage in that battle, what does 1 Corinthians 16:13 call us to do? Can you apply that verse to a specific challenge in your life today?

As we face specific challenges, being watchful means being aware of times when the devil is at work, stirring up trouble and making things worse. We are wise to always remain aware of who the real enemy is. As we face these challenges, we need to stand firm. The devil wants to take us out at the knees, to see us give up. God calls us to stand firm in the face of this. He calls us to remain courageous and strong—not because we have confidence in our own strength, but because of our confidence in *Him*.

4. How do we stand firm in our faith, according to CCC 162?

Quiet your heart and enjoy His presence. . . . "the One who is in you is greater than he who is in the world." (1 John 4:4)

Do you know how terrified the enemy of your soul is of you?

You may think of him and the evil in the world as being powerful and pervasive, and you're right. He is powerful, and it is pervasive. But authority trumps power. *What do I mean by that?*

Think of a policeman directing traffic. An enormous Mack truck could be driving down that road, but if a policeman stepped into the road and held up his hand, that Mack truck would stop. Obviously, the truck driver wouldn't want to run over the policeman. But there is more at play here—it is also the authority *of the policeman that causes the driver to stop. And you have access to the greatest authority in the universe because He is your daddy. And He loves you. And He steps out and fights for you.*

If you can recognize who you are as a child of the King, if you know the truth of Scripture and have it at your fingertips, you can step into the spiritual battle with authority, and Satan will be terrified of you your every waking moment. Men and women who know who they are in Christ are his worst nightmare.

Spend some time meditating on God's authority and power. Thank Him for stepping out and fighting for you.

Day Four
THE CHALLENGE TO STAY CHILDLIKE

With all this focus on the things we need to do (deny ourselves, accept healthy conflict, stand firm), we can think it's all up to us. It's easy to lose sight of the *type* of faith that God wants us to cultivate.

1. Why does it matter if we remain childlike? See Matthew 18:2–4.

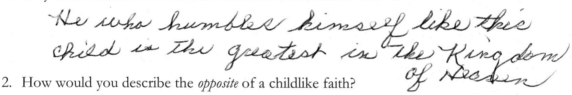

He who humbles himself like this child is the greatest in the Kingdom of Heaven

2. How would you describe the *opposite* of a childlike faith?

3. Childlike faith isn't naive; it's trusting of God. It isn't about being innocent; it's about being dependent. It's a steady acknowledgment that it isn't all up to us. What we can't do ourselves, Jesus will do. It's an acknowledgment that we aren't perfect supersaints, but are spiritual children who desperately need God. For people who like to be strong and self-sufficient, this is a challenge. In what area of your life do you find it most difficult to exhibit childlike faith?

Quiet your heart and enjoy His presence. . . . Come empty and ask Him to fill you.

It's a challenge to make sure our confidence is rooted in God and not in our own abilities and strength. Anytime we find ourselves white-knuckling it[75] in the spiritual battle, trying so hard to be perfect that we are worn out, we have forgotten the secret of the Christian life. What's that secret? God dwells within us through the Holy Spirit, and He wants to do the work in and through us. He wants us to live a life of constant dependence on His care and guidance. God knows that on our own, we are no match for the intensity of the spiritual battle. Anytime we fool ourselves into thinking that we're doing OK without Him, we are setting ourselves up for defeat. Our prayer life indicates just how much we are relying on Him.

---

[75] "White-knuckling it" means that we're doing something in a state of fear and tension. It's a picture of clenching something so tightly that our knuckles turn white.

As we set out to follow Christ, we need to be sure to meet the challenges in God's strength, not in our own.

"Not by might, not by power, but by my spirit, says the LORD *of hosts." (Zechariah 4:6)*

"Finally, be strong in the Lord and in the strength of his *might." (emphasis added) (Ephesians 6:10)*

Take some time to confess any tendency to rely on yourself instead of on God. Reaffirm your faith in His strength and power.

Day Five
SAINT'S STORY

Saint Perpetua and Saint Felicity

Often, we think of saints as those whose faithfulness and devotion were called upon to make the ultimate sacrifice. These saints followed Christ to the point of shedding blood. While not every story ends this way, it did for Perpetua and Felicity.

Perpetua was a Roman noblewoman blessed with beauty, wisdom, and high birth. But more than anything, she was a Christian. And when the time came to choose what defined her most deeply, she declared herself to be a Christian even unto death. Felicity was a slave whose devotion to the Lord and her mistress, Perpetua, led her to follow in Perpetua's footsteps completely.

From Perpetua's life, we learn that martyrdom is not a matter of a moment. It is the crowning second of many days of quiet faithfulness. It is one thing to be heroic in front of a crowded stadium chanting for blood, which eventually happened when she and Felicity faced the wild beasts while singing "Te Deum." But this was only the final chapter of many struggles and many battles. And you, too, have battles that you must fight in the solitude of your own heart, with God and the saints as your witnesses.

Our enemy in this world is not made of flesh and blood. Our battle is against the unseen powers that wage war against our spirits, inside our minds, and in our hearts. What are the enemies that range themselves against us? How are they to be conquered?

One of our greatest foes is fear. There is a fear that worms its way into a woman's heart; it is the devil's envoy, a parasite on God's blessings. Have you ever not trusted that God will take care of you and the ones you love? Have you ever failed to be faithful to God because you were anxious about what other people would think of you? Have you ever shied away from doing something for God or for others because you thought you were not capable, strong, or intelligent enough? Have you ever worried that Jesus might be disgusted with your weakness and your sins of pride and sensuality? Have you ever been tempted to give up and just let it all slide because you thought you could never win? These are your battles, but Jesus and the saints are all on your side, rooting for you, cheering for you, ready to help you at the slightest hint of a prayer.

So how will you conquer this fear? Listen to Saint John, who says, "Perfect love casts out all fear." (1 John 4:18) It is the love of God poured out into your heart that will give you the strength to tread on the serpent's head.

This was how Felicity and Perpetua conquered. Before they entered the arena, Perpetua had several dreams and visions of what would soon come to pass. She saw herself climbing up a ladder to heaven, carefully avoiding the weapons being thrust at them from all sides, and stepping over the head of the devil on her way up. She saw the saints in heaven calling them, cheering them on. In another dream, she saw herself as a gladiator doing battle with an Egyptian in a crowded amphitheater. And in these visions, Perpetua understood that her true enemy was not the wild beasts that were waiting for her in the arena, but the temptations that would dissuade her from her deepest identity as a Christian. Her heavenly reward was worth the trials of the world, but she knew that she and Felicity must resist the urge to shrink back in perceived "safety," away from the Lord's call to battle.

We live in a time of intense spiritual warfare. These are times unlike any other, when the true Christians following in Jesus' way and living lives honoring God will give immense glory to Him. You are blessed; you are gifted with grace. And if God calls you to do battle against these spiritual foes, it is because He knows you can win. Remember the words of Saint Paul and tell yourself that no matter what challenges you face, "I can do all things through him who strengthens me." (Philippians 4:13)

As you read Saint Perpetua and Saint Felicity's story, do you recognize some spiritual foes they faced that you currently struggle with? What can you learn from these saints to help you be victorious in the battle?

Conclusion

"For our struggle is not with flesh and blood but with the principalities, with the powers, with the world rulers of this present darkness, with the evil spirits in the heavens." (Ephesians 6:12)

Most things that are really worthwhile involve some hard work, and the Christian life is no exception. If we choose to live above the level of mediocrity, then we will soon see that the Christian life is a battle, and in this battle, we have some enemies.

We need only look at Christ's words and actions to see that He believes in the existence of the devil (1 John 3:8; Matthew 4:1–11; Mark 1:21–27, 3:11–15, 5:1–20). We need to strike a balance between being aware of Satan's work in our world and giving him more attention than he deserves. C. S. Lewis stated it well when he wrote, "There are two equal and opposite errors into which our race can fall about the devils. One is to disbelieve in their existence. The other is to believe, and to feel an excessive and unhealthy interest in them."[76]

Satan is the tempter, and he tries to keep us from following Jesus in many ways. Like no other time in history, women have the capability to really make a difference in the world. Yet we can be quickly distracted by things that don't matter. These things seem very important in the moment, but if we were to take a step back and think about whether they matter eternally, we might choose to spend our time in different places. Satan tempts us—not to join him, but simply to do nothing, to watch from the sidelines.

When we sit on the sidelines, he's not nearly as interested in us. Why? We aren't getting in his way! We're not having a real effect on the battle. But when we step in and decide that we want to be women who bring change, who make this world a better place for our children and grandchildren—this gets him annoyed. He knows the power of one person's holiness. So he gets out his weapons and makes it challenging to follow Christ and really make a difference in this world.

This reality may make you want to head over to the sidelines, where it seems safer. But if we do that, what will happen to our culture? What will happen to the many hearts that won't be touched by the love of Christ? What will our children be left with?

Jump into the battle. You'll never regret it, because it is there that you will experience God's great power. "The one who is in you [Christ] is greater than the one who is in

---

[76] C. S. Lewis, *The Screwtape Letters* (New York: Touchstone, 1996), 15.

the world [Satan]." (1 John 4:4) In this battle, there are no vacations. But this life of adventure is the only one truly worth living.

"Evil can only exist if good men do nothing." —Edmund Burke

My Resolution

So many of the challenges we face when we decide to follow Christ come from within. We are tempted to live humdrum lives of mediocrity and let others fight the battle for us. May the resolution you make this week help you stand firm as you face down these challenges and remain faithful to Christ.

In what specific way will I apply what I have learned in this lesson?

Examples:

1. I commit this week to living out my baptism to the utmost. When I feel discouragement or self-pity, I won't give in to it. Instead, I'll refocus on what I *can* do: love. Alone, I can do nothing. But with God, all things are possible.

2. I commit to becoming a woman of prayer. I recognize that I am in a battle, and there are no vacations. My greatest weapon is prayer—this unleashes God's power in my life. When I don't pray, I am saying that I can do it all on my own. This self-sufficiency will reduce the flow of grace into my life. Because I believe this, I am going to consistently pray for ten minutes each morning. I will recognize that the quantity of my prayers can sometimes be as important as the quality. I will honestly assess whether I am spending enough time with God to make a real impact on my life.

3. I commit this week to refrain from complaining about my challenges. When I stop focusing on my desire for comfort, I can see the value of challenges. They make me stronger as I exercise the muscles of my will. With each yes to God and each no to self, I am changed, and for the better. I commit this week to a change in attitude: no complaining.

Catechism Clips

CCC 162 Faith is an entirely free gift that God makes to man. We can lose this priceless gift, as St. Paul indicated to St. Timothy: "Wage the good warfare, holding faith and a good conscience. By rejecting conscience, certain persons have made shipwreck of their faith." To live, grow and persevere in the faith until the end we must nourish it with the word of God; we must beg the Lord to increase our faith; it must be "working through charity," abounding in hope, and rooted in the faith of the Church.

CCC 409 This dramatic situation of "the whole world [which] is in the power of the evil one" makes man's life a battle:

> The whole of man's history has been the story of dour combat with the powers of evil, stretching, so our Lord tells us, from the very dawn of history until the last day. Finding himself in the midst of the battlefield man has to struggle to do what is right, and it is at great cost to himself, and aided by God's grace, that he succeeds in achieving his own inner integrity.

Lesson 20

WHAT IS THE RELEVANCE OF THE CHURCH IN MY LIFE?

Introduction

In our individualistic culture, more and more people are questioning why they need the Church. When adult Americans were asked by the Barna Group[77] about the importance of attending church, 49 percent said it is "somewhat" or "very" important, and 51 percent said that it is "not too" or "not at all" important. The stats regarding Millennials (those age thirty and under) paint a grimmer picture. Only two out of ten think church attendance is important.

What has caused this change? Many cite hypocrisy within the Church as a prime reason for their disinterest. They are tired of people saying one thing and doing another. For some, this has gone a step further: They have been hurt by the Church and have walked away because of it. Others feel that everything they hear in the service lacks relevance to the rest of their lives. They have limited time, and they'd rather spend it somewhere else. In addition, we are impacted by the consumerist mind-set of the Western world—we want what we want, when we want it, how we want it. We don't have patience with an experience that irritates us ("I can't stand the music"), bores us ("The homily was too long and had nothing to do with my day-to-day challenges"), or offends us ("Every time I come here they are asking me for money"). We have high standards for the place where we share our most valuable resource: our time.

It's interesting that at the heart of our coming together as the Church we find the Eucharist, which means "thanksgiving" in the original Greek. And perhaps it's that

---

[77] The Barna Group, located in Ventura, CA, is widely considered to be a leading research organization focused on the intersection of faith and culture.

spirit of thanksgiving that's really missing in our analysis of the relevance of the Church today. A couple of years ago, I had the opportunity to travel into the rural countryside in Zambia. Our group was invited to go to church with the villagers. Halfway through the service, we realized that they were following the order of the Mass as well as they could, with no priest present. They were baptized Catholics, but they only had the privilege of a priest visiting once a year. The Eucharist and the other sacraments were considered precious gifts—they certainly didn't take them for granted. Hearing them speak about the celebration that occurred when the priest came annually made me ashamed of the countless times I took for granted what I had available back at home.

In this very moment, Catholics in other parts of the world are literally putting their lives at risk in order to come together and worship. It's similar to the time of the early Church when Christians were fed to lions, beheaded, and imprisoned because they followed Christ. And what was the result of followers of Christ being persecuted in this way? They turned the world upside down. In the words of Jon Tyson, author of *Sacred Roots: Why Church Still Matters in a Post-Religious Era*:

> The growth of the early church is arguably the most remarkable sociological movement in history. The numbers are staggering. In AD 40 there were roughly one thousand Christians in the Roman Empire, but by AD 350 there were almost 30 million. Remarkably, 53% of the population had converted to the Christian faith. What on earth could have compelled half an empire to convert? How could a Jewish political rebel, crucified on a Roman cross, become the Savior of the empire that killed him? The early church leaders didn't have the things we now consider essential for our faith to foster church growth. They didn't have fancy buildings and social media, no celebrity pastors or vision statements. Yet they loved and they served and they prayed and they blessed, and slowly, over hundreds of years, they brought the empire to its knees.[78]

Could it be that it is time for us to overcome our deeply ingrained consumer mentality? Instead of abandoning the Church when it frustrates us, is God calling us to dig in deeper with commitment to the local parish? What can we do together that we cannot do alone? And what does the Church offer us that we cannot get in other places?

---

[78] Barna and Jon Tyson, "Sacred Roots Outline," http://www.bibleresourcelink.com/frames/pdf/sacred-roots-outline.pdf.

"Let us hold unswervingly to the hope we profess, for he who promised is faithful. And let us consider how we may spur one another on toward love and good deeds. Let us not give up meeting together, as some are in the habit of doing, but let us encourage one another." (Hebrews 10:23–25)

Day One
WE NEED TRUTH TO STAND ON

I remember well a restless period of my life when I was learning about many different philosophies and theological perspectives, finding that *all* of them could be quite convincing. I was easily tossed back and forth depending on who made the most sense to me at the time. Because of this, I lacked inner peace, and I hit a wall in terms of my spiritual growth. With time, I learned that Jesus didn't want me to feel frustrated in this way. It wasn't up to me to figure out who had the corner on truth. I could rest, knowing that God wanted me to discover the truth about Him. Jesus had left someone in charge, and I could count on the promise that God would always make sure that His truth was protected. Let's explore the passages of Scripture that brought me to that place of understanding.

Read Matthew 16:13–20.

1. How did Jesus describe Peter in this passage? What did He promise regarding the Church? What did He give to Peter?

2. What was Jesus entrusting to Peter when He gave him the keys to the kingdom? What does the phrase "the power to bind and loose" mean? See CCC 553.

We can gain additional insight into the meaning of "the keys of the kingdom" from Isaiah 22:15–22. In the Old Testament, when a person carried the keys that belonged to the King, he was given a special position of authority. In this reading in Isaiah, we read about a steward who had that authority but who did a bad job. He had been given this special position of authority, but he misused it. As a result, the position he had held wasn't removed, but the keys were given to a successor. As in Isaiah 22, Peter's position was designated not just for him but also for his successors. Some of those successors were less than perfect, to say the least. But in spite of fallible people leading the Church, God has protected the doctrine of the Catholic Church so that we can have a rock to cling to when the storms of our culture threaten to wash us away.

A powerful video encouraging Catholics to "come home" says it well:

> Jesus, Himself, laid the foundation for our faith when He said to Peter, the first pope, "You are rock, and upon this rock I will build my church." For over 2,000 years, we have had an unbroken line of shepherds guiding the Catholic Church with love and truth, in a confusing and hurting world. And in this world filled with chaos, hardship and pain, it's comforting to know that some things remain consistent, true, and strong, our Catholic faith, and the eternal love that God has for all creation.[79]

3. In John 18:37, Jesus said, "Everyone who belongs to the truth listens to my voice." The following commentary from Father John Bartunek sheds light on what being led by truth requires of us. Read his words and write down your reflections on whether or not you find it difficult to be led in this way.

> Whoever lets himself be led by what is true will be drawn into communion with Christ and will hear and heed God's ceaseless invitations to follow Him more closely. **But being led by truth requires humility.** It requires recognizing a higher authority than oneself: if I am obliged to discover, accept, and conform to what is objectively true (morally, physically, historically), then I am not autonomous; I am not the master of my universe; I am not God.
>
> That act of humility, which frees us from the enervating bonds of selfishness, is hard to make. Our fallen human nature tends toward pride, self-sufficiency, control, and dominance. To resist that tendency requires courage. It takes courage to obey the truth and expose oneself to the burning love of God.[80]

---

[79] Catholics Come Home, "2000 Years of Faith: The Truth Behind Our 'Epic' Evangomercial," http://www.catholicscomehome.org/wp-content/uploads/2012/12/CCH-Epic-Factual-Documentation-20121.pdf.

[80] Bartunek, *The Better Part*, 977.

Quiet your heart and enjoy His presence. . . . He is near to all who call upon Him in truth. (Psalm 145:18)

"They exchanged the truth of God for a lie and revered and worshiped the creature rather than the creator." (Romans 1:25)

This exchanging of truth for a lie is so very subtle. It's a slippery slope—a gradual accepting of what the world says matters most. We don't worship creatures in the form of carved-stone idols, but we worship comfort, money, beauty, and prestige. And when we worship them by allowing them a place in our hearts that was meant for God alone, we start to believe all sorts of lies.

It takes a lot of humility and courage to ask the question, "God, where have I exchanged your truth for a lie? Where am I defining truth for myself instead of humbly accepting what you have said is right and wrong?" If there is a teaching of the Church that you find hard to accept, take some time to pray about it with a humble heart. Ask God to reveal to you if pride, self-sufficiency, or a desire for control is getting in the way of you obeying the truth.

Day Two
WE NEED GRACE TO STRENGTHEN US

1. How is Jesus (the Word) described in John 1:14? According to CCC 771, what part does the Church play in Jesus communicating this to the world?

2. According to CCC 774, what are "the signs and instruments by which the Holy Spirit spreads the grace of Christ"? What role does the Church play in this?

Many of us feel especially close and connected to God when we are in nature. Whether it's the magnificence of the mountains or the ocean, or the quiet of the woods, there's something in the beauty of the outdoors that can draw our hearts to the One who created it all in a special way. For others it's the beauty of music or of art that causes the soul to soar toward heaven. Because God is omnipresent (He is everywhere), we can certainly experience His presence in countless places. But it is only in the Mass and in the tabernacle that we experience His presence not just spiritually, but physically as well. If you long to be strengthened, filled, and sustained by the grace of Christ, there is no better place to receive it than at the Mass.

3. Look up the following verse and Catechism Clips to explore how Christ is present both spiritually and physically at the Mass. Record any thoughts below.

   Matthew 18:20

   CCC 1548

   CCC 1392

4. Saint Teresa of Calcutta said, "The Mass is the spiritual food that sustains me—without which I could not get through one single day or hour in my life." Has this ever been your experience?

Quiet your heart and enjoy His presence. . . . "Grace is nothing else but a certain beginning of glory in us." —Saint Thomas Aquinas

Are you feeling weak? In need of guidance? Do you feel discouraged? Do you need a reminder that you are loved? Jesus waits for you—longing to shower you with strength, wisdom, hope, and unconditional love. The most powerful way you can experience His grace and presence is in the Mass. He is present there, spiritually and physically.

"Do you want the Lord to give you many graces? Visit Him often. Do you want Him to give you few graces? Visit Him rarely. Do you want the devil to attack you? Visit Jesus rarely in the Blessed Sacrament. Do you want him to flee from you? Visit Jesus often. Do you want to conquer the devil? Take refuge often at the feet of Jesus. Do you want to be conquered by the devil? Forget about visiting Jesus. My dear ones, the visit to the Blessed Sacrament is an extremely necessary way to conquer the

devil. Therefore, go often to visit Jesus and the devil will not come out victorious against you."
—*Saint John Bosco*

Day Three
WE NEED EACH OTHER

1. What insights do the following verses give in terms of our innate need for connection and belonging?

   Genesis 2:18

   Ecclesiastes 4:9–12

2. What was the early Church doing when its members came together in community? See Acts 1:14, 2:42–47, and 4:32.

The early Christians loved in a way that was truly radical. It captured the attention and the hearts of an empire, and the world was changed. Jesus said His followers would be known by their fruits (Matthew 7:16), and they have been. That revolutionary kind of love has continued to be at the core of the Church's activities as the centuries have passed.

The Catholic Church started hospitals and orphanages, and is the largest charitable organization in the world.[81] More children have been educated by the Catholic school system than by any other scholarly or religious institution.[82] The Catholic Church has

---

[81] Catholics Come Home, "2000 Years of Faith."
[82] Center for Applied Research in the Apostolate, "Frequently Requested Church Statistics," http://cara.georgetown.edu/CARAServices/requestedchurchstats.html.

made significant contributions to science: Catholics developed the scientific method[83] and laws of evidence.[84] The Catholic Church created the university system.[85] She continues to defend the dignity of all human life and the importance of the family. Her extraordinary contributions to art and architecture have brought inspiration, beauty, and hope to the world for centuries.

Yet today, so many of us feel ashamed of our story. We don't know how to articulate the beauty of what the Church has contributed and continues to contribute to the world. Yes—the sexual scandals and corruption within the Church are a part of who we are. But it isn't our whole story.

Perhaps part of the problem lies in the fact that for too many of us, our experience of parish life is totally different from the experience of the early Christians. I know that many of their circumstances were completely unlike ours today, so there's little point in making those comparisons. But what made the early Christians stand out was their radical love. And that type of love is as needed today as it ever has been. I believe the outpouring of love, mercy, and practical help that the Church became known for is still active and strong today. What I believe is missing, however, is an experience of that revolutionary love on a personal level. Is this what people feel when they walk through the doors on an average Sunday at Mass? Think about the deep sense of community and belonging that the early Christians experienced. Think about their strong sense of family. Then think about this: That is our heritage. That is what we should be experiencing today. But far too many people walk through the doors to Mass, and walk out again at the end feeling unknown, unloved, unimportant. Will anyone notice whether or not they come next week?

3. In Galatians 6:2, we're told to "bear one another's burdens, and thus fulfill the law of Christ." What do you think can be done in our parishes to create a community where people feel they belong to a family, that they matter—that their presence matters and this is the safe place to land?

Quiet your heart and enjoy His presence. . . . Let His love fill you and overflow into the lives of your brothers and sisters in Christ.

---

[83] New Advent, "Science and the Church," Kevin Knight, 2012, http://www.newadvent.org/cathen/13598b.htm.
[84] Thomas E. Woods Jr., *How the Catholic Church Built Western Civilization* (Washington, DC: Regenery Publishing, 2012), 187, 198, 201.
[85] New Advent, "Universities," Kevin Knight, 2012, http://www.newadvent.org/cathen/15188a.htm.

"Now you are Christ's body, and individually parts of it." (1 Corinthians 12:27)

We need one another. Just as the head needs the neck, the leg needs the hip, and the fingers need the hand, we do not do well cut off from the body. To live as a family—as the body of Christ—will take a conscious choice. We live in a highly individualistic society that encourages us to stand on our own two feet, to rely on no one, to be confident in our own strength. To participate in a faith community—"doing life together," as opposed to merely attending a religious service together—takes time and sacrifice. When we draw close to one another, we receive the comfort of another's presence, but we also see each other's faults a little more clearly. But that's what it means to be in a family.

Our family spans the globe and includes every race, the rich and the poor, the educated and the simple. We are diverse. We are full of complex differences. But what draws us together is a love for Jesus and for His body—the Church.

Spend some time talking to the Lord about how it feels to walk into your parish. Ask Him to open your eyes to ways in which you can be His hands and feet, bringing His warmth, His grace, His provision, and His love to the aching souls that come to Mass week after week. Ask Him to help you see people as He sees them. And ask for the courage to step out of your comfort zone to radically love those God has called to be your Church family.

"If the Church was a body composed of different members, it couldn't lack the noblest of all; it must have a Heart, and a Heart burning with love. *And I realized that* this love alone *was the true motive force which enabled the other members of the Church to act; if it ceased to function, the Apostles would forget to preach the gospel, the Martyrs would refuse to shed their blood.* Love, in fact, is the vocation which includes all others; it's a universe of its own, comprising all time and space—it's eternal!"[86] *—Saint Thérèse of Lisieux*

Day Four
WE NEED TO GIVE BACK

When we look at church as a destination—a place that we *go*—we inadvertently develop the mind-set of a consumer. We go there to have our needs met. We go there to be filled. We go there to receive. That is *part* of what the Church does for us, but it is only a portion of the whole picture. The way in which needs are met in the Church is not only through receiving the sacraments. Needs are also met through the hands and hearts of God's people—through the ways in which we minister to one another. This means that each one of us has a part to play. When we were baptized, we were

---

[86] Thérèse of Lisieux, *Autobiography of a Saint*, trans. Ronald Knox (London: Harvill, 1958), 235.

anointed as priests, prophets, and kings. Each one of us has a mission within the Church, and when we do not step up and do our part, the body of Christ suffers.

1. What does Saint Paul encourage us to do in Galatians 6:9–10? How does he suggest that we prioritize where we spend our time "giving back" to our needy world?

2. What problem did Jesus describe in Matthew 9:36–38?

3. Why are there so few "laborers in the fields"? There are all sorts of reasons that we give for standing on the sidelines instead of stepping in and getting our hands dirty in building up the Church. We can call them reasons, but sometimes they really are just excuses. Read the following excuses, and record any insights you gain from the corresponding Bible verses.

   A. "I have given up hope that this parish can change. My pastor/DRE/music minister [you fill in the blank] gets in the way."

   Ephesians 3:20 and Mark 11:22–23

   B. "I'm not that good at anything. What do I have to offer?"

   1 Corinthians 12:4–7

No one is overlooked. God gives these spiritual gifts to *each of His children*. When He handed out spiritual gifts, He did not skip you.

C. "I'm too busy. I don't have time."

Psalm 78:3–4

Matthew 10:8

Hebrews 12:15

These are the charges that are given to us. This is what God is asking of us. Hand it on to the next generation. Freely give away what you have spiritually received. See to it that no one misses the grace of God. We hear these instructions, we nod our heads, but *far too many of us do nothing in response.*

I get it. We're busy. We're stressed out. We already have more on our plates than we can keep up with. But what if our schedules are filled up with things that aren't really going to matter in the long run? And by long run, I mean eternity. What if when we stand before God and explain to Him what we've done with the time and talent He's given us, we realize that we used it selfishly or for superficial pursuits?

I understand that so many of us feel we have nothing to offer. And I truly can relate to that feeling of inadequacy. I feel as if God is constantly asking me to do things that are far, far beyond my abilities. I look at the tasks, and I look at my limitations, and I recognize that I don't have what it takes. So if bringing renewal to the Church depended on our abilities, then I'd have to say, "Fair point—we can't do it." But it doesn't. God isn't so concerned with how skilled we are, but He's very concerned with how obedient we are. As has been wisely said, "God doesn't call the equipped. He equips the called." And make no mistake—He is calling you.

Quiet your heart and enjoy His presence. . . . He wants to fill you with all you need to step out.

God has been pouring His Spirit and His grace into you throughout this study. You are now faced with a choice. You can turn your focus inward and be so glad for this spiritual awakening. You can become a "spiritual consumer" who is always looking for the next thing you need to feel spiritually "high." Or you can embrace the power of the word and. You can keep doing the things that help you grow spiritually and you can turn your focus outward. We aren't here to form a spiritual club, to be a part of a holy huddle. It's time to step out.

Where is God calling you? It doesn't need to be some big mission or project. Start small. Just be obedient and respond to the needs that God places in front of you. What is driving you crazy in your parish? Can you step in and be a part of the change that you want to see?

Go to the Lord in prayer. Offer Him your hands and feet. Commit to Him to stop focusing on your limitations and the barriers in your way. Fix your eyes instead on Him and on His immeasurable power.

Day Five
SAINT'S STORY

Saint Anysia Walks the Line

Every Christian should love the Church with the same heartbeats with which he or she loves Christ Himself. The Church is Christ's own mystical body, His bride, and the chosen instrument of salvation. Saint Paul calls it "God's household—that is, in the Church of the living God, pillar and support of the truth." (1 Timothy 3:15) The New Testament sums up Christ's entire mission by saying that "Christ loved the Church and sacrificed Himself for her." (Ephesians 5:25) And this is why so many saints and martyrs have preferred to suffer horrible persecution before cutting themselves off from the Church. Saint Anysia was one of these.

Anysia was a Christian girl who grew up in the fourth century in Thessalonica, which is known as Macedonia today. She was just a girl when her parents died. She used her considerable inheritance to benefit the poor and destitute throughout the city, and she never lacked for friends because of it. But soon a cruel persecution broke out in the city. The governor ordered that no Christians would be allowed to worship, on pain of death, lest they displease the local pagan gods. Displaying incredible courage, Christians continued to gather in secret for Mass on Sundays, knowing that it was worth risking their bodies to save their souls.

Anysia was surprised and confronted by a city guard while on her way to one of these celebrations. He asked her (none too nicely) where she was going. She was frightened and made the sign of the cross on her forehead, and the guard seized her, demanding to know who she was and where she was going. She boldly answered, "I am a servant of Jesus Christ, and I am going to the Lord's assembly." The infuriated guard reacted violently and tried to drag her to the pagan sacrificial service instead, but she resisted, whereupon he drew his sword and killed her, right there in the street. Such, sometimes, are the risks of being a faithful member of the Catholic Church.

Even more than her courageous death, it is her words to the guard that are so striking. In her mind and heart, as she made her way to assist at Mass, she was thinking of that sacred celebration of worship as a gathering of the Lord's servants with their Lord. It was no empty formula for her, no dry and soulless duty, no mechanical obedience to a nonsensical Church ordinance; it was a living encounter with the risen Lord, together with all her brothers and sisters in Christ.

Anysia recognized that her faith was not just a "me-and-Jesus" type thing. She knew that being a Christian meant being part of a visible, structured body of believers. Being there, being an active member of the Church, meant more to Saint Anysia than life itself. She clearly recognized Christ's presence in and purpose for His Church.

Why do you think Anysia risked everything to worship with the body of believers? Does her determination and courage make you think about your own level of commitment to the Church?

Conclusion

I owe a great deal to a wise woman who told me the truth at a time when I really just wanted someone to feel sorry for me. I had been a disillusioned, disgruntled, confused Catholic for about ten years. The Catholic faith hadn't been explained to me in a way that really made sense, I had felt mistreated by Church leaders who were operating out of their own places of hurt and brokenness (not that I could really see that at the time), and week after week, I'd wonder why I was even bothering to go to Mass.

As I sat with this woman, sharing all my complaints, I finished off the litany with the strong statement, "I just *can't* worship God in the Catholic Church." I looked at her expectantly, waiting for her to nod her head in sympathetic agreement. She was, after all, a Protestant Bible study leader. Surely she would advise me to cut the ties and come back to a Church that would meet my needs a little better. Instead, she said this: "It sounds to me like this isn't so much a problem with the Catholic Church. It's a problem with you."

I was shocked. Where was the sympathy? Where was the soothing response? She thought the problem was with *me*?

She continued, "You can actually worship God wherever you are. There's nothing that can get in the way of that. If you want to see change in the Church, *be that change*." Then she got up and left.

That was a pivotal moment for me. I lifted up my head and started looking around at Sunday Mass. I wasn't the only one who was walking out the parish door still with burdens, still with questions, wondering if it even mattered if I went to church at all. And God began to whisper in my head. What if change could happen for just a small group of us? What if we got together and started creating a community that met our need to belong and helped us unpack the truths that the Catholic Church had protected all these centuries? What if, in our little sphere of influence, we could see change, transformation, and healing?

The failure to engage people at the pressure points of their lives has an enormous impact. We have got to meet people where they are and offer real-life solutions for today's challenges. The gates of hell will not prevail against the Church, but the goal of the Church cannot be just to survive. If we want the Church to thrive, then we have got to say yes when Jesus calls us to step out of our comfort zones. We need to be the change we want to see.

There is a price we pay when we don't shrink back from this call—when instead we say, "Here I am, Lord. Use me." There are times when we will doubt if God can possibly work through someone like us. There will be times of weariness. There will be barriers that make forward progress slow. But bit by bit, step by step, arm in arm, we can push back the darkness. We can bring Christ's light and hope to a world that desperately needs to know that there is more to this life than how much money is in the bank, where your kid is going to college, and where you're going for your next vacation. All of that could be gone in an instant. There is more—*Christ* is the more, and it's up to us to share that truth with the world.

When we determine to *be* the Church instead of simply *go to* church, a fire will be lit in our hearts that spreads from one soul to another. It will burn up our frustration, reveal the truth, and help those in need in a way that will not only change us, it will transform the world.

My Resolution

In what specific way will I apply what I have learned in this lesson?

1. Instead of looking at my parish with a critical eye, I'll look for a specific opportunity to serve there. I'll recognize that I don't need to serve in a way that brings me accolades. In humility, I need to be willing to serve in whatever way is needed.

2. I may not have time that I can offer to a parish ministry, but I can always offer my love and warmth when I attend Mass. I will make an extra effort to smile at people as they come in, to give a compliment to someone as we walk out, and to thank my pastor for all he does to serve our parish.

3. If my parish doesn't have a Walking with Purpose Bible study, I will prayerfully consider whether or not God is calling me to gather with a small group of women to offer it.

My Resolution:

Catechism Clips

CCC 553 Jesus entrusted a specific authority to Peter: "I will give you the keys of the kingdom of heaven, and whatever you bind on earth shall be bound in heaven, and whatever you loose on earth shall be loosed in heaven." The "power of the keys" designates authority to govern the house of God, which is the Church. Jesus, the Good Shepherd, confirmed this mandate after his Resurrection: "Feed my sheep." The power to "bind and loose" connotes the authority to absolve sins, to pronounce doctrinal judgments, and to make disciplinary decisions in the Church. Jesus entrusted this authority to the Church through the ministry of the apostles and in particular through the ministry of Peter, the only one to whom he specifically entrusted the keys of the kingdom.

CCC 771 "The one mediator, Christ, established and ever sustains here on earth his holy Church, the community of faith, hope, and charity, as a visible organization through which he communicates truth and grace to all men."

CCC 774 The seven sacraments are the signs and instruments by which the Holy Spirit spreads the grace of Christ the head throughout the Church which is his Body. The Church, then, both contains and communicates the invisible grace she signifies.

CCC 1392 What material food produces in our bodily life, Holy Communion wonderfully achieves in our spiritual life. Communion with the flesh of the risen Christ, a flesh "given life and giving life through the Holy Spirit," preserves, increases, and renews the life of grace received at Baptism. This growth in Christian life needs the nourishment of Eucharistic Communion, the bread for our pilgrimage until the moment of death, when it will be given to us as viaticum.

CCC 1548 In the ecclesial service of the ordained minister, it is Christ himself who is present in his Church as Head of his Body, Shepherd of his flock, high priest of the redemptive sacrifice, Teacher of Truth. This is what the Church means by saying that the priest, by virtue of the sacrament of Holy Orders, acts *in persona Christi Capitis*.

Lesson 21

HOW DO I READ THE BIBLE IN A MEANINGFUL WAY?

Introduction

As we come to the end of *Opening Your Heart: The Starting Point*, you may be wondering how you can keep reading the Bible in a meaningful way on your own. You've seen the difference it makes to spend time with God in the pages of Scripture. But what should you do without the help of the guided questions in this study? You want to keep growing spiritually, but perhaps you could use some tips on how to structure time alone with Jesus. This lesson will focus on the how-to of spending quality time with the lover of your soul.

It may make you nervous to think of opening up the Bible on your own without a study guide alongside. You may be wondering if you're allowed to approach Scripture in this way or if this is something reserved for the clergy or people with theology degrees. If that's where you're at, you can rest assured knowing that the Catechism teaches us that "The Church forcefully and specifically exhorts all the Christian faithful . . . to learn 'the surpassing knowledge of Jesus Christ,' by frequent reading of the divine Scriptures." (CCC 133)

That being said, the Second Vatican Council gave three criteria for interpreting Scripture. These guidelines aren't given to discourage us from opening up the Bible on our own. They are meant to prevent us from setting ourselves up as the supreme authority, wrongly drawing conclusions from the Bible that God never intended. We find the three criteria in CCC 112–114. Here's a summary:

CCC 112 *"Be especially attentive 'to the content and unity of the whole Scripture.'"*
In other words, interpret Scripture in light of the overall message of the
Bible—the story of God's plan of salvation. Don't take verses out of context.
Pay attention to the literary form that's being used. Is it poetry? A letter of
instruction? Prophecy? Historical narrative? Knowing what kind of writing it is
will help you read it in the way it is meant to be read.

CCC 113 *"Read the Scripture within 'the living Tradition of the whole Church." According
to a saying of the Fathers, Sacred Scripture is written principally in the Church's heart rather
than in documents and records, for the Church carries in her Tradition the living memorial of
God's Word."*
Because the Catholic Church existed before the entire Bible was penned, we
believe in the importance of the oral teaching that has been passed down to us.
As Catholics, we have at our disposal the teaching of the early Church fathers
and the magisterium. (The early Church fathers were the earliest teachers in the
Church. The magisterium is the teaching office of the Church, made up of the
pope and the bishops, and it lays out what is the authentic teaching of the
Church.) Our interpretation of Scripture should not conflict with those
teachings.

CCC 114 *"Be attentive to the analogy of faith."*
This means that when we encounter a difficult text, the teachings of tradition
and the analogy of faith lead the way. Analogy of faith is "the Catholic doctrine
that every individual statement of belief must be understood in the light of the
Church's whole objective body of faith."[87]

As we read the Bible, we need to remember that while it is God's love letter to us, it is
primarily about Him. We are in the story, but it is *His* story. This means that we
should ask, "What does this mean?" before we ask, "What does this mean to me?"
We must seek to understand what a passage meant *then* (in context) before
determining what it means *now*. Some parts of the Bible won't make sense if we read
them thinking it's all about us instead of looking at the big picture of God's
overarching plan of redemption for mankind.

But we don't just approach Scripture intellectually. We approach God's Word with
our emotions, too. God wants *all of us*. He looks at each one of us as a whole. He
doesn't just want to engage our minds—He cares deeply about the state of our hearts.
Because of this, we can come to Scripture with our emotions in a hot mess, praying
that God will guide us to a better place. In the words of Bible teacher Hayley Morgan,

---

[87] John A. Hardon, *Modern Catholic Dictionary* (Bardstown, KY: Eternal Life, 2000).

"We approach Scripture emotionally—that we would be restored to God's best way of handling those emotions." In doing so, we bring our humanity under God's authority, and ask Him to refine our humanness. We go to His Word saying, "Relieve the troubles of my heart, bring me out of my distress." (Psalm 25:17)

Pick up your Bible. You hold in your hands the story of God's relentless love for you. It's a love story about the Prince of Peace, who came to rescue you, His bride. It's a story about your spiritual family, your heritage. The whole lot of us have been up and down in our faithfulness to God. But God has always remained steady. He's never wavered in His love for a single person in the Bible, or a single one of His children who came afterward. God waits to speak to your heart every day. Don't let a single one pass by without hearing His voice.

Day One
GETTING STARTED

This week, you'll need your Bible and a prayer journal. I'm giving you an excuse to go shopping. You're welcome. You won't actually need the journal until tomorrow, but I thought you might like to give it some time so you can choose one that's really fabulous.

1. Although you can pray and read the Bible at any time of the day, what special benefits might there be in spending quality time with Jesus in the morning? See Psalm 90:14 and Mark 1:35.

If we're going to spend time alone with Jesus, we've got to come up with a time and a place when we can be by ourselves. For many of us, this seems like an insurmountable task. I really relate to this challenge. I have found that if I don't wake up a half hour earlier than my family, getting time alone becomes almost impossible.

We all love sleep. Getting up earlier in order to spend time with God can seem like a tall order. But could you start small? Could you give up just ten minutes of sleep so that your first thoughts could be of God?

You may be in a season of life when it feels impossible to get up even ten minutes earlier. If that's the case, I encourage you to look for the first pocket of quiet in your day, and reserve it for God. At some point, a pocket of quiet will come. What will you do with it? Check e-mails? Catch up on Facebook? Unload the dishwasher? Or open your Bible? The choice is yours.

2. Regardless of what time of day you decide to meet with God, I encourage you to consider it an appointment. Put it on your calendar, and then honor it just as you would any other commitment.

   The best time for my appointment with God is:

   The best place for my appointment with God is:

   What are some external obstacles I need to overcome to stay committed to the best time and place in order to concentrate well?

3. Why should you always begin your time with God by inviting the Holy Spirit to come and be your teacher? See John 16:13–14 and 2 Peter 1:20–21.

Quiet your heart and enjoy His presence. . . . Meet Him early, and begin with prayer.

Take a moment to think about this mind-blowing truth: The maker of the universe is with you. He's listening to you.

Begin your time with the Lord with a simple prayer like Psalm 119:18: "Open my eyes to see clearly the wonders of your law." Invite the Holy Spirit to be your teacher. Ask Him to convict you of anything that needs to change, to comfort you when your heart is aching, and to direct you when you feel confused.

Day Two
PREPARING YOUR HEART

When God looks at you, He looks at you as a whole. He considers your heart (your emotions, dreams, desires, fears, hurts, etc.) to be an integral part of who you are. He longs to see you experience interior freedom and peace.

We read in Luke 6:45 that "out of the overflow of the heart the mouth speaks." This means that whatever is deep in our hearts will eventually come out. The safest place to explore our feelings is in the presence of God.

Beginning your time with God by prayer journaling allows you to bring your emotions to Him, inviting Him to help you sort through them all. It helps identify where you need forgiveness, healing, and guidance. This is different from self-focused navel gazing because while you are sorting through what's in your heart, you are keeping your focus on God.

There's no "right" way to journal your prayers. The following format is provided as a springboard, a loose guide—a starting point.

1. I'm especially grateful to you, God, for these three things:

2. Instead of racing through life, I want to be fully present in the moment. This is when I've felt the most soul-satisfied recently:

3. Lord, I know you created me with a specific purpose in mind. I want my life to have meaning. I don't want to miss your plan for me. This is something I'm dreaming of right now:

4. God, please free me from the following fear:

5. Please forgive me for the following way in which I have failed to love you:

6. Recently, I noticed your glory in the following way:

7. Mother Mary, please mother me in this specific way:

Quiet your heart and enjoy His presence. . . . Come before Him wholeheartedly, holding nothing back.

"To you O Lord I lift up my soul, my God, in you I trust." (Psalm 25:1-2)

When you think about it, it's a little silly that we think we can hide our emotions from God. He sees everything, into the very depths of who we are. All the things we manage to conceal from people around us are totally visible to Him. And guess what? What He sees doesn't make Him run away. When He looks within each one of us, He actually draws closer in love. So we don't need to worry about presenting some cleaned-up version of ourselves to Him. We can be real. Reverent, because there's no one greater, but real because we are His beloved daughters, and He says, "Come as you are."

Day Three
THE DEVOTIONAL METHOD OF BIBLE STUDY EXPLAINED

Once you have prepared your heart to listen to God speak through the Scriptures, it's time to dive in! But where do you begin? This section of the lesson will show you how to prayerfully think about a passage of the Bible. The purpose of this method of study is to form a practical application from what you have read. As you read, you'll ask yourself the question, "What am I going to do with what I've learned?"

There are a number of different ways to read the Bible devotionally. You can use just one, or if you have more time, you can do them all. As is the case with everything, the more you put into it, the more you'll get out of it. You can record your study notes in the same journal you used for Day Two.

Ways to Read the Bible Devotionally:

1. Place Yourself in the Scene
    Picture yourself in the midst of the Biblical scene. What would you have felt? What would you have done? Think about the historical context of the story. How would that change what you would have experienced if you were actually there? This way of meditating on a passage can make the people come alive to you.

2. Word Emphasis
    Read a Bible verse multiple times, and each time, emphasize a different word. Each emphasis will give a new meaning. For example, 2 Corinthians 5:17 could be read in this way:

    "**If** anyone is in Christ, he is a new creation."
    "If **anyone** is in Christ, he is a new creation."
    "If anyone **is** in Christ, he is a new creation."
    "If anyone is **in** Christ, he is a new creation."
    "If anyone is in **Christ**, he is a new creation."
    "If anyone is in Christ, **he** is a new creation."
    "If anyone is in Christ, he **is** a new creation."
    "If anyone is in Christ, he is a **new** creation."
    "If anyone is in Christ, he is a new **creation**."

3. Paraphrase the Bible Passage

This means that you take the Bible passage and put it into your own words. When you summarize what you've read in this way, the core lesson often comes to the surface.

4. Personalize the Bible Passage

You can personalize Scripture by putting your name in place of certain nouns and pronouns in the Bible passage. For example, in 1 Corinthians 13:4–7, you can replace the word *love* with your name:

"*Lisa* is patient, *Lisa* is kind. She is not jealous, she is not pompous, she is not inflated. *Lisa* is not rude, she does not seek her own interests, she is not quick-tempered, she does not brood over injury. *Lisa* does not rejoice over wrongdoing, but rejoices with the truth. *Lisa* bears all things, believes all things, hopes all things, endures all things." (Hmm . . . it's rather convicting.)

The final step after studying this passage is the most important. Ask yourself, "Now what am I supposed to do with this information? How can it help me to live more like Christ?" You can use this simple acrostic to tease out a personal application from the passage:

Is there a(n) . . .
Promise to claim?
Example to follow?
Attitude to change?
Command to obey?
Error to avoid?

Write your application down in your journal, and end your time with the Lord by prayerfully responding to what you have studied. The passage may lead you in prayer to praise, confess, or commit to a new path.

To reflect on why it's important to read and *apply* the Bible (this is what the devotional method does), record your thoughts on the following verses.

A. Matthew 7:24–27

B. James 4:17

C. 1 Corinthians 8:1

Quiet your heart and enjoy His presence. . . . Let the Holy Spirit guide you toward transformation.

Just knowing a lot about the Bible doesn't necessarily translate into the kind of transformed life that pleases God. The Sadducees were the priestly aristocracy, well versed in the Scriptures. They were the conservatives of the day, and highly esteemed the written law. Yet when Jesus spoke to them, He said, "You are misled because you do not know the scriptures or the power of God." (Matthew 22:29) They knew the Scriptures intellectually, but failed to apply the overall message. Their long-awaited Messiah, the source of salvation, stood right in front of them. For all their academic knowledge, they failed to recognize the truth.

Dear Lord,

I pray that you will never say to me what you said to the Sadducees: "You are misled because you do not know the scriptures or the power of God." I want to know both! Help me to live out James 1:22, to "be [a] doer of the word and not [a] hearer only, deluding [myself]."

Day Four
GIVE IT A TRY!

Let's dive in and give this a whirl. *You can do this,* and you'll feel so empowered when you realize that truly all you need is your Bible, a journal, and a teachable heart.

Be sure to start by preparing your heart with prayer (remember Day Two). Then choose the passage you'd like to study. Here are some suggestions:

Psalm 139 (my favorite Psalm to read if I feel lonely or insignificant)

Isaiah 43:1–7 (powerful verses for when you feel overwhelmed; let these truths sink in *deep*)

Luke 1:46–55 (This is the "Magnificat," Mary's hymn of praise to the Lord; I love it. It's very interesting to think about what the Blessed Mother was feeling when she prayed these words.)

John 3:16–21 (when you need truth that's good and solid)

Philippians 4:4–8 (great when an attitude adjustment is needed)

James 1:19–27 (or maybe even a portion of this passage—it's so loaded with things that convict my heart, lots of times an application jumps out at me after just one verse)

Revelation 2:2–5 (Read this when you need a kick in the pants. Because sometimes we do. This is a great one to reflect on when you know that something has been competing for Jesus' place in your heart.)

Revelation 21:3–7 (when you need hope)

My Bible passage for today:

My study notes:
(Place yourself in the scene, emphasize certain words, paraphrase the passage, and personalize it.)

My application:

Quiet your heart and enjoy His presence. . . . Just you and the Lord. You're making Him so happy right now.

When we open up the Bible and ask the Holy Spirit to teach us, the Lord is absolutely thrilled. When we take the next step and obey what He's pointed out to us, He feels loved. Obedience is His love language.

This is where the rubber meets the road. What do we do with all we've learned? The Holy Spirit is working on us from within, giving us the desire and the power to change. But our part is to step out and be doers of the Word.

Not always, but often, that means doing the opposite of what we feel like. That's when our love is the most pure, because it's sacrificial. But be assured, not one little sacrifice goes unnoticed by the Lord. He sees. He remembers.

Dear Lord,

In John 15:5, you said, "I am the vine, you are the branches. He who abides in me, and I in him, he it is that bears much fruit, for apart from me you can do nothing." Someone was once asked how to spell abide *with four letters. The reply? O-B-E-Y. So I ask for your help in this. Obedience isn't easy. But I claim your promise in Philippians 4:13: "I can do all things through Christ who strengthens me." Apart from you, there's not a lot I can do, but with you, there's no limit to how sacrificial my love can be.*

Day Five
SAINT'S STORY

Saint Edith Stein

Saint Edith Stein's story is unusual. Born a Jew, she lived her youth as an atheist, worked as a philosopher, converted to the Catholic faith, and was martyred as a Carmelite nun in the gas chamber at Auschwitz in 1942.

Saint Edith Stein wasn't born a saint. Known to be iron-willed and headstrong, she went through a period of radical feminism and spent many years as an atheist. She struggled through a period of depression in her youth, and at the age of fourteen, she consciously and freely decided to give up praying and stopped practicing her Jewish religion. Instead, she immersed herself in study, pursuing truth through philosophy.

It took many years, but by the mercy of God, this profound thirst for truth led her back to Him in a deeper way. As she began to pore over the words of the New Testament, her heart was called home to the Catholic Church through its words.

Every soul hears the song of another homeland deep in the heart. Ultimately, we all yearn for heaven. Whether we realize it or not, we all thirst to see the face of Christ. Reading Scripture is one of the ways we can quench our "homesickness." It gives us a reminder of God's sovereignty—that He has always had a plan and continues to be the supreme authority over all, even when it seems like everything is out of control. Through its pages, we hear His voice of love, comfort, and strength.

When Edith was a laywoman living in the world, already Catholic, she used to go by herself to a chapel in the city where she worked. There, she would kneel before the tabernacle for hours at a time. She would close her eyes and go deep inside her heart and soul. Sometimes she would say nothing at all. It was an experience of deep stillness in God, of silence, and of letting go and offering herself over and over again without words.

What resulted from Saint Edith Stein's deep devotional life was a total surrender of her heart. She let herself be filled with His will like an empty vessel is filled with the choicest of ointments. And when the time came for the vessel to be broken, the perfume of her surrender filled the Church and the world with its fragrance.

Don't assume that such obedience is beyond you. It is always within reach, because every surrender is a work of the Holy Spirit within us. It is God Himself within you who knits your heart to Christ and strengthens His life within you. You pray in your words; He prays in His with "unspeakable groanings," as Saint Paul says in Romans 8:26.

When you prayerfully read Scripture, Jesus is able to enter your life in a deeper way, healing wounds that you didn't even know you had. He enters your soul with gentleness and understanding, working silently while you think nothing is happening. He enlarges your capacity to love and adorns you with grace.

That is why we must never judge our prayers or get discouraged, thinking, "I can't pray. I can't read the Bible. I don't feel anything. Nothing is happening." This is not for us to judge. Must the canvas understand everything the Divine Artist is painting? Perhaps some brushstrokes are so light that they escape notice. And yet, those details may be the most beautiful of all.

The spiritual life is a relationship between a lover and His beloved. It is not a personal resolution for self-perfection or a business contract. It is a friendship full of trust and affection, a bond of love that deepens into the ultimate gift of self. This is what your time reading the Bible can become: a conversation that draws you ever deeper into the heart of Christ.

And when the time comes for your soul to return to its maker, you will find that death is nothing to be feared. Because you have prayed and touched the face of Christ in darkness, the unveiling will be an occasion of great joy.

And when you do see His face, you will realize that you have finally come home.

Can you find ideas in the spiritual life of Saint Edith Stein that can enliven your own?

Conclusion

"And we, who with unveiled faces all reflect the Lord's glory, are being transformed into his likeness with ever-increasing glory, which comes from the Lord, who is the Spirit." (2 Corinthians 3:18)

Unveiled faces reflecting God's glory.

These words make me think of a woman making sure that nothing is getting between her and her God. She holds out her heart to Him, just as it is. She comes into His presence, full of emotions and needs, and asks Him to sort it all out. And He does. And she is utterly transformed, from the inside out. As a result, she reflects Him to a world in desperate need of His touch.

Everywhere she goes, she spreads "the fragrance of the knowledge of him . . . [she is] the aroma of Christ." (2 Corinthians 2:14–15) That aroma is described by She Reads Truth founder Amanda Williams in this way:

> *An aroma is something experienced.* It transforms the air simply because of what it is.
> **Sisters, we are the aroma of Christ.**
> Not peddlers of a way of life.
> Not salespeople for a system of beliefs.
> **We are those commissioned by God to transform the very air in which we live, not because of who we are but because of who He is . . .**
> It truly is all about Him. And what *He's* all about is love.
> Mercy. Grace. Wholeness. Justice. Redemption. Hope. These are the things that should come from our steeping our souls in God's Word. We are not to

wield it as a weapon to beat the unbelieving into submission. **We are simply to hold out Christ.**[88]

We've come to the end of our study, but it's only the beginning of a beautiful journey for you. Day by day, as you turn to God and spend time with Him in prayer and the Scriptures, you are being changed into His likeness. You are no longer defined by your past mistakes. A fresh path stretches before you. As you run toward Him, the old you is stripped away and you are changed. What remains is all that is *the best of you*. You bear the image of God, and the more you are with Him, the more you become like Him.

This is my prayer for each one of us—that we would come before the Lord with unveiled faces, and then go out, giving everyone we meet a little glimpse of who He is.

My Resolution

In what specific way will I apply what I have learned in this lesson?

Examples:

1. I'll set up a spot in my house where I'll spend time alone with God each day. It'll help me to diligently keep that appointment if I make sure all the things I need (Bible, journal, pen) are there.

2. I will set my alarm ten minutes early every day this week in order to spend time alone with God.

3. I'll ask a friend to hold me accountable for living out the personal application I find each day in my Bible reading.

My Resolution:

---

[88] Amanda Bible Williams, "It Is a Merciful Fragrance," She Reads Truth, March 4, 2014, http://shereadstruth.com/2014/03/04/merciful-fragrance/.

Catechism Clips

The Second Vatican Council indicates three criteria for interpreting Scripture in accordance with the Spirit who inspired it.

CCC 112 *Be especially attentive "to the content and unity of the whole Scripture".* Different as the books which compose it may be, Scripture is a unity by reason of the unity of God's plan, of which Christ Jesus is the center and heart, open since his Passover.

> The phrase "heart of Christ" can refer to Sacred Scripture, which makes known his heart, closed before the Passion, as the Scripture was obscure. But the Scripture has been opened since the Passion; since those who from then on have understood it, consider and discern in what way the prophecies must be interpreted.

CCC 113 *Read the Scripture within "the living Tradition of the whole Church".* According to a saying of the Fathers, Sacred Scripture is written principally in the Church's heart rather than in documents and records, for the Church carries in her Tradition the living memorial of God's Word, and it is the Holy Spirit who gives her the spiritual interpretation of the Scripture ("... according to the spiritual meaning which the Spirit grants to the Church").

CCC 114 *Be attentive to the analogy of faith.* By "analogy of faith" we mean the coherence of the truths of faith among themselves and within the whole plan of Revelation.

NOTES

Lesson 22: Connect Coffee Talk

OUTSIDE ACTIVITIES – SET THE WORLD ON FIRE

Accompanying DVD can be viewed by disc or please visit our website at walkingwithpurpose.com/videos and select *Opening Your Heart* Bible Study, click through to select Videos.

Key verse:

"Then I heard the voice of the Lord saying, 'Whom shall I send? Who will go for us?' 'Here I am,' I said. 'Send me!'" (Isaiah 6:8)

The world needs you, so . . .

1. **Begin with Balance**

   A balanced woman is well formed in the four main areas of Christian living:

   A. _____ life

   "I am the vine, you are the branches. Whoever remains in me and I in him will bear much fruit, because without me you can do nothing." (John 15:5)

   B. Human _____

   "Put on then, as God's chosen ones, holy and beloved, heartfelt compassion, kindness, humility, gentleness, and patience, bearing with one another and forgiving one another . . . and over all these put on love . . . and let the peace of Christ control your hearts." (Colossians 3:12–15)

C. _____ of the faith

"Do not conform yourselves to this age but be transformed by the renewal of your mind, that you may discern what is the will of God, what is good and pleasing and perfect." (Romans 12:2)

D. _____ activity

"For the Son of Man did not come to be served but to serve and to give his life as a ransom for many." (Mark 10:45)

2. Recognize the Battle

"For our struggle is not with flesh and blood but with the principalities, with the powers, with the world rulers of this present darkness, with the evil spirits in the heavens." (Ephesians 6:12)

3. Light Your Fire

A. Identify your holy discontent

B. Feed on it

4. Keep It Burning

A. Take risks

B. Don't lose hope

"With God, all things are possible." (Matthew 19:26)

"The one who is in you is greater than the one who is in the world." (1 John 4:4)

C. Remember your first love

"I know your works, your labor, and your endurance, and that you cannot tolerate the wicked; you have tested those who call themselves apostles but are not, and discovered that they are impostors. Moreover, you have endurance and have suffered for my name, and you have not grown weary. Yet I hold this against you: you have lost the love you had at first. Realize how far you have fallen. Repent, and do the works you did at first. Otherwise, I will come to you and remove your lampstand from its place, unless you repent." (Revelation 2:2–5)

Questions for Discussion

1. If you could help any group of people in the world, who would it be, and what would you do?

2. What woman has most inspired you through her response to her holy discontent?

3. What are some ways we can prevent burnout when serving those in need?

NOTES

Appendices

NOTES

Appendix 1
SAINT THÉRÈSE OF LISIEUX
Patron Saint of Walking with Purpose

Saint Thérèse of Lisieux was gifted with the ability to take the riches of our Catholic faith and explain them in a way that a child could imitate. The wisdom she gleaned from Scripture ignited a love in her heart for her Lord that was personal and transforming. The simplicity of the faith that she laid out in her writings is so completely Catholic that Pope Pius XII said, "She rediscovered the Gospel itself, the very heart of the Gospel."

Walking with Purpose is intended to be a means by which women can honestly share their spiritual struggles and embark on a journey that is refreshing to the soul. It was never intended to facilitate the deepest of intellectual study of Scripture. Instead, the focus has been to help women know Christ: to know His heart, to know His tenderness, to know His mercy, and to know His love. Our logo is a little flower, and that has meaning. When a woman begins to open her heart to God, it's like the opening of a little flower. It can easily be bruised or crushed, and it must be treated with the greatest of care. Our desire is to speak to women's hearts no matter where they are in life, baggage and all, and gently introduce truths that can change their lives.

Saint Thérèse of Lisieux, the little flower, called her doctrine "the little way of spiritual childhood," and it is based on complete and unshakable confidence in God's love for us. She was not introducing new truths. She spent countless hours reading Scripture and she shared what she found, emphasizing the importance of truths that had already been divinely revealed. We can learn so much from her:

> The good God would not inspire unattainable desires; I can, then, in spite of my littleness, aspire to sanctity. For me to become greater is impossible; I must put up with myself just as I am with all my imperfections. But I wish to find the way to go to Heaven by a very straight, short, completely new little way. We are in a century of inventions: now one does not even have to take the trouble to climb the steps of a stairway; in the homes of the rich, an elevator replaces them nicely. I, too, would like to find an elevator to lift me up to Jesus, for I

am too little to climb the rough stairway of perfection. So I have looked in the books of the saints for a sign of the elevator I long for, and I have read these words proceeding from the mouth of eternal Wisdom: "He that is a little one, let him turn to me" (Proverbs 9:16). So I came, knowing that I had found what I was seeking, and wanting to know, O my God, what You would do with the little one who would answer Your call, and this is what I found:

"As one whom the mother caresses, so will I comfort you. You shall be carried at the breasts and upon the knees they shall caress you" (Isaiah 66:12–13). Never have more tender words come to make my soul rejoice. The elevator which must raise me to the heavens is Your arms, O Jesus! For that I do not need to grow; on the contrary, I must necessarily remain small, become smaller and smaller. O my God, You have surpassed what I expected, and I want to sing Your mercies. (Saint Thérèse of the Infant Jesus, *Histoire d'une Ame: Manuscrits Autobiographiques* [Paris: Éditions du Seuil, 1998], 244.)

Appendix 2
WALKING WITH PURPOSE LETTERHEAD STATIONERY FOR YOUR LETTER TO JESUS

 NOTES

Appendix 3
CONVERSION OF HEART

The Catholic faith is full of beautiful traditions, rituals, and sacraments. As powerful as they are, it is possible for them to become mere habits in our lives, instead of experiences that draw us close to the heart of Christ. In the words of Saint John Paul II, they can become acts of "hollow ritualism." We might receive our first Communion and the sacraments of confession and confirmation, yet never experience the interior conversion that opens the heart to a personal relationship with God.

Pope Benedict XVI has explained that the "door of faith" is opened at one's baptism, but we are called to open it again, walk through it, and rediscover and renew our relationship with Christ and His Church.[89]

So how do we do this? How do we walk through that door of faith so we can begin to experience the abundant life that God has planned for us?

GETTING PERSONAL

The word *conversion* means "the act of turning." This means that conversion involves a turning away from one thing and a turning toward another. When you haven't experienced conversion of heart, you are turned *toward* your own desires. You are the one in charge, and you do what you feel is right and best at any given moment. You may choose to do things that are very good for other people, but the distinction is that *you are choosing*. You are deciding. You are the one in control.

Imagine driving a car. You are sitting in the driver's seat, and your hands are on the steering wheel. You've welcomed Jesus into the passenger's seat, and have listened to His comments. But whether or not you follow His directions is really up to you. You may follow them or you may not, depending on what seems right to you.

When you experience interior conversion, you decide to turn, to get out of the driver's seat, move into the passenger's seat, and invite God to be the driver. Instead of seeing Him as an advice giver or someone nice to have around for the holidays, you give Him control of every aspect of your life.

---

[89] Pope Benedict XVI, *Apostolic Letter: Porta Fidei*, for the Indiction of the Year of Faith, October 11, 2011.

More than likely, you don't find this easy to do. This is because of the universal struggle with pride. We want to be the ones in charge. We don't like to be in desperate need. We like to be the captains of our ships, charting our own courses. As William Ernest Henley wrote, "I am the master of my fate: I am the captain of my soul."

Conversion of heart isn't possible without humility. The first step is to recognize your desperate need of a savior. Romans 6:23 states that the "wages of sin is death." When you hear this, you might be tempted to justify your behavior, or compare yourself with others. You might think to yourself, "I'm not a murderer. I'm not as bad as this or that person. If someone were to put my good deeds and bad deeds on a scale, my good ones would outweigh the bad. So surely I am good enough? Surely I don't deserve death!" When this is your line of thought, you are missing a very important truth: Just one sin is enough to separate you from a holy God. Just one sin is enough for you to deserve death. Even your best efforts to do good fall short of what God has required in order for you to spend eternity with Him. Isaiah 64:6 says, "All our righteous acts are like filthy rags." If you come to God thinking that you are going to be accepted by Him based on your "good conduct," He will point out that your righteousness is nothing compared to His infinite holiness.

Saint Thérèse of Lisieux understood this well, and wrote, "In the evening of my life I shall appear before You with empty hands, for I do not ask You to count my works. All our justices are stained in Your eyes. I want therefore to clothe myself in Your own justice and receive from Your love the eternal possession of Yourself."[90]

She recognized that her works, her best efforts, wouldn't be enough to earn salvation. Salvation cannot be earned. It's a free gift. Saint Thérèse accepted this gift, and said that if her justices or righteous deeds were stained, then she wanted to clothe herself in Christ's own justice. We see this described in 2 Corinthians 5:21: "God made him who had no sin to be sin for us, so that in him we might become the righteousness of God."

How did God make Him who had no sin to be sin for you? This was foretold by the prophet Isaiah: "But he was pierced for our transgressions, he was crushed for our iniquities; the punishment that brought us peace was upon him, and by his wounds we are healed." (Isaiah 53:5)

---

[90] Saint Thérèse of Lisieux, "Act of Oblation to Merciful Love," June 9, 1895.

Jesus accomplished this on the cross. Every sin committed, past, present, and future, was placed on Him. Now, *all the merits of Jesus can be yours*. He wants to fill your empty hands with His own virtues.

But first, you need to recognize, just as Saint Thérèse did, that you are little. You are weak. You fail. You need forgiveness. You need a savior.

When you come before God in prayer and acknowledge these truths, He looks at your heart. He sees your desire to trust Him, to please Him, to obey Him. He says to you, "My precious child, you don't have to pay for your sins. My Son, Jesus, has already done that for you. He suffered, so that you wouldn't have to. I want to experience a relationship of intimacy with you. I forgive you.[91] Jesus came to set you free.[92] When you open your heart to me, you become a new creation![93] The old you has gone. The new you is here. If you will stay close to me, and journey by my side, you will begin to experience a transformation that brings joy and freedom.[94] I've been waiting to pour my gifts into your soul. Beloved daughter of mine, remain confident in me. I am your loving Father. Crawl into my lap. Trust me. Love me. I will take care of everything."

This is conversion of heart. This act of faith lifts the veil from your eyes and launches you into the richest and most satisfying life. You don't have to be sitting in church to do this. Don't let a minute pass before opening your heart to God and inviting Him to come dwell within you. Let Him sit in the driver's seat. Give Him the keys to your heart. Your life will never be the same again.

---

[91] "If we acknowledge our sins, he is faithful and just and will forgive our sins and cleanse us from every wrongdoing." 1 John 1:9

[92] "So if the Son makes you free, you will be free indeed." John 8:36

[93] "So whoever is in Christ is a new creation: the old things have passed away; behold, new things have come." 2 Corinthians 5:18

[94] "I will sprinkle clean water over you to make you clean; from all your impurities and from all your idols I will cleanse you. I will give you a new heart, and a new spirit I will put within you. I will remove the heart of stone from your flesh and give you a heart of flesh." Ezekiel 36:25, 26

NOTES

Appendix 4
CONFESSION BY THE NUMBERS

Pope Benedict XVI is emphatic about confession. "The renewal of the Church in America depends on the renewal of the practice of penance and the growth in holiness which that sacrament both inspires and accomplishes," he said at Nationals Stadium in Washington, D.C.

Saint John Paul II was also emphatic. He spent his last years as Pope pleading for more confession. He made it one the Church's two top priorities in 2001's "at the beginning of the New Millennium." In 2002's *Misericordia Dei* he sought to correct abuses of it. In 2003's encyclical *Ecclesia de Eucharistia*, he used formal language to declare its necessity.

Pope Benedict XVI shares both John Paul's urgency and his compassionate love for the sacrament of mercy.

"The liberating power of this sacrament," Benedict told Americans, "in which our honest confession of sin is met by God's merciful word of pardon and peace, needs to be rediscovered and reappropriated by every Catholic."

Use this guide to rediscover, and help others rediscover, this crucial sacrament.

2 SATURDAY AFTERNOONS
1. The Grateful Penitent
Here's a story from a Connecticut parish.

A nicely dressed man who looked anxious and upset walked into a church, squinted at the confessional, and couldn't tell if there was a priest in it or not. "Is there a priest in there?" he asked a woman. He didn't care what priest – he just needed a priest. Any priest.

"Yes," came the answer. He barely acknowledged the help, and hurriedly entered the confessional. After a few minutes, he emerged, looking like a different person. Gone was the haunted expression on his face. Gone was the urgency and anxiety. He was a man set free.

He smiled at the person who had merely pointed out the obvious and said, "Thank you," with the gratitude of someone who had just been handed an antidote to rattlesnake poison.

2. The Ultimate Therapy
Here's a story from a California parish.

A teenage girl's whole character suddenly seemed to change. She was moody and preoccupied for weeks, so her parents took her to a counselor.

Therapy sometimes does wonders for people who suffer from mental anxiety. In this case, it didn't help. Their daughter had seasons of improvement, but always ended up back in her distracted unhappy state. This continued through college, and afterward.

By coincidence, the therapist met her outside near a Catholic church one rainy Saturday afternoon. Stepping out of the rain, they saw someone leaving the confessional.

The girl asked if she should go to confession, too. The therapist advised against it. She ducked in anyway. She emerged smiling, the first smile the therapist had ever seen on her young patient. The therapist noted that in the days, weeks, and months that followed, the girl was no longer troubled with her old moodiness and unhappiness.

The therapist started to look into confession more, and then decided to enter the Church. Now, she counsels regular confession for all her Catholic patients.

9 CONFESSIONAL PROMISES

According to the Catechism of the Catholic Church, confession gives you...

1. Pardon and mercy

"Those who approach the sacrament of penance obtain pardon from God's mercy for the offence committed against him." (1422)

2. Reconciliation

Confession reconciles us with the Church, with God, and helps us reconcile with others. (1424)

3. A Welcome from the Father

Comparing our journey to the story of the prodigal son, the Catechism calls confession "the first step in returning to the Father." (1423)

4. A second "Baptism"

We are first "converted" and become Christians at our baptism, but a second "conversion" is needed. Said St. Ambrose: "There are water and tears: the water of baptism and the tears of repentance." (1428-9)

5. Interior change

Peace comes from a "radical reorientation of our whole life, a return, a conversion with God with all our heart, and end of sin, a turning away from evil." (1431)

6. A new heart

"The human heart is heavy and hardened, "says the Catechism. "God must give man a new heart... it is in discovering the greatness of God's love that our heart is shaken by the horror and weight of sin." (1432)

7. A just penance

The penance that the priest gives "must correspond as far as possible with the gravity and nature of the sins committed. It can consist of prayer, an offering, works of mercy, service to neighbor, voluntary self-denial, sacrifices, and above all the patient acceptance of the cross we must bear." (1460)

8. The strictest secrecy

"Every priest who hears confessions is found under very severe penalties to keep absolute secrecy regarding the sins that his penitents have confessed to him. He can make no use of the knowledge that confession gives him about penitents' lives." (1467) "It is a crime for a confessor in any way to betray a penitent by word or in any other manner or for any reason." (2490)

9. Strength for the battle

Confession improves us, offering "spiritual strength for the Christian battle." (1496) It's a rescue boat "after the shipwreck which is the loss of grace." (1446)

10 REASONS TO CONFESS
5 Human Reasons

1. Sin aggravates you.
Sin leads to depression and anxiety. It violates the plan for happy living that's built into our very being by God.

2. Sin makes you aggravating.
The ancient philosopher Aristotle said that we are defined by our choices. He was right. Our sins become part of who we are. They shape our personality, bending us one way or another, unless we fix them.

3. We need to say it.
If you break something that's important to a friend, you wouldn't feel satisfied with a general feeling of regret. You want to say, "I'm sorry," and try to replace the loss. Sin is no different.

4. Confessing helps you know yourself.
We get ourselves wrong: We convince ourselves that we are righteous and great, or we obsess about our faults and blow them out of proportion. Confession forces us to look at our lives objectively, with the priest.

5. Confessing strengthens us.
When we are stronger: When we avoid thinking of our sins, or when we confront them, deal with them, and move on? As the Catechism puts it, "Sin creates proclivity to sin." (1865) Confessing stops the cycle.

5 Spiritual Reasons

1. Freedom means choices count.
The world tries to tell us that freedom means your choices don't matter. In reality, freedom means your choices count. As the Catechism points out, mortal sin, unconfessed, "causes exclusion from Christ's Kingdom and the eternal death of hell, for our freedom has the power to make choices forever, with no turning back." (1861)

2. Confessing makes you freer.
After confession, people smile like a heavy burden was lifted from their shoulders. The guilt is gone. They can now make new choices count: choices for God, not against him.

3. Confessing is a personal encounter with Christ.
In confession, it's Christ that heals and forgives us, through the ministry of the priest. We have a personal encounter with Christ in the confessional. Just like the shepherds and Magi at the crèche, we find awe and humility. And just like the saints at the crucifixion, we find gratitude, repentance, and peace.

4. Confessing mortal sin is required.
You can't go to Communion – or be at peace with God – without confessing mortal sins. This is bare-minimum Christianity, one of the precepts of the Church: You must confess sins once a year, and as soon as possible when you are aware of committing a mortal sin.

Mortal sin definition: "One commits a mortal sin when there are simultaneously present: grace matter, full knowledge, and deliberate consent" (Compendium of the Catechism, 395).

Some common sins that constitute grace matter, according to "Happy Are Those Who Are Called to His Supper" (U.S. Bishops, 2006).

Missing Mass – "Failing to worship God by missing Mass on Sundays and holy days of obligation without a serious reason such as sickness or the absence of a priest."

Abortion or Euthanasia – "Committing murder, including abortion and euthanasia, harboring deliberate hatred for others."

Any extramarital sexual activity – "Engaging in sexual activity outside of the bonds of a valid marriage."

Theft – Including, "serious fraud, or other immoral business practices."

Pornography – "Producing, marketing, or indulging in pornography."

Slander, hatred, and envy – "speaking maliciously or slandering people in a way that seriously undermines their good name."

5. You also tidy "venial" messes in your house.

Even if you aren't conscious of a serious sin, it is still highly recommended that you go to confession regularly, say, once a month.

As Pope Benedict XVI put it: "We clean our homes, our rooms, at least once a week, even if the dirt is always the same; in order to live in cleanliness, in order to start again. Otherwise, the dirt might not be seen, but it builds up. Something similar can be said about the soul."

7 THINGS EXPECTED FROM YOU IN CONFESSION

1. Be contrite
The Catechism calls contrition "sorrow of the soul and detestation for the sin committed, together with the resolution not to sin again." (1451)

Perfect contrition "arises from a love which God is loved above all else."

Imperfect contrition is "born of the consideration of sin's ugliness or the fear of eternal damnation." (1452-1453) Either works.

2. Examination of conscience
The Catechism says that the sacrament "ought to be prepared for by an examination of conscience made in the light of the word of God." (1454)

3. Disclosure of sin
A penitent "looks squarely at the sins he is guilty of, takes responsibility for them, and thereby opens himself again to God and the communion of the Church in order to make a new future possible." (1455)

4. Confession to a priest
"All mortal sins of which penitents after a diligent self-examination are conscious must be recounted by them in confession." (1456)

5. Confession before Communion
"After having attained the age of discretion each of the faithful is bound by an obligation faithfully to confess serious sins at least once a year. Anyone who is aware of having committed a mortal sin must not receive holy Communion, even if he experiences deep contrition, without having first received sacramental absolution, unless he has a grave reason for receiving Communion and there is no possibility of going to confession. Children must go to the sacrament of "penance before receiving holy Communion for the first time." (1457)

6. Satisfaction
"One must do what is possible in order to repair the harm of sins (e.g. return stolen goods, restore the reputation of someone slandered, pay compensation for injuries)." (1459)

7. Penance

"Absolution takes away sins, but it does not remedy all the disorders sin has caused. Raised from sin, the sinner must sill recover his full spiritual health by doing something more." (1459)

CONFESSION IN 6 STEPS

1. You always have the option to go to confession anonymously, that is, behind a screen. You may have the option of going to confession face-to-face only if the priest offers it.

2. After the priest greets you in the name of Christ, make the sign of the cross. He may choose to recite a reading from Scripture, after which you say, "bless me, Father, for I have sinned. It has been (state how long) since my last confession. These are my sins."

3. Tell your sins simply and honestly to the priest. You might even want to discuss the circumstances and root causes of your sins and ask the priest for advice or direction. However, avoid explanations that are really excuses or rationalizations for your sins. You are here to own up to what you have done. The best confessions are honest and to the point.

4. Listen to the advice the priest gives you and accept the penance from him. Then make an act of contrition for your sins.

5. The priest will then absolve you, using these words, "I absolve you from your sins, in the name of the Father, and the Son, and the Holy Spirit." Then he will dismiss you, sometimes with a prayer. You may respond by saying "Thanks be to God."

6. Spend some time with Our Lord thanking and praising him for the gift of his mercy. Perform your penance as soon as possible; in the church, if you can. All heaven is rejoicing with you!

6 WAYS TO EXAMINE YOUR CONSCIENCE

1. Look at your life

Says the Catechism: "The reception of this sacrament ought to be prepared for by an examination of conscience made in the light of the word of God. The passage best suited to this can be found in the moral catechesis of the Gospels and the apostolic letters, such as the Sermon on the Mount [Matthew 5-7ff] and the apostolic teachings." (1454)

The Two Commandments of Love

1. You should love the Lord your God with all your heart, with all your soul, and with all your mind.
2. You should love your neighbor as yourself.

The Golden Rule (Matthew 7:12)

Do to others as you would have them do to you.

The Beatitudes (Matthew 5:3-12)

Blessed are the poor in spirit, for theirs is the kingdom of heaven.

Blessed are they who mourn, for they will be comforted.

Blessed are the meek, for they will inherit the earth.

Blessed are the merciful, for they will be shown mercy.

Blessed are the pure of heart, for they will see God.

Blessed are the peacemakers, for they will be called children of God.

Blessed are those persecuted for righteousness' sake, for this is the kingdom of heaven.

Blessed are you when people revile you and persecute you and utter all kinds of evil against you falsely on my account.

Rejoice and be glad, for your reward will be great in heaven.

The Five Precepts of the Church

1. You shall attend Mass on Sundays and on holy days of obligation and remain free from work or activity that could impede the sanctification of such days.
2. You shall confess your sins at least once a year.
3. You shall receive the sacrament of Eucharist at least during the Easter season.
4. You shall observe the days of fasting and abstinence established by the Church.
5. You shall help to provide for the needs of the Church.

The Six Capital Sins

1. Pride
2. Covetousness
3. Lust
4. Anger
5. Gluttony
6. Envy
7. Sloth

2. Look at your love

Read 1 Corinthians 13:4-7. Ask of each word, "Is this me?"

"Love is patient, love is kind. It is not jealous, love is not pompous, it is not inflated, it is not rude, it does not seek its own interests, it is not quick-tempered, it does not brood over injury, it does not rejoice over wrongdoing but rejoices with truth. It bears all things, believes all things, hopes all things, endures all things."

3. Look at Christ

Read Colossians 3:1-10. Ask, "Do I indulge these?"

"If then you were raised with Christ, seek what is above, where Christ is seated at the right hand of God…"

"Put to death, then, the parts of you that are earthly: immortality, impurity, passion, evil desire, and greed that is idolatry. Because of these wrath of God is coming upon the disobedient. By these you too once conducted yourselves, when you lived in that way."

"But now you must put them all away: anger, fury, malice, slander, and obscene language out of the mouths. Stop lying to one another, since you have taken off the old self with its practices and have put on the new self, which is being renewed, for knowledge, in the image of its creator."

4. Look at your Relationships

My relationship with God

- Am I generous in the way I live the precepts of the Church?
- Did I skip Sunday Mass? Did I try to make the most of it, even if distracted? Did I tune it out and not try to tune back in?
- Have I been "saying" my prayers instead of praying them?
- Do I send God away and block him out of certain areas of my life – social life, leisure life, work life, studies, etc.?

My relationship with others

- Am I generous in the way I live the Golden Rule?
- Do I put myself at the service to others, or do I more or less use them?
- Do I show my spouse love in words and actions?
- Do I respect my spouse enough to be honest?
- How am I with my children? Am I careful about the example I set? Do I try to build their character, or is my discipline all reactive?
- How am I with my friends? Do I always make things go my way? Do I go along with them, even in what is morally offensive? Do I initiate or participate in gossip?
- How am I with my employer? Do I make the best use of my time? Do I treat my employer with gratitude for employing me?
- How about my parents and others in my family? Do I honor them all with the respect they deserve?

Relationship with myself

- Do I battle the seven capital sins?
- Am I another person when I am alone? Am I another person in my thoughts? Do I think things about others I would never say? Or do I strive to live the Golden Rule, even in my heart?
- Do I live my Christian principles when no one is watching? Online? At work? In what I read? In what I watch? In what I listen to? In the car?
- Every Sunday I confess to faults "in what I have done and in what I have failed to do." What good have I failed to do?

5. Look at the Commandments

6. Look at your Kids

21 QUESTIONS FOR KIDS

1. Did I pay attention at Mass? Have I fooled around at church?
2. Did I say my prayers every day?
3. Did I say mean things to my mom or dad?
4. Did I always say "thank you" to people?
5. Am I hard to get along with (during school, at Grandma's, at home)?
6. Did I do what my mom and dad told me to do? My teacher?
7. Was I lazy around the house? Did I do my chores?
8. Did I hurt other people's feelings by calling them bad names?
9. Have I started fights with my brothers and sisters at home?
10. Have I blamed other people for things I do? Did I get other people into trouble?
11. Do I hit people when I get mad?
12. Have I forgiven people, or am I holding a grudge?
13. Have I cheated or been unfair in games?
14. Did I refuse to play with someone for no good reason?
15. Was I lazy about my schoolwork?
16. Did I fail to do my homework?
17. Did I cheat in school?
18. Did I ever lie to my parents? My teacher? My friends?
19. Did I take anything that didn't belong to me?
20. Did I avoid medicine? Did I refuse to eat food I didn't like?
21. Did I watch or look at something I wasn't supposed to?

7 WAYS TO PROMOTE CONFESSION

1. Go regularly yourself.
Our example evangelizes more than we know; people notice. We also give the priest the shot of hope he needs to stay in the confessional each Saturday. (It doesn't hurt to thank him for being there.)

2. Bring your family – especially children and the elderly.
Confession can give children a place to unburden themselves without fear; a place to get kindly adult advice when they are worried about speaking to their parents. Many families make confession an outing, followed by ice cream or coffee.

3. Mention it to others.
We often think of confession as unmentionable. But there's no reason not to tell people that we've gone to confession. It's an appropriate answer to the question, "What did you do last weekend?" Also, when discussing plans, feel free to say: "I won't be able to make it until later, because I want to get to confession."

4. Learn more, and spread your knowledge.
There are many books and pamphlets on confession. Buy books for your parish's pamphlet rack, with your pastor's permission. Have some material on hand to give to others as the opportunity arises. Two good books: Father Richard Rego's *A Guide to Conscience*; Scott Hahn's *Lord, Have Mercy: The Healing Power of Confession*; The National Catholic Register's reader-friendly "*How and Why to Go to Confession*" is available at NCRegister.com for free. Click on Resources, and then on the Confessional Guides.

5. Follow the Pope.
Pope Benedict XVI is an eloquent spokesman for confession. "How can one recognize in our age... that confession must be rediscovered and proposed anew? How many people in difficulty seek the comfort and consolation of Christ? How many penitents find in confession the peace and joy that they sought for so long?" He also recommends the Divine Mercy devotion, which places a special emphasis on confession.

6. Children, use your power.
Kids have led their families into all sorts of healthy practices, from recycling to quitting smoking. Why not confession? When a girl asked Pope Benedict if she could take the initiative in leading her parents back to the sacraments, he told her: "With a daughter's respect and love, you could say to them: 'Dear Mommy, dear Daddy, it is so important for us, even for you, to meet Jesus. This encounter enriches us. It is an important element in our lives. Let's find a little time together; we can find an opportunity. Perhaps there is also a possibility where Grandmas lives.'"

7. Mention it as kind of "excuse."
If someone invited you on a walk through the mud, you'd say, "No thanks, I don't want to have to clean my shoes and clothes." When someone begins to engage in denigrating gossip, or wants you to watch an objectionable movie, or suggests plans that make it impossible to go to Mass on Sunday, the same answer is available. "No thanks, I would have to figure out how to get to confession again before my regularly scheduled time!"

10 COMMANDMENTS

1. **I am the Lord your God. You shall not have strange gods before me.**
   - Does God's law come first in my major decisions? Are there other "gods" – money, security, power, people, etc. in my life?
   - Do I dabble with things that can harm my faith, such as the occult, out of curiosity?
   - Have I received Communion in a state of mortal sin?
   - Have I deliberately told a lie or withheld sins in confession?

2. **You shall not take the name of the Lord your God in vain.**
   - Have I used God's name in vain either lightly or carelessly?
   - Do I tell jokes that profane sacred things or insult sacred persons?

3. **Remember to keep holy the Lord's Day.**
   - Have I deliberately missed Mass on Sundays or holy days of obligation?
   - Do I indulge mental distractions during Mass?
   - Have I tried to observe Sunday as a family day and a day of rest?
   - Do I do needless work on Sunday?

4. **Honor your father and your mother.**
   - Do I obey my parents?
   - Do I honor them if I am an adult?
   - Have I neglected my duties to my spouse and children?
   - Have I given my family good religious example?
   - Do I try to bring peace into my home life?

5. **You shall not kill.**
   - Have I had an abortion or encouraged or helped anyone to have an abortion?
   - Have I engaged, in any way, in sins against human life such as artificial insemination or in vitro fertilization?
   - Have I participated in or approved of euthanasia?
   - Have I physically harmed anyone? Have I insulted them?
   - Have I abused alcohol or drugs?
   - Have I been angry or resentful? Have I harbored hatred in my heart?
   - Have I mutilated myself through any form of sterilization?
   - Have I encouraged or condoned sterilization?

6. **You shall not commit adultery.**
   - Have I been faithful to my marriage vows in thought and action?
   - Have I engaged in any sexual activity outside of marriage?
   - Have I used any method of contraception or artificial birth control in my marriage?
   - Have I been guilty of masturbation? Do I control my thoughts and imaginations? Do I indulge in pornography?
   - Have I been guilty of any homosexual activity?

7. **You shall not steal.**
   - Have I stolen what is not mine? Have I returned or made restitution for what I have stolen?
   - Have I cheated anyone out of what is justly theirs, for example creditors, insurance companies, big corporations?
   - Do I waste time at work, school, and/or home?

- Do I gamble excessively, thereby denying my family of their needs?
- Do I pay my debts promptly?

8. **You shall not bear false witness against your neighbors.**
   - Have I lied? Have I gossiped? Do I speak badly of others behind their back?
   - Am I sincere in my dealings with others? Am I critical, negative, or uncharitable in my thoughts of others?
   - Have I shared what should be kept confidential?
   - Have I injured the reputation of others by slander?

9. **You shall not desire your neighbor's wife.**
   - Have I consented to impure thoughts? Have I caused them by impure reading, pornography, movies, television, conversation, or curiosity?
   - Have I behaved in an appropriate ways with members of the opposite sex: flirting, encouraging flirtation, etc.?
   - Am I careful to dress modestly?

10. **You shall not desire your neighbor's goods.**
    - Do I envy the families or possessions of others?
    - Am I greedy or selfish? Are material possessions the purpose of my life?
    - Do I share with the poor?

Walking with Purpose wishes to extend a special 'thank you' for this wonderful synopsis.
CONFESSION BY THE NUMBERS
Reprinted with Permission from *Faith and Family Magazine*.
Originally published January/February 2009.

Answer Key

NOTES

Lesson 2, Day One

1. **A.** We are to follow Jesus. This means imitating and obeying Him. In the words of the Blessed Mother, "Do whatever He tells you." (John 2:5) Jesus' example and instructions are meant to lead us safely through this life, and into His loving presence for all eternity.

   B. We can know what is true. All knowledge and all mysteries are held in Christ. Because He is the source of truth and is willing to share it with me, I can know the workings of the   universe. I can know the longings of the human heart. I don't have to figure out and define   my own version of truth. I can trust that He knows all things and will faithfully reveal to me   whatever I need to know for my present circumstances.

   C. In Christ, we can hope for and expect to experience "fullness of life." Isn't this what we all long for? If we want to be fully alive, tasting life in all its depth, breadth, and height, we need to be connected to the source of life, Jesus.

2. Answers will vary.

Lesson 2, Day Two

1. **Luke 17:25 (fulfillment of Isaiah 53:3)** Jesus was despised and rejected.

   2 Corinthians 5:21 (fulfillment of Isaiah 53:4–5) Jesus bore the punishment that was due us so that we could be whole.

   Mark 15:4–5, Luke 23:8–9, John 1:29 (fulfillment of Isaiah 53:7) Jesus was silent before His accusers. He was the lamb sacrificed in our place to take away the sins of the world.

2. **Matthew 1:22–23** As prophesied, Mary bore a son who was God in the flesh— Emmanuel.

   Matthew 2:1 As prophesied, Jesus was born in Bethlehem.

Lesson 2, Day Three

1. The name Jesus means "God saves." His name expresses His identity and mission "because he will save his people from their sins." (Matthew 1:21)

2. No. We all have sinned. If we claim that we are without sin, we are deceiving ourselves. Answers will vary.

   The wages, or consequence, of sin is death.

3. The solution God offered for our hopeless situation was to have Jesus die for our sins, in our place. He did this for us when we were still sinners. He doesn't wait until we're cleaned up and "worthy" before we can accept this gift from Him. He offers it to us when we are helpless.

4. Love was the motivation. God loved the world (and that means each one of us) so much that He gave His only Son so that we wouldn't perish and be separated from Him. Instead, we can have eternal life.

Lesson 2, Day Four

1. **Colossians 1:15** Jesus is the exact representation of God and reveals God to us. If we want to know what God is like, we need only look at Jesus. Jesus is God made visible.

   Colossians 1:16 Everything in all of creation was created through Jesus and for Jesus.

Colossians 1:17 Jesus sustains everything in the world. He holds it all together and keeps creation from spiraling into chaos. We live and breathe because He chooses to sustain us.
Colossians 1:18 Jesus is the head of the Church. He is the firstborn of all of us who will be resurrected to new, eternal life after we experience earthly death. Jesus is to have first place in all things, most of all in our thoughts and hearts. The alternative is giving Him a little corner of our hearts. But if we make this choice, we'll never make room for the fullness of His grace.
Colossians 1:19 While Christ is fully human, He is also fully divine. He is not half-human, half-divine.

2. **John 1:2–3** Jesus was there at the beginning. Everything was created through Him. Without Him, nothing was created.
   John 1:14 Jesus became flesh and came to live on earth, revealing the glory of God as His only Son. He was full of grace and truth.
   John 1:18 No one has ever seen God, but Jesus revealed Him when He came to earth. Jesus is now at the Father's side.

3. When the title Lord is used in Scripture, it's referring to God's sovereignty (His supreme power and authority). Jesus referred to Himself by this title and revealed that it was fitting by proving to be more powerful than nature, demons, sin, and death.

Lesson 3, Day One

1. Personal reflection.
2. Answers will vary.
3. God will never leave you alone. There is nowhere you can go to escape His loving presence. He is with you right now.
4. God's love for you is everlasting, steadfast, and faithful.

Lesson 3, Day Two

1. Answers will vary.
2. **Jeremiah 29:13** We are promised in Scripture that if we seek God, we will find Him, as long as we seek Him with our whole hearts. All too often, we want Him, but not as much as we want other things. This verse encourages us to purify our motives and to long to know God more than we long for anything else.
   Proverbs 3:5–6 As we choose to trust in Christ instead of ourselves, our relationship with Him will deepen and grow. This process isn't easy. A leap of faith always involves risk, and we tend to prefer being in control. But as we acknowledge that God's ways are better than ours, we'll grow in intimacy with Him.
   John 14:23 If we love Jesus, we'll obey Him. As we take the time to figure out what He asks of us, we get to know Him better. When we prove to be faithfully obedient in little things, He'll reveal bigger things to us and, most important, more about who He is.
3. Answers will vary.

Lesson 3, Day Three

1. **A.** If we are Jesus' friends, we'll do what He commands.
   B. Love God. Love people. It's that simple, and that hard.

2. If we are going to come after Jesus (and this is what He requires of His friends), then we have to deny ourselves, take up our cross daily, and follow Him.

3. Answers will vary.

Lesson 3, Day Four

1. Heaven is described as the heavenly Father's house, which has many rooms. Jesus has gone ahead of us there to prepare a place for us. He's going to come back and take us to Himself, so that we can be where He is.

2. We are to believe in Jesus Christ to have eternal life. This belief is more than a cerebral agreement as to His existence. It's believing that He is who He said He is. It's a belief that requires action. We need to listen to Jesus' words, believe they are true, and live according to those beliefs. The alternative to receiving eternal life is receiving eternal condemnation.

3. Answers will vary.

Lesson 4, Day One

1. Answers will vary.

2. We often consider our feelings to be just as important as our reasoning, but if we allow ourselves to be led by our emotions, we'll rarely pray. God wants to know how we are feeling in prayer. In that sense, feelings are very important. He wants a relationship with the real you—not some inauthentic version of you. But when we let our feelings guide our decisions, we'll take the easy way out far too often, and miss out on being transformed into the women God created us to be.

3. According to CCC 572, prayer is a battle because we are fighting against ourselves, our surroundings, and the Tempter (Satan). Satan is doing all he can to keep us from praying. As easy as it is to give up, it's worth it to persevere in prayer because "we live as we pray." Nothing will transform us the way prayer does. Prayer increases our trust in God.

Lesson 4, Day Two

1. A. Jesus tells us that unless we turn and become like little children, we won't enter heaven. He values childlike dependence, not self-sufficiency that lives as if He is an add-on or someone   who is nice to have around for the holidays.

   B. They talk without pretense. What you see is what you get; they haven't yet learned to live behind a mask. They ask for the moon without worrying how hard it would be for you to deliver it. They trust that you are more powerful than they are, and worth running to when they are scared. They believe you can make it all better, just by your presence.

2. These teachings on prayer highlight the importance of persistence. Children ask, and ask, and ask. Luke 11:5–8 encourages us to be steadfast and persistent in our prayer.

3. Answers will vary.

Lesson 4, Day Three

1. John 3:16 He gave His only Son so we could be saved.

   Ephesians 1:7 He gave us redemption through Christ's blood; He gave us forgiveness for our sins.

Ephesians 1:13 He gave us the Holy Spirit.

1 Peter 1:3–4 He gave us a new birth to a living hope through Jesus' Resurrection and an inheritance that is being kept for us in heaven.

2. Answers will vary.

Lesson 4, Day Four

1. God can do absolutely anything. Nothing is impossible for Him. This verse suggests that our prayers should be bold, and that tame, hesitant, doubt-filled prayers might make Jesus think we are lacking faith in His ability and power.

2. Jesus boldly asked God to come up with a different plan instead of the cross. He didn't hold back or hesitate. He begged God for a way out. But even as He honestly shared what He was feeling with God, He surrendered completely to God's will.

3. We do not have the mind of God. His ways are better and beyond our own. His wisdom surpasses ours. He can see into the future; we cannot. We can imagine how life would be if He answered our prayers in a certain way, but He can see how answering them would impact other people and other unforeseen events in our lives.

Lesson 6, Day One

1. According to CCC 685, "the Holy Spirit is one of the persons of the Holy Trinity, consubstantial with the Father and the Son." He is of the same substance or essence as God the Father and Jesus. He is worshipped and glorified with them. He is equal to them. He is fully divine.

2. A mighty wind was sweeping over the waters.

   Ezekiel 36:26–27 They were told that they were going to be given new hearts, and God's Spirit was to be *put inside them*. This Spirit would help them to do all the things God had been asking of them, to help them keep His laws. This was mind-blowing stuff; it was unheard of.

   Joel 3:1–2, NAB They were told that God's Spirit was going to be poured out on them—not just the super religious and powerful, but even the women and the servants would experience it. At a time when women and servants were considered property, this was incredible. This outpouring of the Holy Spirit would cause them to prophesy, dream supernatural dreams, and see visions. What an unimaginable manifestation of God's presence and power.

Lesson 6, Day Two

1. **Luke 1:15** John the Baptist was filled with the Holy Spirit even when he was within his mother's womb.

   Luke 1:34–35 The Holy Spirit came upon Mary, the Blessed Mother, and she conceived Jesus.

   Luke 3:21–22 The Holy Spirit descended on Jesus at His baptism and anointed Him.

2. Underlined phrases: comprehends the thoughts of God, reveals God, makes known to us Christ, has spoken through the prophets, makes us hear the Father's Word, reveals the Word to us, disposes us to welcome him in faith, "unveils" Christ to us, dwells with them.

Circled phrases: does not speak of himself, we do not hear the Spirit himself, will not speak on his own, divine self-effacement.

3. **John the Baptist: John 3:30** John said of Jesus, "He must increase, I must decrease."
   Mary, the Blessed Mother: Luke 1:47–48 The Blessed Mother described herself as a lowly handmaid of the Lord.
   Jesus: Philippians 2:6–8 Jesus didn't grasp at His equality with God. He emptied Himself, and became a slave. He humbled Himself, even to the point of dying in our place for sins He didn't commit.
   Humility.
4. Answers will vary.

Lesson 6, Day Three

1. He could speak a new language (Acts 2:4–12), he spoke with boldness (Acts 2:14–39), and his words had power and led people to repentance.
2. He told them to repent and be baptized, and they'd receive the gift of the Holy Spirit.
3. The promise was made to all the people in Jerusalem whom Peter was addressing and their descendants, and to all those far off, whomever God calls.
4. Answers will vary.

Lesson 6, Day Four

1. When the Holy Spirit took up residence inside me, He brought along love, joy, peace, patience, kindness, goodness, faithfulness, gentleness, and self-control. This means that I always have these good character qualities at my disposal. If I'm not feeling patient, I can ask the Holy Spirit to be patient *in me*, to replace my impatience with His presence—with His patience.
2. I don't have to pray perfectly. I can just talk to God as I would a friend, and ask the Holy Spirit to intercede for me, communicating within the Trinity in a way that I don't understand, but in a way that asks perfectly for what I truly need.
3. When I am heading into a conversation and I'm not sure what to say, or I'm aware of how important it is that my words be the right ones, the Holy Spirit is willing to *speak through me*. I just need to ask Him. I can pray, "Give me the right words! Please speak through me. Please keep me from saying the wrong thing," and He will do it.
4. I am never alone. If I need to be comforted, encouraged, or strengthened, the Holy Spirit is always there, just waiting to be asked for help. He's the quiet guest of my heart.

Lesson 7, Day One

1. Answers will vary.
2. Answers will vary.
3. Answers will vary.
4. **Isaiah 40:8** Grass withers and flowers wilt, but God's words will stand forever.
   Mark 13:31 Heaven and earth will pass away, but God's words will not.

Lesson 7, Day Two

1. **A.** Scripture is useful for **teaching**. It can teach us that we know God's truth and His will for our lives. It can teach us about His character, which will help us to trust Him.

B. Scripture is useful for **rebuking**. It can rebuke us by making it really clear what God expects. We compare ourselves to His ideal (which is always shown to us so that we can be fulfilled and happy) and we see where we're missing the mark.

C. Scripture is useful for **correcting**. It can help us correct our motives, attitudes, and behaviors.

D. Scripture is useful for **training in righteousness**. Jesus wants us to be trained in righteousness because He knows that many people will never read the Bible; they will read our lives. Our lives should reflect Him. We should look like Him. But this is a training *process*. It's not instant. It requires us to get back up and try again when we fail.

E. Scripture is useful for **equipping us for every good work**. When God created us, He created us with a purpose. There are specific works that He wants us to do, and He only calls us to do things that He equips us for. Many of the tools we need to answer and live out that call are found in Scripture.

2. **A.** We should respond by obeying what we've read.
   B. Answers will vary.
3. Answers will vary.

Lesson 7, Day Three

1. Answers will vary.
2. Answers will vary.
3. Answers will vary.
4. Answers will vary.

Lesson 8, Day One

1. Conversion is the first work of the grace of the Holy Spirit. It is grace that moves man to turn toward God and away from sin.
2. Justification is not only the remission of sins but also the sanctification and renewal of the interior man. Justification *detaches man from sin*. It purifies his heart of sin. It reconciles man with God. It frees him from the enslavement to sin. Justification heals.
3. We are saved through the bath of rebirth and renewal by the Holy Spirit. The bath of rebirth is baptism. He poured out the Holy Spirit on us so we could be justified by His grace and become heirs in hopes of eternal life.
4. As we saw in question 3, according to Titus 3:4–7, we need to experience rebirth and renewal by the Holy Spirit (baptism) to experience all the benefits of justification. We read in CCC 1991 that we also need to accept "God's righteousness through faith in Jesus Christ." This is what we do when we "make our faith our own." We receive God's grace in baptism. But many of us walked away from Him at some point, and are trying to find our way back to Him. This is why we need to experience conversion of heart, a true turning back to God. We ask Him to pour His faith, hope, and love into our hearts. We ask for Him to fill us. We recognize that it's God's righteousness that we need, because our own just isn't enough.

Lesson 8, Day Two

1. We cannot earn the grace of salvation. It is a gift from God.

2. Our salvation (justification) comes at an enormous cost: Christ's life. "Justification has been merited for us by the Passion of Christ . . ." (CCC 1992)

3. The charity (or love) of Christ *in us* is the source of all our merits before God. Grace is what unites us to Christ in love. It ensures that our acts have supernatural impact and value.

4. Perhaps we simply have difficulty with the concept of something being given that is truly undeserved. Even as we accept Christ's forgiveness and gift of salvation, we remain aware of the things we have done that were good. Our tendency to self-justify and feel a little superior to others is strong. At the same time, we're quick to attribute ill motive to others and to notice when we think they don't deserve mercy or help. This is what Jesus was talking about when He asked, "How can you say to your brother, 'Brother, let me take the speck out of your eye,' when you yourself fail to see the plank in your own eye?" (Luke 6:42)

Lesson 8, Day Three

1. Sin is not to have power over us because we are not under the law but under grace.

2. The law was given so that every mouth would be silenced and the whole world stands accountable to God. We become conscious of our own sin through the law.

3. The new law is the grace of the Holy Spirit.

4. Answers will vary for the first two questions. Lack of prayer is always an indication that we are relying on ourselves instead of on God.

Lesson 8, Day Four

1. God told Saint Paul that His grace was sufficient for him, because God's power was made perfect in weakness.

2. We receive grace through the sacraments.

3. Saint Paul was content with the thorn in his life—not just this particular thorn but also weaknesses, insults, hardships, persecution, and constraints, because he had learned that when he was weak, he was actually strong; his dependence on the Lord unleashed God's power within him.

Lesson 9, Day One

1. Jesus addressed the parables to the Pharisees.

2. Jesus was welcoming sinners and eating with them.

3. Each of the parables in Luke 15 deals with something that has been lost and then found.

4. It's important to remember that the Pharisees spent all their time keeping the moral code. They didn't consider themselves the "one sinner who repents." They considered themselves one of "the righteous people." To hear that there would be more rejoicing over one sinner repenting than over their fastidious rule keeping likely offended them.

Lesson 9, Day Two

1. When the younger son asked for his inheritance while his father was still living, he showed great disrespect. It was as if he said, "I don't want you; I want your stuff. I'd be better off if you were dead. So why not just give me the money now?"

2. He was asking to be treated as one of the hired workers. He wasn't asking to be accepted as a son. He knew he didn't deserve that kind of treatment. But being hired as a worker would allow him to earn his keep.

3. When he was still a long way off, the father caught sight of him and began to run. Even before the son had a chance to offer his full apology, the father had asked that his best robe, sandals, and a ring be placed on his son. He asked that the fattened calf be slaughtered and a feast be prepared in his son's honor.

4. Answers will vary.

Lesson 9, Day Three

1. He was angry because he had stayed home, following the rules and working hard while his brother squandered his inheritance. His brother didn't deserve to be treated this way. The older son felt that if anyone had earned a party, he had. Instead of responding in anger, the older son might have expressed joy and relief that his brother was home.

2. The father came out and pleaded with him, inviting him to come in to the feast.

3. He said that all these years, he had served his father and never once disobeyed his orders, yet the father had never thrown a feast for him.

Lesson 9, Day Four

1. God will never give up on us. His patience will never wear thin. He seeks us out and calls us home.

2. The only reason God forgives us is out of "His sheer gratuitous love." (CCC 218) God's love for us is stronger than a mother's love for her children. It is the highest possible degree of love. God's love will be victorious over even the worst infidelities. He loves us so much that He gave what was most precious to Him, His Son, so that we could be forgiven (CCC 219). God's love is everlasting and steadfast (CCC 220).

3. Answers will vary.

Lesson 11, Day One

1. The 9 Confession Promises are pardon and mercy, reconciliation, a welcome from the Father, a second "baptism," interior change, a new heart, a just penance, the strictest secrecy, and strength for the battle.

2. Answers will vary.

3. **Exodus 34:6** God's very character is grace and mercy. He has consistently been slow to anger and overflowing with love and faithfulness. It was true as far back as the Old Testament, and it's still true today.

   Isaiah 49:15 I'm imagining the strength, power, and steadfastness of a mother's love. Then I'm imagining something more faithful still. This is God's love for me, and He will never, ever forget me.

   Ephesians 2:4–5 God didn't wait for us to clean ourselves up before determining that we were worth dying for. When we were spiritually dead and hopeless, His love for us caused Him to send His Son, Jesus, to pay the price for our sins. Because of His grace, His unmerited favor, we have been offered mercy and made spiritually alive.

Lesson 11, Day Two

1. **A.** Sin aggravates you.
   B. Sin makes you aggravating.
   C. We need to say it.
   D. Confessing helps you know yourself.
   E. Confessing strengthens us.
2. Answers will vary.
3. **A.** Freedom means choices count.
   B. Confession makes you freer.
   C. Confession is a personal encounter with Christ.
   D. Confessing a mortal sin is required.
   E. Confession allows you to tidy "venial" messes in your house.
4. Answers will vary.

Lesson 11, Day Three

1. The whole power of the sacrament of penance consists in (is based on) restoring us to God's grace and joining us with Him in an intimate friendship.
2. In the beginning, God wanted an intimate relationship with His children. This is what was experienced in the Garden of Eden when Adam and Eve looked at God and walked with Him. Everything changed when sin entered the world. Shame filled their hearts, and they hid their faces from God.
3. Answers will vary.

Lesson 11, Day Four

1. We become enslaved to sin.
2. We receive an increase in spiritual strength for the Christian battle.
3. Where the Spirit of the Lord is, there is freedom.

Lesson 12, Day One

1. **A.** Each family had to get a year-old, unblemished, male sheep or goat. On the fourteenth day   of the month, they were to slaughter it during the evening twilight, and take some of its   blood and put it on the doorposts and lintels of their homes. Then they were to eat its meat   with unleavened bread and bitter herbs.
   B. John the Baptist called Jesus the Lamb of God, who takes away the sins of the world.
   C. He gave them bread and told them to take it and eat it, that it was His body. Then He gave them a cup and told them it was His blood, shed for the forgiveness of sins. The Catholic Church has always taught that this was the institution of the sacrament of the Eucharist.
2. God rained down bread from heaven. It was called manna and was like "coriander seed, white, and it tasted like wafers made with honey." (Exodus 16:31)
3. They probably were confused, and it would have tested their trust in Jesus to be open to looking at things in a new way.

Lesson 12, Day Two

1. Jesus claimed to be the bread of life, saying that whoever came to Him would never hunger, and the one who would believe in Him wouldn't ever be thirsty. This made the people complain about Him, saying, "Isn't this just Jesus? A man just like you or me? We know his mom. We know his dad. How can he claim to have come down from heaven?"

2. Jesus said, "I am the bread of life." He talked about the manna that had given short-term sustenance to the Israelites, but reminded His listeners that everyone who ate the manna died. Jesus said that anyone who would eat the bread that comes down from heaven (Him) would not die. Whoever ate the bread (Him) would live forever. He said that the bread He was talking about was His flesh. The people argued after this, talking about how it would be impossible for Jesus to give them His flesh to eat.

3. Jesus said that unless they ate the flesh of the Son of Man and drank His blood, they wouldn't have life within them. He promised that whoever would eat His flesh and drink His blood would have eternal life. He said His flesh was true food, and His blood was true drink, and that whoever ate His flesh and drank His blood would remain in Him and live forever.

4. Many of His disciples returned to their former way of life and no longer accompanied Him.

Lesson 12, Day Three

1. This structure has persevered throughout the centuries: "the gathering, the liturgy of the Word, with readings, homily, and general intercessions; the liturgy of the Eucharist, with the presentation of the bread and wine, the consecratory thanksgiving, and communion." (CCC 1346)

2. One meaning of eating and drinking without "discerning the body" is receiving the Eucharist without really believing that you are in fact receiving the body and blood of Jesus. It also has to do with having respect for whom we are receiving—having confessed mortal sin and having prepared our hearts.

3. Answers will vary.

Lesson 12, Day Four

1. The principal fruit of receiving the Eucharist is an intimate union with Christ Jesus.

2. The Eucharist strengthens our charity (which is love) and wipes away our venial sins. When Jesus gives Himself to us in the Eucharist, He revives our love and enables us to break our disordered attachments to creatures and root ourselves in Him.

3. Answers will vary.

Lesson 13, Day One

1. Peter took his eyes off of Jesus and focused on the waves. He was saved from drowning because Jesus reached out His hand and caught him.

2. He's given us a spirit of power, love, and self-control.

3. Answers will vary.

Lesson 13, Day Two

1. No. Jesus said that in this world we'll actually have trouble. But He encouraged us to take heart, because He has overcome the world.

2. She learned that everything passes; our troubles have an end date. Only God never changes. If we are patient in our difficulties, we'll learn that God alone is enough.

3. **A.** We don't walk alone. This passage encourages us to be strong and steadfast; to have no fear, for it is the Lord, our God, who marches with us; He will never fail us or forsake us.

    B. In Jesus' presence, we are never in darkness. He is our light and He promises to save us. Because He is with us, we don't need to be afraid.

    C. God is always with us. He promises to always strengthen and uphold us.

    D. Nothing can separate us from the love of God. Nothing.

4. Answers will vary.

Lesson 13, Day Three

1. It's described as a snare.

2. **Romans 8:31** Ultimately, it's only God's opinion that matters. And the Creator of the universe is *for us*.

    Galatians 1:10 We have a choice. We can either seek to please people or seek to please God. We can't have it both ways.

    Colossians 3:23 Whatever we do, our motive for doing it should be to please God, not to try to meet the expectations of people around us.

3. Answers will vary.

Lesson 13, Day Four

1. **John 10:10** It's described as an abundant life.

    1 Timothy 6:17 It's described as a life in which all the things God has provided for us are for our enjoyment.

    Isaiah 30:18 It's described as a life in which the Lord is waiting to be gracious to us, to show us mercy.

2. Answers will vary.

3. Answers will vary.

Lesson 15, Day One

1. **Isaiah 55:8–9** God's ways and thoughts are beyond us. We are not capable of understanding the mind of God or all His plans.

    Proverbs 3:5 We're told not to "lean on our own understanding" and to trust God instead.

2. Only at the end, when our partial knowledge ceases, when we see God face-to-face, will we understand His ways. This will only happen in heaven.

3. Answers will vary.

4. They are described as people who know God's name.

Lesson 15, Day Two

1. **Psalm 16:11** Abounding joy is found in God's presence. When He shows us the "path to life," we start to discover our purpose. That direction brings us joy.

   James 1:2 James says that joy comes through encountering trials—not because the trials are fun, but because they are worth it. They make our faith stronger as we learn to persevere.

   1 Peter 1:8–9 This passage says that indescribable and glorious joy comes when we "attain the goal of [our] faith," which is our eternal salvation.

2. Jesus focused on the joy that would come in the future if He obeyed in the present. His obedience was painful and costly, leading to the worst suffering imaginable. But the joy of knowing that His sacrifice would purchase our salvation helped Him obey His Father's will.

3. In this verse, Jesus was talking to the disciples, and acknowledging that they were in anguish. But He promised that He would return, and that no one would be able to take away their joy.

Lesson 15, Day Three

1. **A.** He disciplines the one He loves.

   B. He disciplines us for our benefit, so that we can grow in holiness.

   C. The peaceful fruit of righteousness will come to those who are disciplined and are trained by it.

2. Answers will vary.

3. Answers will vary.

Lesson 15, Day Four

1. Personal reflection.

2. Answers will vary.

3. **Psalm 100:5** God is good, merciful, and faithful. *Always.*

   Romans 8:31–32 God is *for us*. There is nothing He has held back from us that is for our good. He handed over His own Son *for us.*

   2 Peter 3:9 God is patient. He wants everyone to spend eternity with Him, and so He continues to intersect our lives with opportunities to let go of the things in the world that don't satisfy so we can fill our hearts with Him.

Lesson 16, Day One

1. **A.** He calls her "favored one."

   B. We are given saving, transforming grace. We're given redemption by Christ's blood, and forgiveness because of the rich grace God has lavished on us.

2. In Luke 1:28, the angel Gabriel told Mary that God was with her. Because of God's promised presence, she was told to not be afraid. Throughout Scripture, whenever God called someone to a great mission—one that would require courage and faith—the assurance He gave them was always *His presence*. He rarely gave the plan. Instead, He gave this promise.

3. She said, "I am the handmaid of the Lord. May it be done to me according to your word."

4. Answers will vary.

Lesson 16, Day Two

1. Elizabeth described Mary as being blessed because she believed that what was spoken to her would be fulfilled.

2. A. John 11:40 promises that if we believe, we'll see the glory of God.

   B. Mary believed in what the angel said, and clung to that truth even when it appeared that everything was spinning out of control. Because she believed, she was able to see Jesus resurrected from the dead, full of glory. She is able to see Him now, honored in heaven, sitting at the right hand of God. There were certainly times when she couldn't understand why God was allowing what He did, but in the end, she was able to see the beautiful tapestry that He was weaving—our salvation.

3. The testing of our faith produces perseverance.

4. Answers will vary.

Lesson 16, Day Three

1. She said, "My soul proclaims the greatness of the Lord; my spirit rejoices in God my savior." Some translations say, "My soul magnifies the Lord."

2. Simeon prophesied that Jesus was "destined for the fall and rise of many in Israel" and that a sword would pierce Mary's heart.

3. Her heart was pierced when she saw her Son suffering and dying on the cross.

4. Answers will vary.

Lesson 16, Day Four

1. Romans 3:23 All have sinned and fall short of the glory of God.

Romans 6:23 The wages (or consequences) of sin is death, but the gift of God is eternal life in Christ Jesus.

Romans 5:8 God proved His love for us in this: While we were still sinners, Christ died for us.

2 Corinthians 5:21 Our sins were placed on Christ—He became sin for us—so that in exchange, He could give us His righteousness.

The consequence of sin is death. Death is what is due each one of us, because we all are sinners. Justice required that a death occur in payment for sin. Justice was satisfied when Christ paid the price for our sins. All our sins were placed on Him, and He died for us. In doing so, He showed us total mercy, because we didn't deserve this help. There is nothing we have done to earn the gift of our salvation.

2. We are described as "the objects of God's merciful love." Through Mary, the Holy Spirit begins to bring men into communion with Christ. The humble are the first to accept Him.

3. We have to recognize that we need mercy, that we need forgiveness, that we are sinful. We aren't saved because of any righteous deeds we have done, but simply because of God's mercy. If we don't recognize this, we'll try to save ourselves, and in doing so, consciously or unconsciously, we'll reject Christ's offer to pay the price for us. And only His sacrifice will satisfy God the Father.

Lesson 17, Day One

1. Answers will vary.
2. **A.** It says that sin is not to have any power over me.
   B. We are under grace.
3. The law of the Spirit of life has set us free from the law of sin and death.

Lesson 17, Day Two

1. Our weapons are described as "not of flesh," as "enormously powerful," and as "capable of destroying fortresses."
2. The weapons of our battle are capable of destroying fortresses, arguments, and every pretension raising itself against the knowledge of God.
3. Answers will vary.
4. Answers will vary.

Lesson 17, Day Three

1. **A.** Our loins are girded in truth, righteousness is our breastplate, our feet are shod in readiness for the gospel of peace, faith is our shield, our salvation is our helmet, and the Word of God is our sword.
   B. Answers will vary.
2. Our second offensive weapon is prayer.
3. **A.** This is where it all begins. In baptism, we become adopted daughters of God with access to all the grace mentioned in this catechism passage: belief in, hope in, and love for God; the power to act as the Holy Spirit leads us; and the ability to grow in goodness through moral virtues.
   B. The Eucharist strengthens us to love heroically and to break disordered attachments to people and things that keep us from obeying God fully.
   C. When we take responsibility for our sins in the sacrament of penance, we are wielding a weapon that sends the devil running. We receive grace that will help us to resist sinning in the future.

Lesson 17, Day Four

1. We learn in 1 Corinthians 15:33 that bad company corrupts good character.
2. According to Colossians 3:1–10, we should be seeking things that are above and setting our minds on things that are above, not on things that are on earth. This is a description of the things that will matter in the long run—in eternity. We're to put to death sexual immorality, impurity, passion, evil desire, and covetousness, which is idolatry, anger, wrath, malice, slander, obscene talk, and lies.
3. "The way of perfection passes by way of the Cross."

Lesson 19, Day One

1. Jesus said that if anyone wanted to follow Him, he had to deny himself and pick up his cross daily.
2. Answers will vary.
3. Answers will vary.
4. If we are willing to lose our lives for Christ's sake, we will actually save our lives.

Lesson 19, Day Two

1. Jesus never promised that following Him would make our relationships more peaceful; in fact, He promised that it would often cause conflict and division.
2. We are supposed to love our parents and children. Jesus never contradicted Himself, and countless times in Scripture we are commanded to love sacrificially in the same way He did. This verse tells us that our love for Jesus should be greater than our love for our parents and children.
3. **Ephesians 4:2** We are to be completely humble, gentle, and patient, bearing with one another in love.

   Ephesians 4:26 It's not a sin to be angry, but we are to make sure that in our anger, we aren't sinning. We are to resolve our conflicts right away, not letting the issues fester.

   Ephesians 4:29 We are to check our words, making sure that "no unwholesome talk is coming out of our mouths," but only words that are helpful for building others up according to their needs.

   Ephesians 4:32 We are to be kind and compassionate, forgiving each other.

Lesson 19, Day Three

1. We have a very real enemy, who seeks our destruction. He wants to take us out at the knees because he hates us and is afraid of what we can do through God's power.
2. The whole of man's history has been the story of our combat with the powers of evil. We find ourselves in the midst of this battle, struggling to do what is right, at great cost to ourselves and aided by God's grace.
3. We are called to be watchful, to stand firm in our faith, to be courageous and strong.
4. To stand firm in our faith, we need to pay attention to our conscience. Ignoring the prick of the conscience leads us to sin, which weakens us in battle. We live, grow, and persevere in our faith by nourishing it with the Word of God and begging the Lord to increase our faith. Faith needs to be working through charity (love in action), abounding in hope, and rooted in the faith of the Church.

Lesson 19, Day Four

1. Jesus said that unless we become like children, we won't enter the kingdom of heaven.
2. Faith in our own abilities rather than faith in what God can do; self-sufficiency; a desire or need for control; a lack of trust.
3. Answers will vary.

Lesson 20, Day One

1. Jesus described Peter as the rock on whom He would build the Church. Jesus promised that the gates of Hades would not prevail against the Church. He gave Peter the keys to the kingdom of heaven.
2. When Jesus gave Peter the keys to the kingdom, He was entrusting him with a specific authority. The "power of the keys" designates authority to govern the house of God, which is the Church. The power to "bind and loose" means the authority to absolve sins, to pronounce doctrinal judgments, and to make disciplinary decisions in the Church.
3. Answers will vary.

Lesson 20, Day Two

1. In John 1:14, Jesus is described as "full of grace and truth." The Church, as a community of faith, hope, and charity, is the visible organization through which Jesus communicates His truth and grace.
2. The seven sacraments are the signs and instruments by which the Holy Spirit spreads the grace of Christ. We receive the sacraments through the Church. Without the Church, we wouldn't have access to the sacraments.
3. **Matthew 18:20** Where two or three are gathered in Christ's name, Christ is there in the midst of them.

    CCC 1548 Christ is present in a sacramental way through the person of the priest. This is what is meant by the phrase *in persona Christi.*

    CCC 1392 Christ is present in the Eucharist. What material food does for us physically, the Eucharist does for us spiritually. In it, we are communing with the actual flesh of the risen Christ. This preserves, increases, and renews the life of grace that we receive at baptism.
4. Answers will vary.

Lesson 20, Day Three

1. **Genesis 2:18** One of the first things God said to man was, "It is not good for the man to be alone."

    Ecclesiastes 4:9–12 Two are better than one. If one falls, the other can help him up. One alone can be overcome, but two together can easily resist. And a cord of three is not easily broken.
2. They devoted themselves with one accord to prayer, to the teaching of the apostles, to living a communal life, and to the breaking of the bread. They shared all their possessions—selling property and possessions and then dividing the proceeds among themselves. They met together in the temple area every day. They were of one heart and mind.
3. Answers will vary.

Lesson 20, Day Four

1. He tells us not to grow weary in doing good, because in due time we will reap a harvest if we don't give up. We are to continue to do good to all, but especially to those who belong to the family of the faith. This indicates that our highest priority should be to give back to "the family of the faith."
2. Jesus was moved to pity when He looked at the crowds of people, because they were troubled and abandoned, like sheep without a shepherd. He observed that the harvest was abundant—the problem wasn't that people weren't open or interested in being helped; the problem was that there were so few laborers who were willing to go out and do the work in the fields.
3. **A.** We serve a God who is able to do immeasurably more than all we can ask or imagine. The same power that raised Jesus from the dead is within us. Mountains can be moved. Barriers can come down. We are not weak and powerless to bring change.

    B. The Holy Spirit is given to each individual child of God, equipping him or her with spiritual gifts that God wants him or her to use for the benefit of the Church.

C. **Psalm 78:3–4** We are to pass on our faith to the next generation.
   Matthew 10:8 What we've been given freely, we are to give away, not hoarding it for ourselves.
   Hebrews 12:15 We are to see to it that no one misses the grace of God.

Lesson 21, Day One

1. Psalm 90:14 says, "Fill us at daybreak with your mercy that all our days we may sing for you." Beginning the day with time alone with God sets the tone for the whole day. It resets our minds and reorients our priorities to better reflect what He wants for us. Even Jesus rose before it was light out in order to spend time alone with His Father.
2. Answers will vary.
3. Why wouldn't we welcome the input of the author of the Bible? One of the Holy Spirit's primary roles today is to guide us to truth. He takes the words of our heavenly Father and makes them known (and understandable) to us.

Lesson 21, Day Two

1. Answers will vary.
2. Answers will vary.
3. Answers will vary.
4. Answers will vary.
5. Answers will vary.
6. Answers will vary.
7. Answers will vary.

Lesson 21, Day Three

1. If we listen to God's words and act on them, we're like a wise man who builds his house on the rock. We'll have a foundation to stand on. No matter what hits us, we'll have something firm to cling to. But if we listen to those same words and don't act on them, we'll be standing on shifting sand. When crisis comes, we'll be vulnerable.
2. If we know the good we should do (after all, we just read about it), but fail to do it, we are in sin.
3. "Knowledge inflates with pride, but love builds up." When we build up a store of biblical knowledge, we can become prideful. The best antidote to this is to keep living out what we've read, growing more and more sacrificial in our love.

Lesson 21, Day Four

Answers will vary.
Answers will vary.
Answers will vary.

NOTES

Looking for more material? We've got you covered!
Walking with Purpose meets women where they are in
their spiritual journey. From our Opening Your Heart
22-lesson foundational Bible study to more advanced
studies, we have something to help each and every
woman grow closer to Christ. Find out more:

www.walkingwithpurpose.com

Prayer Pages

NOTES

walking with purpose

Come, Holy Spirit

Come, Holy Spirit, fill the hearts of Your faithful,
and kindle in them the fire of Your love.
Send forth Your Spirit and they shall be created,
and You shall renew the face of the earth.

O God, who by the light of the Holy Spirit,
did instruct the hearts of Your faithful,
grant that by the gift of the same Spirit,
we may be truly wise and always
rejoice in His consolation,
through Christ our Lord,
Amen.

Prayer Requests

Date: 2-7-2019

Discernment answered.
Let go - Let God
Open mind & heart for relationship
Wisdom
Let go.
Comfort to know - recognize
All have calmness
More Spirituality w/ husband
Acceptance - of friend who hurt
Joy among busyness
Wisdom - right decisions

Date: Help to "Feed my Sheep"

My Mother's mind
Awareness for helpfulness.
Patience - w/ details
Better Listener
Trust - Life's Plan
Listening + acting on it.
More Patience
Patience vs diligence balance
Grief - miscarriage - Peace in heart for
God's will

Prayer Requests

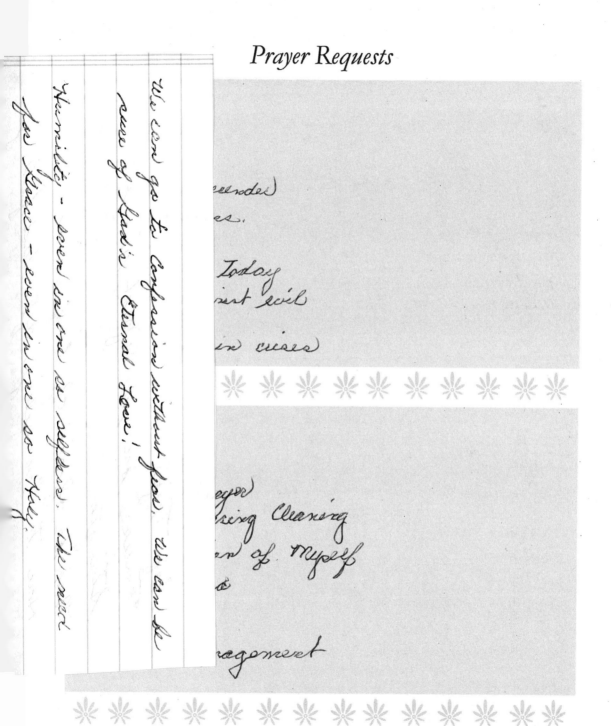

Prayer Requests

Date: 3/21

Safe Travels
Sleep better
Clarity for a relationship for her child - Girl Scouts
Openess to be the best I can be.
Brooding less - acting more
Daughter - go to Church
Babies
Awareness to discern

Date: 4/4

• Acts Retreat Team - preparation
• Intentional w/ my time
• Good feed back on Acts Team
• Attention
• 3 Parishes in town
• Focus on Easter
• Dilution of Love of Church

Prayer Requests

Date: 4-11

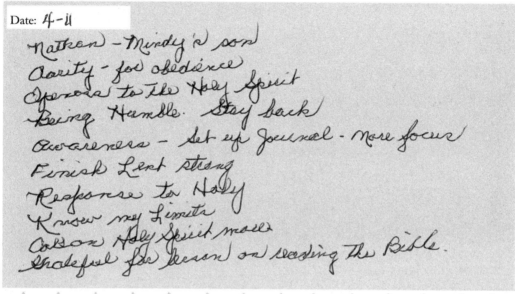

Nathan - Mindy's son
Clarity - for obedience
Openess to the Holy Spirit
Being Humble. Stay back
Awareness - Set up Journal - More focus
Finish Lent strong
Response to Holy
Know my Limits
Colson Holy Spirit move
Grateful for lesson on reading the Bible.

Date:

Prayer Requests

Date:

Date:

Prayer Requests

Date:

Date:

Prayer Requests

Date:

Date:

Prayer Requests

Date:

Date:

Prayer Requests

Date:

Date:

Prayer Requests

Date:

Date:

Prayer Requests

Date:

Date:

"For to the one who has, more will be given"
Matthew 13:12

CHRIST'S LOVE IS ENDLESS.

And the journey doesn't end here.

Walking With Purpose is more than a Bible study, it's a supportive community of women seeking lasting transformation of the heart. And you are invited.

Walking With Purpose believes that change happens in the hearts of women – and, by extension, in their families and beyond – through Bible study and community. We welcome all women, irrespective of faith background, age, or marital status.

Connect with us online for regular inspiration and to join the conversation. There you'll find insightful blog posts, Scriptures, and downloads.

For a daily dose of spiritual nourishment, join our community on Facebook, Twitter, Pinterest and Instagram.

And if you're so moved to start a Walking With Purpose study group at home or in your parish, take a look at our website for more information.

walkingwithpurpose.com
The Modern Woman's Guide to the Bible.

walking with purpose

❊ DEEPEN YOUR FAITH ❊ OPEN YOUR ARMS ❊ ❊ BROADEN YOUR CIRCLE ❊

When your heart opens, and your love for Christ deepens, you may be moved to bring Walking With Purpose to your friends or parish. It's rewarding experience for many women who, in doing so, learn to rely on God's grace while serving Him.

If leading a group seems like a leap of faith, consider that you already have all the skills you need to share the Lord's Word:

- Personal commitment to Christ
- Desire to share the love of Christ
- Belief in the power of authentic, transparent community

The Walking With Purpose community supports you with:

- Training
- Mentoring
- Bible study materials
- Promotional materials

Few things stretch and grow our faith like stepping out of our comfort zone and asking God to work through us. Say YES, soon you'll see the mysterious and unpredictable ways He works through imperfect women devoted to Him.

Remember that if you humbly offer Him what you can, He promises to do the rest.

"See to it that no one misses the grace of God" Hebrews 12:15

Learn more about bringing Walking with Purpose to your parish.
Visit us at walkingwithpurpose.com
The Modern Woman's Guide To The Bible.

walking with purpose

INTRODUCING 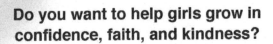 blaze THE MODERN GIRL'S GUIDE TO THE BIBLE.

Do you want to help girls grow in confidence, faith, and kindness?

The Lord is calling for women like you to speak truth into the hearts of young girls – girls who are understandably confused about their true worth and beauty. Blaze is a fun and engaging program developed especially for 7th and 8th grade girls to counteract the cultural forces that drive them to question their value, purpose, and faith.

Like Walking With Purpose, Blaze makes the wisdom of the Bible relevant to today's challenges. Blaze teaches girls to recognize the difference between the loving, affirming voice of their heavenly Father and the voices that tell them they aren't good enough.

Would you like to be a positive influence on the girls you know? Start a Blaze program in in your parish or community.

It's easy and convenient to share God's word with a Leader's Guide and Blaze kit that includes:

- Blaze Prayer Journals
- Truth vs. Lie Cards
- Fun gifts for the girls
- Facebook and Instagram messaging to maintain connection and amplify the message

Additional resources to nurture girls' spiritual growth:

- Discovering My Purpose – a 6-session Bible study that leads girls on an exploration of their own spiritual gifts
- Between You & Me – a 40-day conversation guide for mothers and daughters

 walking with purpose

For more spiritual inspiration or to learn more about Blaze and Walking With Purpose, visit us at walkingwithpurpose.com/BLAZE

You're also invited to join our community on Facebook, Twitter, Pinterest and Instagram.

"Be who God meant you to be and you will set the world on fire." - Saint Catherine of Siena

walking with purpose

These transformative full-length Bible studies are created to help women deepen their personal relationship with Christ. Each study includes many lessons that explore core themes and challenges of modern life through the ancient wisdom of the Bible and the Catholic Church.

INTRODUCTORY LEVEL

Opening Your Heart

A thoughtful consideration of the fundamental questions of faith – from why and how to pray to the role of the Holy Spirit in our lives and the purpose of suffering.

Living In the Father's Love

Gain a deeper understanding of how God's unconditional love transforms your relationship with others, with yourself, and most dearly, with Him.

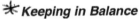

INTERMEDIATE LEVEL

* Keeping in Balance

Discover how the wisdom of the Old and New Testaments can help you live a blessed lifestyle of calm, health, and holiness.

Touching the Divine

These thoughtful studies draw you closer to Jesus and deepen your faith, trust, and understanding of what it means to be God's beloved daughter.

ADVANCED LEVEL

Discovering Our Dignity
Modern-day insight directly from women of the Bible presented as a tender, honest, and loving conversation—woman to woman.

Beholding His Glory
Old Testament Scripture leads us directly to our Redeemer, Jesus Christ. Page after page, God's awe-inspiring majesty is a treasure to behold.

Beholding Your King
This study of King David and several Old Testament prophets offers a fresh perspective of how all Scripture points to the glorious coming of Christ.

Grounded In Hope
Anchor yourself in the truth found in the New Testament book of Hebrews, and gain practical insight to help you run your race with perseverance.

Fearless and Free
This study is for any woman confronting the reality that life isn't easy through six compassionate lessons to flourish in Christ's love.

Walking With Purpose is a supportive community of women seeking lasting transformation of the heart through Bible study. We welcome all women, irrespective of faith, background, age, or marital status. For a daily dose of spiritual nourishment, join our community on Facebook, Twitter, Pinterest and Instagram.

walkingwithpurpose.com

Mission

Walking with Purpose transforms the hearts
and lives of women by providing Bible studies
that enable women to know Christ
through Scripture and the teachings of the
Roman Catholic Church.

 ## Vision

To enable every Catholic woman
in America to experience our life-changing
Bible study, **Opening Your Heart.**

Join us in transforming the hearts and lives of women.
Make a gift to Walking with Purpose today!

walkingwithpurpose.com/donate